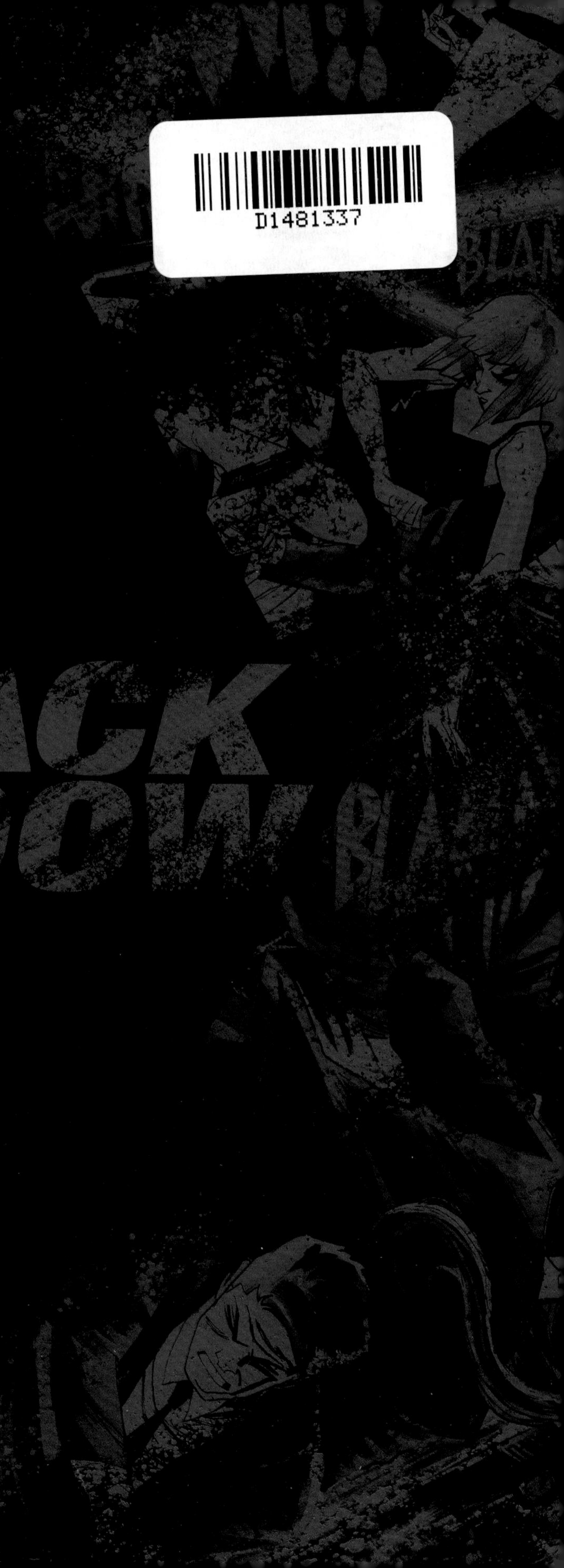

BLACK WIDOW

NO RESTRAINTS PLAY

NO RES

Je

VC's Joe Caramag
LET

Lindsey Cohick
ASSISTANT EDITOR

COLLECTION EDITOR: JENNIFER GRÜ
ASSISTANT EDITOR: CAITLIN O'T
ASSOCIATE MANAGING EDITOR: KATERI
EDITOR, SPECIAL PROJECTS: MARK D. I
VP PRODUCTION & SPECIAL PROJECTS: JEFF YOU
BOOK DESIGNER: ADAM

BLACK WIDOW: NO RESTRAINTS PLAY. Contains material originally published in maga

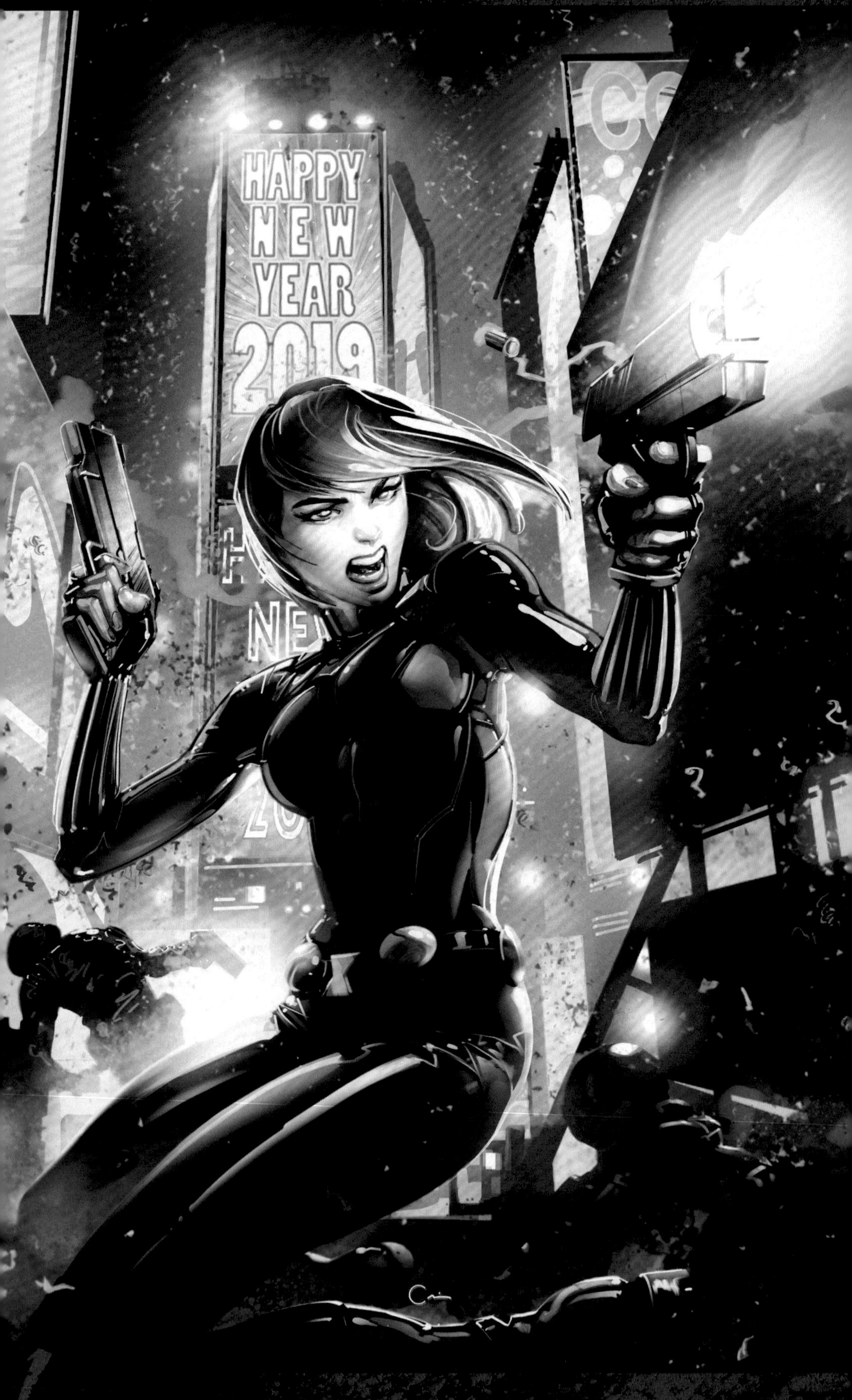
HAPPY
NEW
YEAR
2019

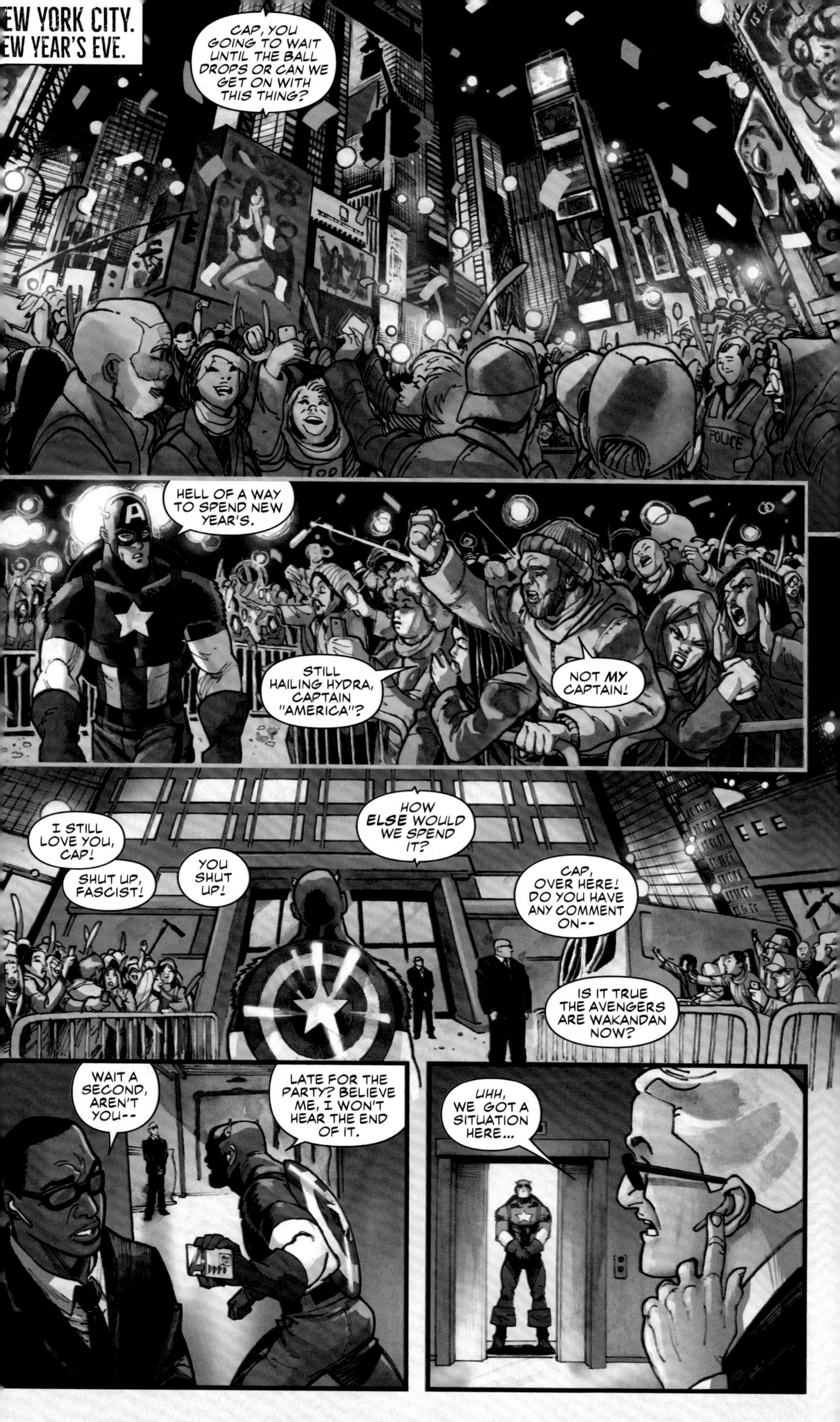

EW YORK CITY.
EW YEAR'S EVE.
CAP, YOU GOING TO WAIT UNTIL THE BALL DROPS OR CAN WE GET ON WITH THIS THING?
POLICE
HELL OF A WAY TO SPEND NEW YEAR'S.
STILL HAILING HYDRA, CAPTAIN "AMERICA"?
NOT MY CAPTAIN!
I STILL LOVE YOU, CAP!
SHUT UP, FASCIST!
YOU SHUT UP!
HOW ELSE WOULD WE SPEND IT?
CAP, OVER HERE! DO YOU HAVE ANY COMMENT ON--
IS IT TRUE THE AVENGERS ARE WAKANDAN NOW?
WAIT A SECOND, AREN'T YOU--
LATE FOR THE PARTY? BELIEVE ME, I WON'T HEAR THE END OF IT.
UHH, WE GOT A SITUATION HERE...

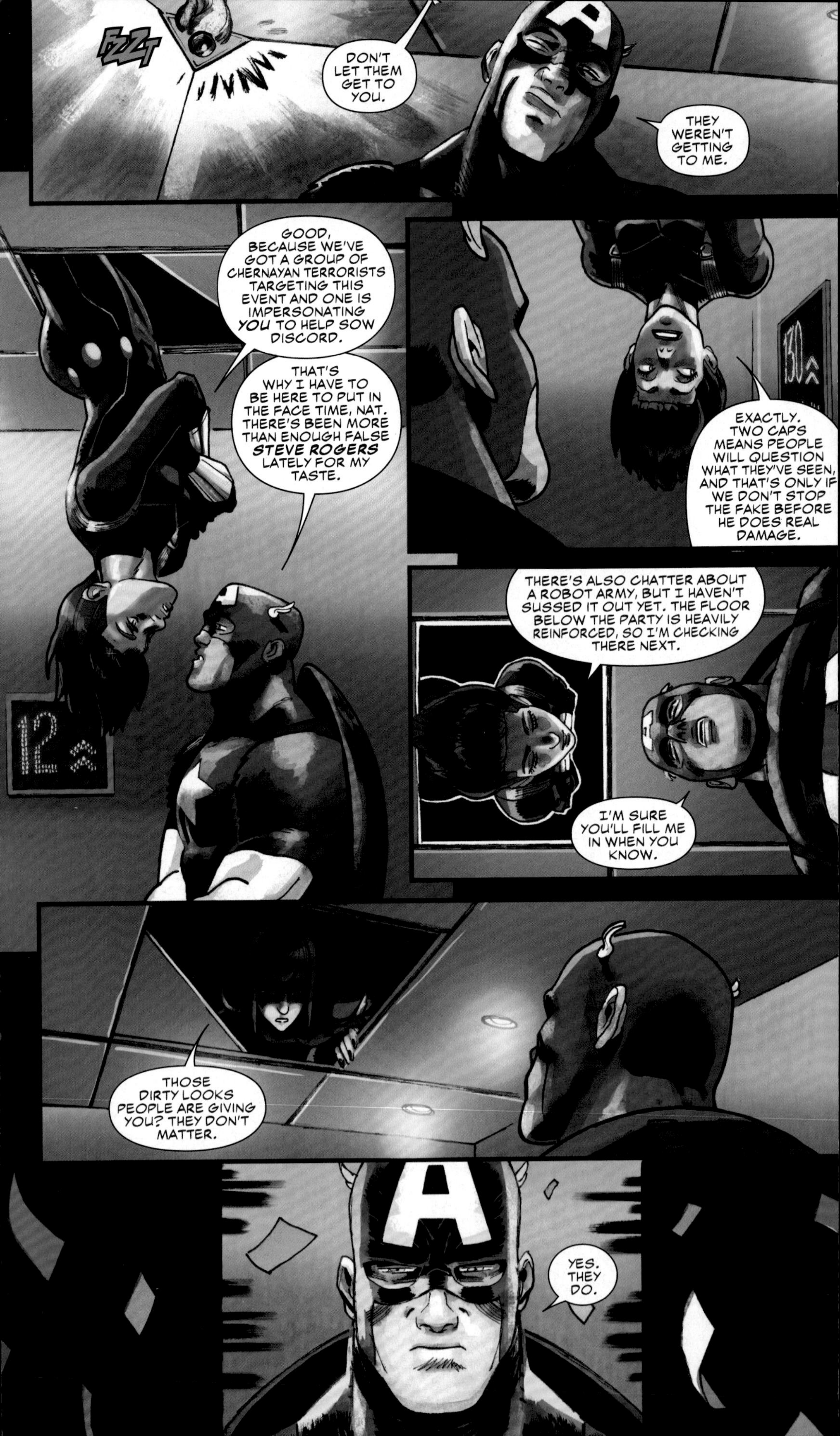
FZZT
DON'T LET THEM GET TO YOU.
THEY WEREN'T GETTING TO ME.
GOOD, BECAUSE WE'VE GOT A GROUP OF CHERNAYAN TERRORISTS TARGETING THIS EVENT AND ONE IS IMPERSONATING YOU TO HELP SOW DISCORD.
THAT'S WHY I HAVE TO BE HERE TO PUT IN THE FACE TIME, NAT. THERE'S BEEN MORE THAN ENOUGH FALSE STEVE ROGERS LATELY FOR MY TASTE.
12
EXACTLY. TWO CAPS MEANS PEOPLE WILL QUESTION WHAT THEY'VE SEEN, AND THAT'S ONLY IF WE DON'T STOP THE FAKE BEFORE HE DOES REAL DAMAGE.
13
THERE'S ALSO CHATTER ABOUT A ROBOT ARMY, BUT I HAVEN'T SUSSED IT OUT YET. THE FLOOR BELOW THE PARTY IS HEAVILY REINFORCED, SO I'M CHECKING THERE NEXT.
I'M SURE YOU'LL FILL ME IN WHEN YOU KNOW.
THOSE DIRTY LOOKS PEOPLE ARE GIVING YOU? THEY DON'T MATTER.
YES. THEY DO.

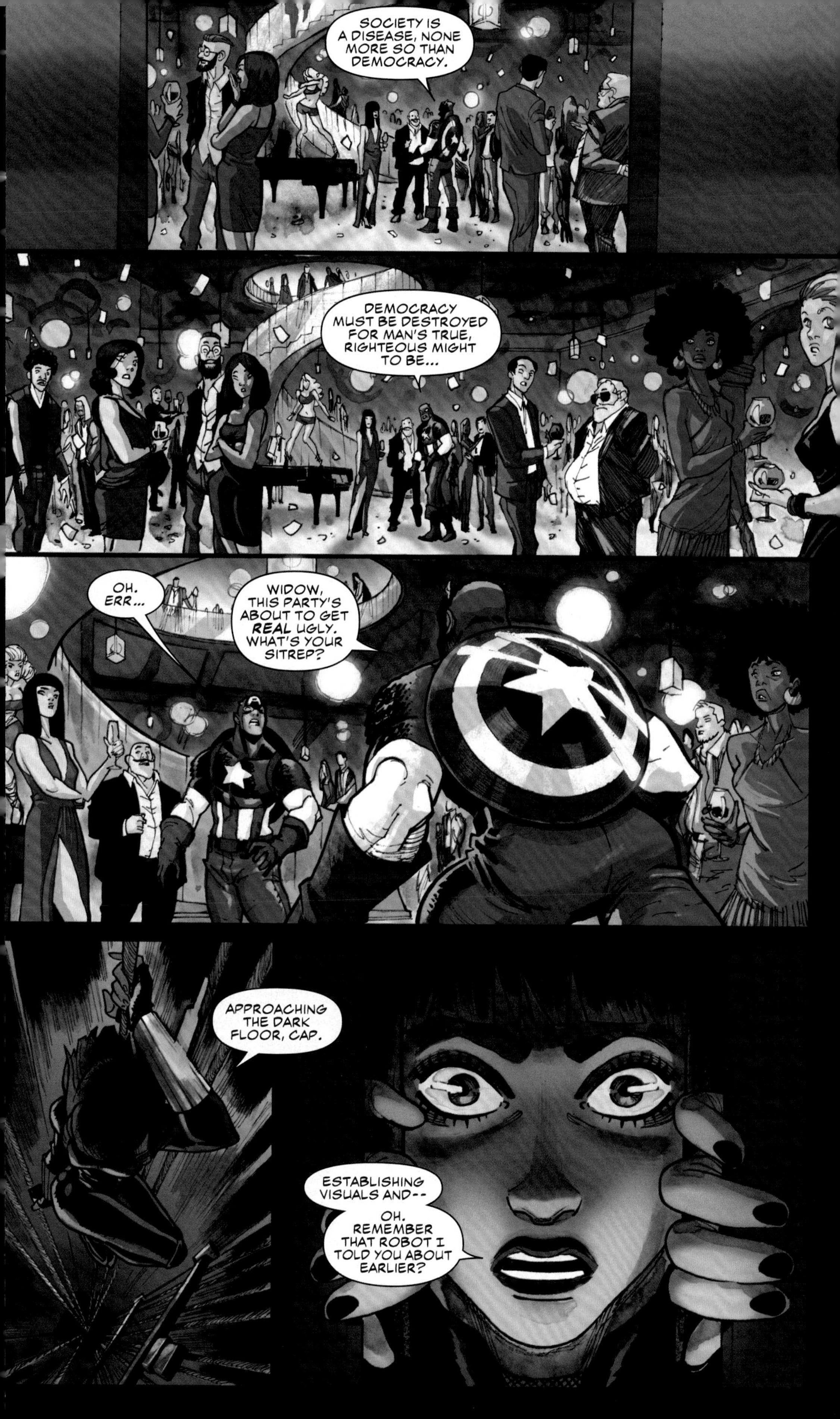
SOCIETY IS A DISEASE, NONE MORE SO THAN DEMOCRACY.
DEMOCRACY MUST BE DESTROYED FOR MAN'S TRUE, RIGHTEOUS MIGHT TO BE...
OH. ERR...
WIDOW, THIS PARTY'S ABOUT TO GET **REAL** UGLY. WHAT'S YOUR SITREP?
APPROACHING THE DARK FLOOR, CAP.
ESTABLISHING VISUALS AND--
OH. REMEMBER THAT ROBOT I TOLD YOU ABOUT EARLIER?

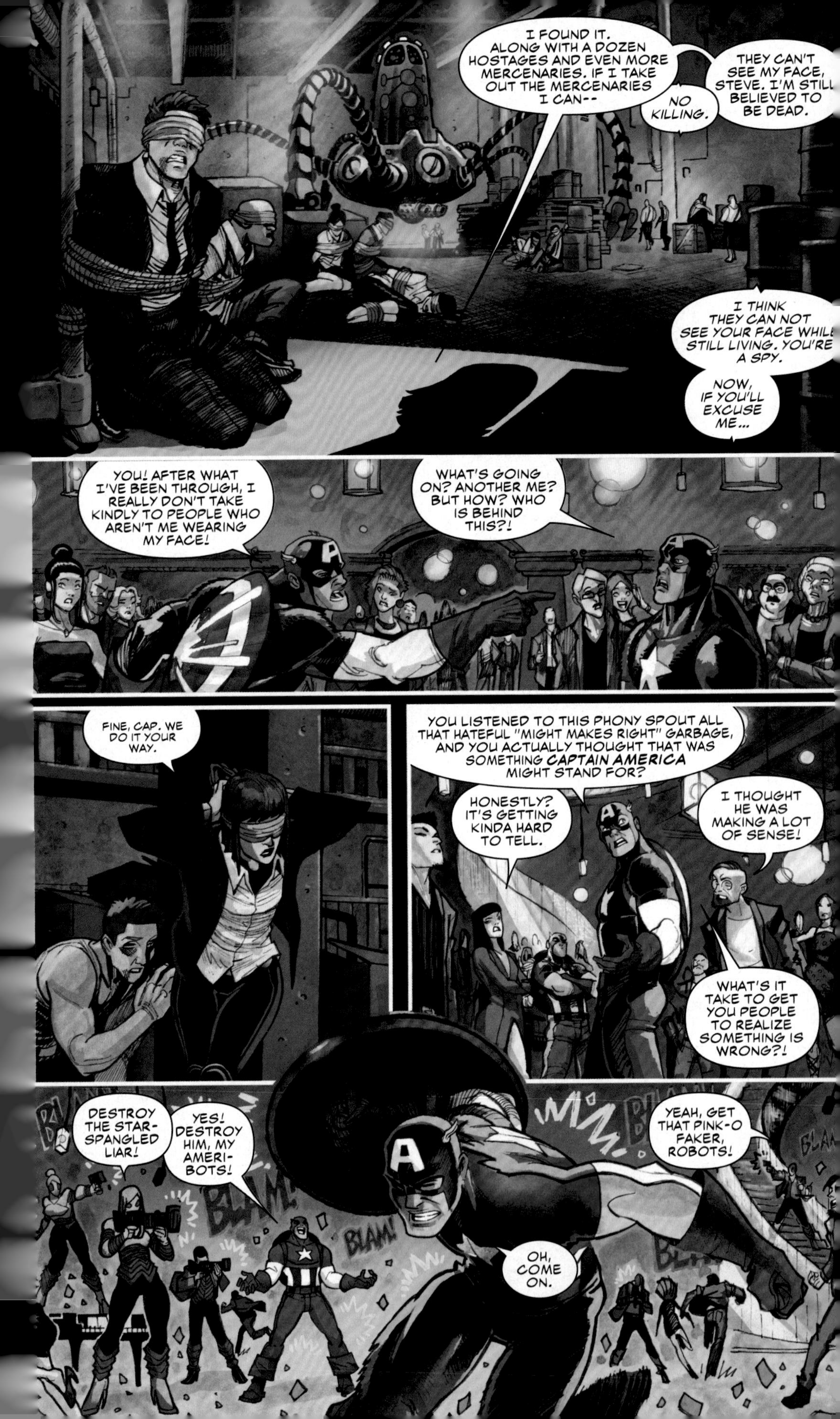
I FOUND IT. ALONG WITH A DOZEN HOSTAGES AND EVEN MORE MERCENARIES. IF I TAKE OUT THE MERCENARIES I CAN--
NO KILLING.
THEY CAN'T SEE MY FACE, STEVE. I'M STILL BELIEVED TO BE DEAD.
I THINK THEY CAN NOT SEE YOUR FACE WHILE STILL LIVING. YOU'RE A SPY.
NOW, IF YOU'LL EXCUSE ME...
YOU! AFTER WHAT I'VE BEEN THROUGH, I REALLY DON'T TAKE KINDLY TO PEOPLE WHO AREN'T ME WEARING MY FACE!
WHAT'S GOING ON? ANOTHER ME? BUT HOW? WHO IS BEHIND THIS?!
FINE, CAP. WE DO IT YOUR WAY.
YOU LISTENED TO THIS PHONY SPOUT ALL THAT HATEFUL "MIGHT MAKES RIGHT" GARBAGE, AND YOU ACTUALLY THOUGHT THAT WAS SOMETHING CAPTAIN AMERICA MIGHT STAND FOR?
HONESTLY? IT'S GETTING KINDA HARD TO TELL.
I THOUGHT HE WAS MAKING A LOT OF SENSE!
WHAT'S IT TAKE TO GET YOU PEOPLE TO REALIZE SOMETHING IS WRONG?!
DESTROY THE STAR-SPANGLED LIAR!
YES! DESTROY HIM, MY AMERI-BOTS!
YEAH, GET THAT PINK-O FAKER, ROBOTS!
BLAM!
BLAM!
OH, COME ON.

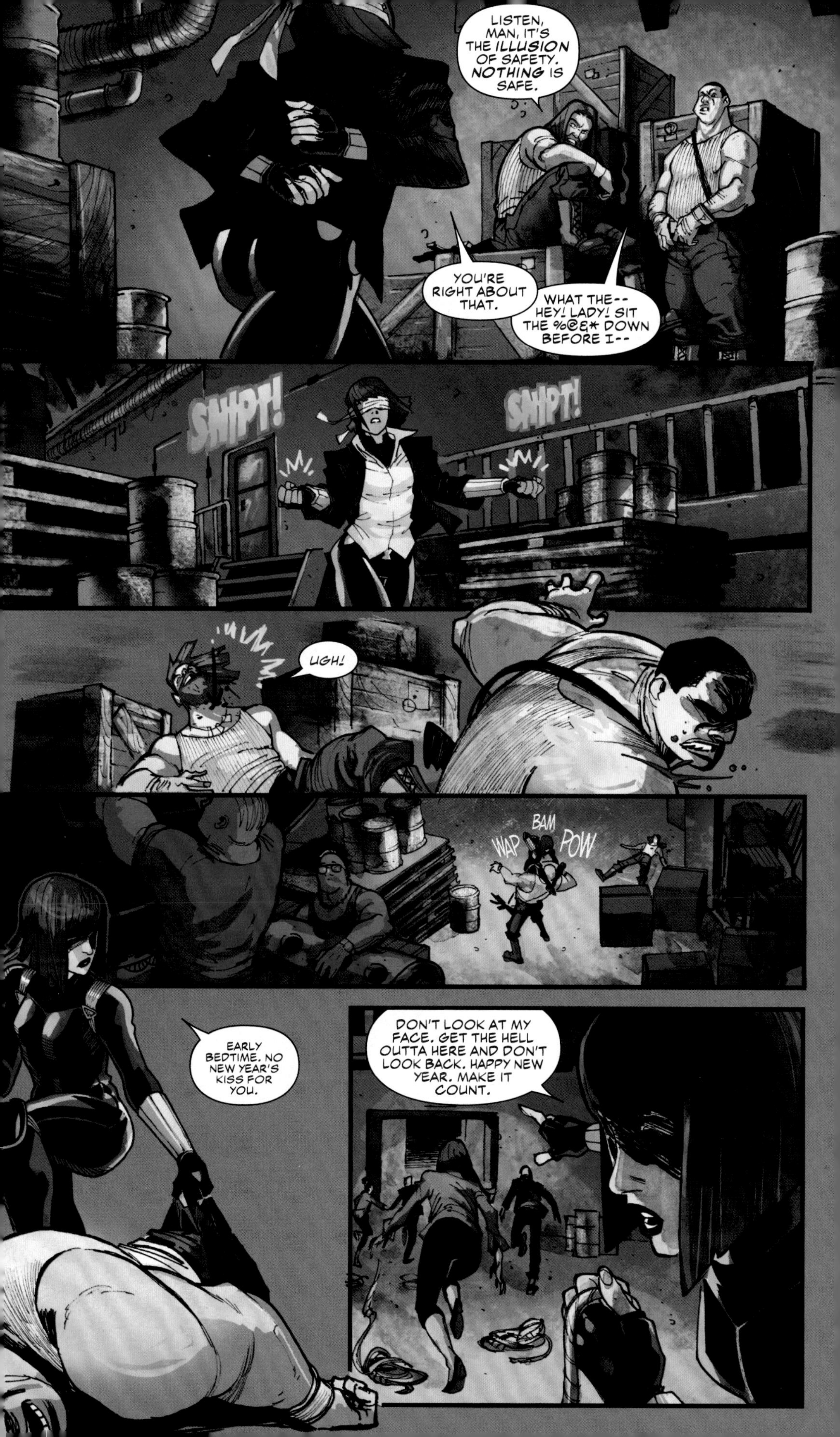
LISTEN, MAN, IT'S THE ILLUSION OF SAFETY. NOTHING IS SAFE.
YOU'RE RIGHT ABOUT THAT.
WHAT THE-- HEY! LADY! SIT THE %@&* DOWN BEFORE I--
SHIPT!
SHIPT!
UGH!
WAP
BAM
POW
EARLY BEDTIME. NO NEW YEAR'S KISS FOR YOU.
DON'T LOOK AT MY FACE. GET THE HELL OUTTA HERE AND DON'T LOOK BACK. HAPPY NEW YEAR. MAKE IT COUNT.

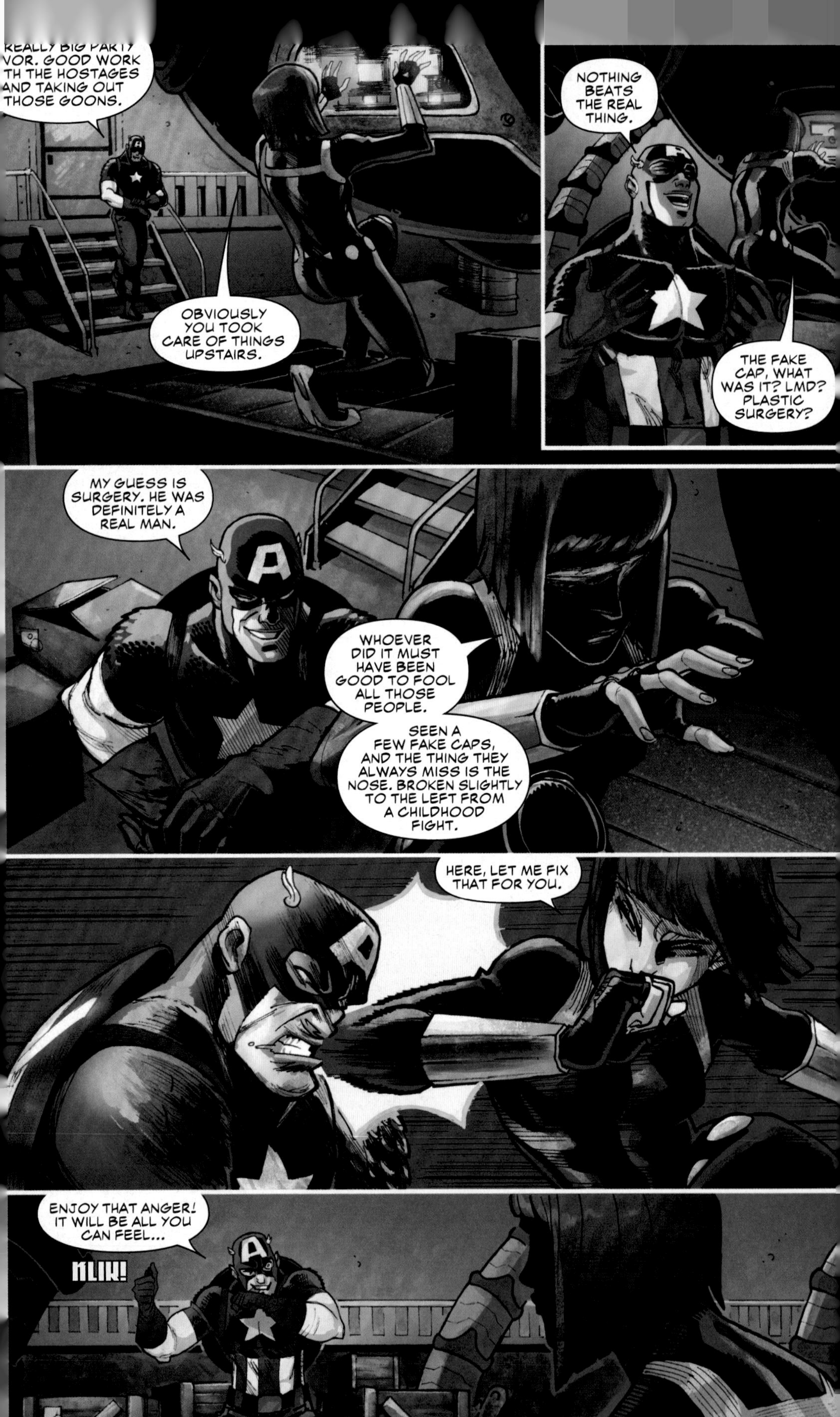

REALLY BIG PARTY
VOR. GOOD WORK
TH THE HOSTAGES
AND TAKING OUT
THOSE GOONS.
OBVIOUSLY YOU TOOK CARE OF THINGS UPSTAIRS.
NOTHING BEATS THE REAL THING.
THE FAKE CAP, WHAT WAS IT? LMD? PLASTIC SURGERY?
MY GUESS IS SURGERY. HE WAS DEFINITELY A REAL MAN.
WHOEVER DID IT MUST HAVE BEEN GOOD TO FOOL ALL THOSE PEOPLE.
SEEN A FEW FAKE CAPS, AND THE THING THEY ALWAYS MISS IS THE NOSE. BROKEN SLIGHTLY TO THE LEFT FROM A CHILDHOOD FIGHT.
HERE, LET ME FIX THAT FOR YOU.
ENJOY THAT ANGER! IT WILL BE ALL YOU CAN FEEL...
KLIK!

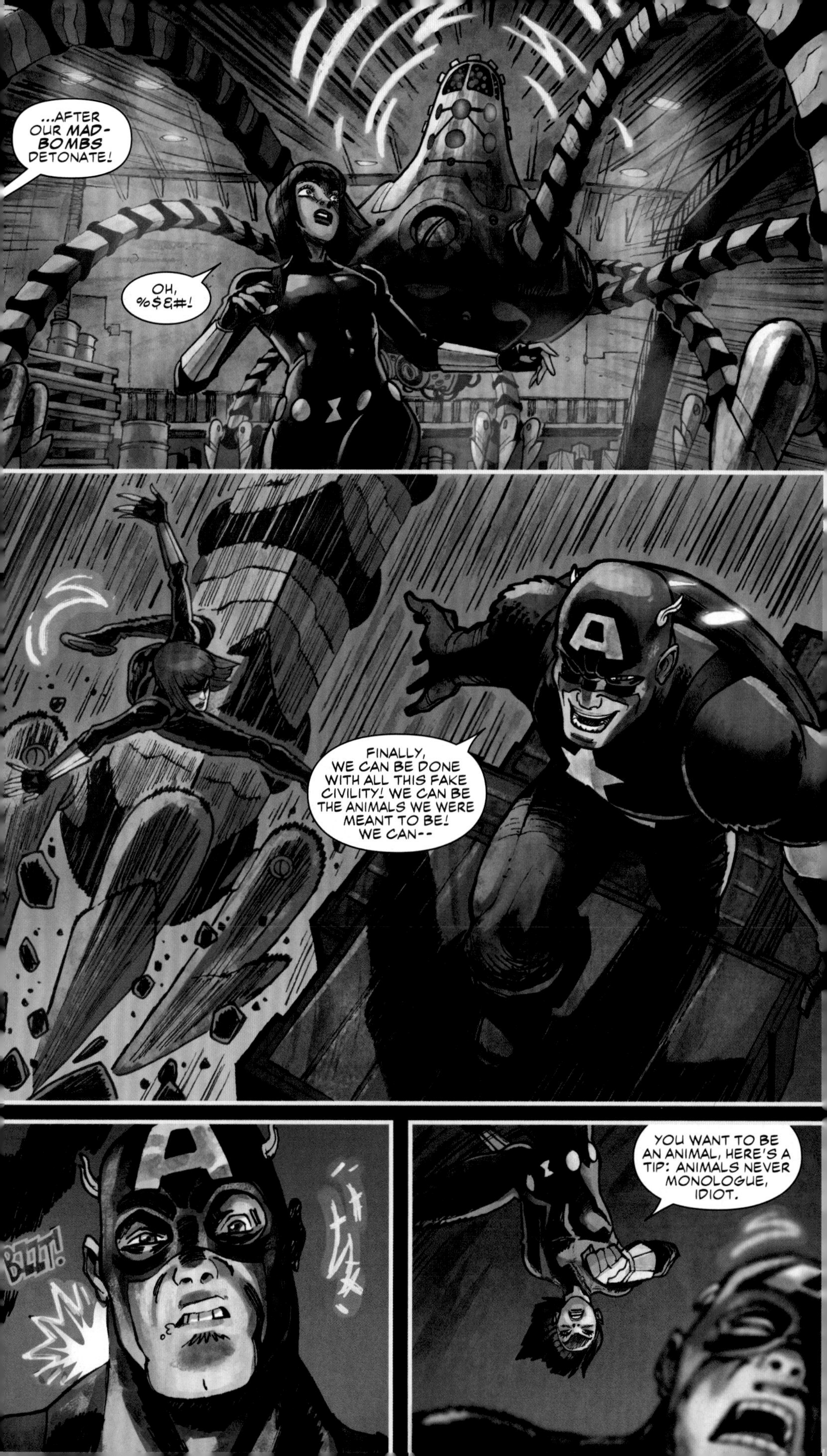
...AFTER OUR MAD-BOMBS DETONATE!
OH, %$&#!
FINALLY, WE CAN BE DONE WITH ALL THIS FAKE CIVILITY! WE CAN BE THE ANIMALS WE WERE MEANT TO BE! WE CAN--
YOU WANT TO BE AN ANIMAL, HERE'S A TIP: ANIMALS NEVER MONOLOGUE, IDIOT.

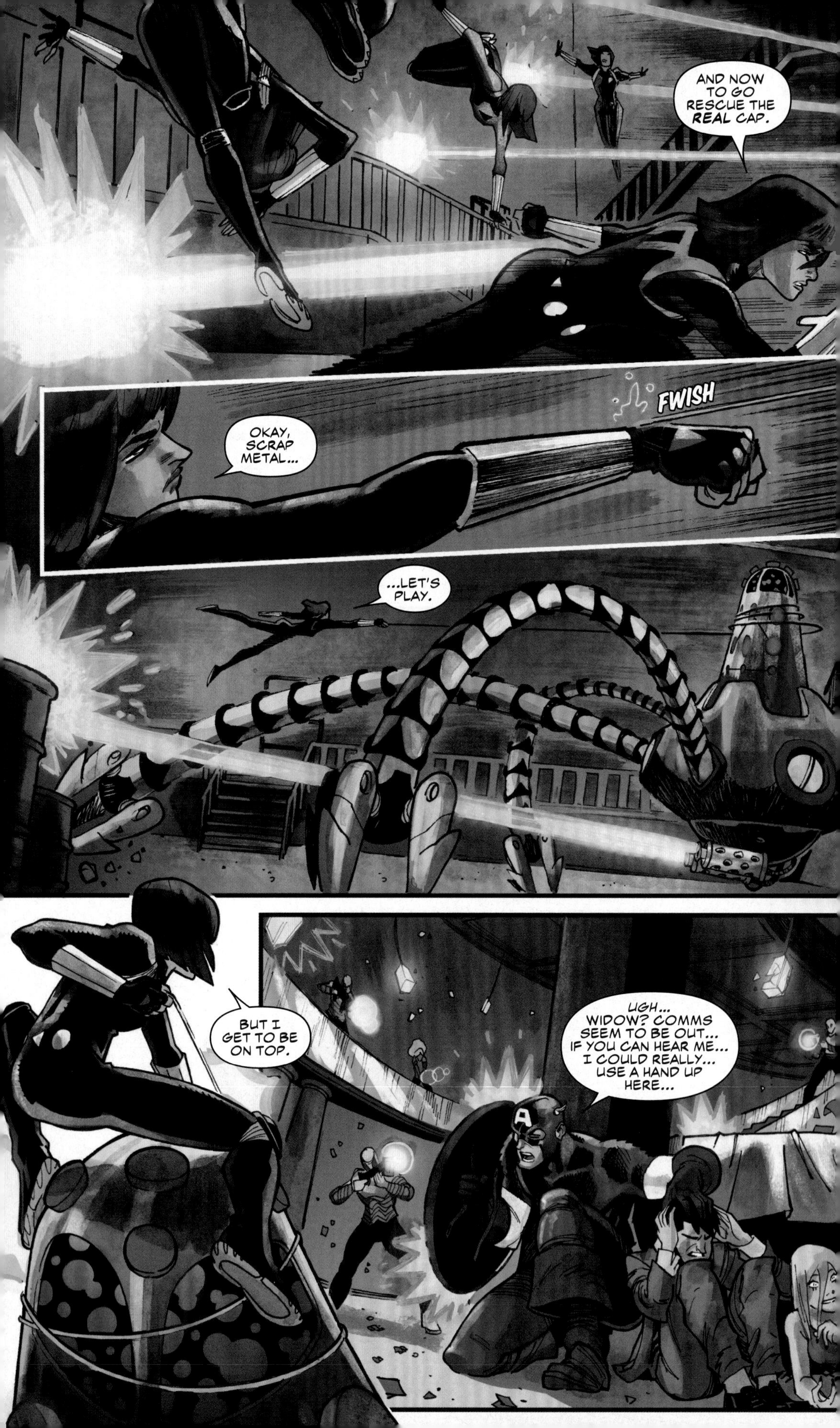
AND NOW TO GO RESCUE THE REAL CAP.
FWISH
OKAY, SCRAP METAL...
...LET'S PLAY.
BUT I GET TO BE ON TOP.
UGH... WIDOW? COMMS SEEM TO BE OUT... IF YOU CAN HEAR ME... I COULD REALLY... USE A HAND UP HERE...

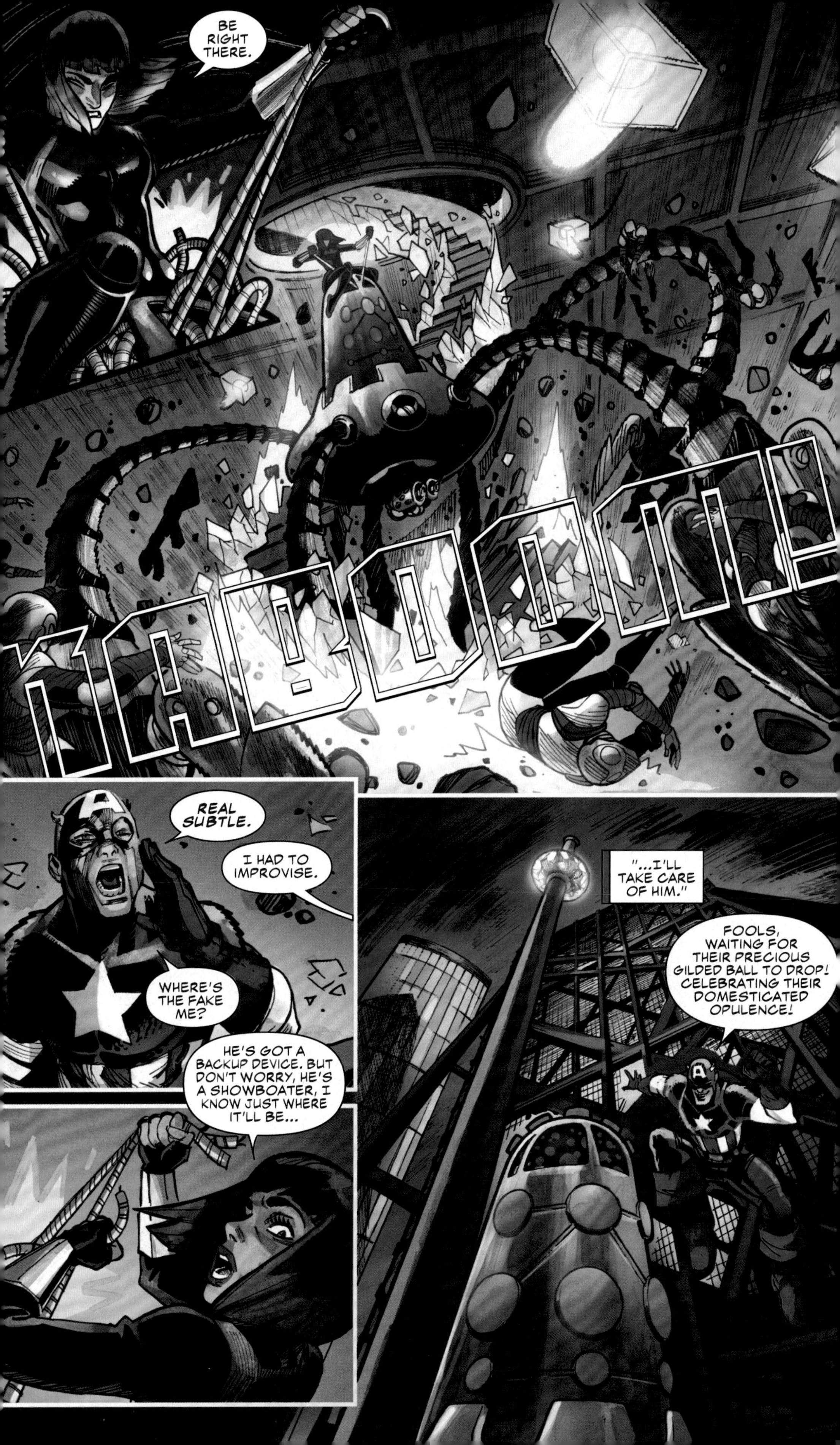
BE RIGHT THERE.
KABOOM!
REAL SUBTLE.
I HAD TO IMPROVISE.
WHERE'S THE FAKE ME?
HE'S GOT A BACKUP DEVICE. BUT DON'T WORRY, HE'S A SHOWBOATER, I KNOW JUST WHERE IT'LL BE...
"...I'LL TAKE CARE OF HIM."
FOOLS, WAITING FOR THEIR PRECIOUS GILDED BALL TO DROP! CELEBRATING THEIR DOMESTICATED OPULENCE!

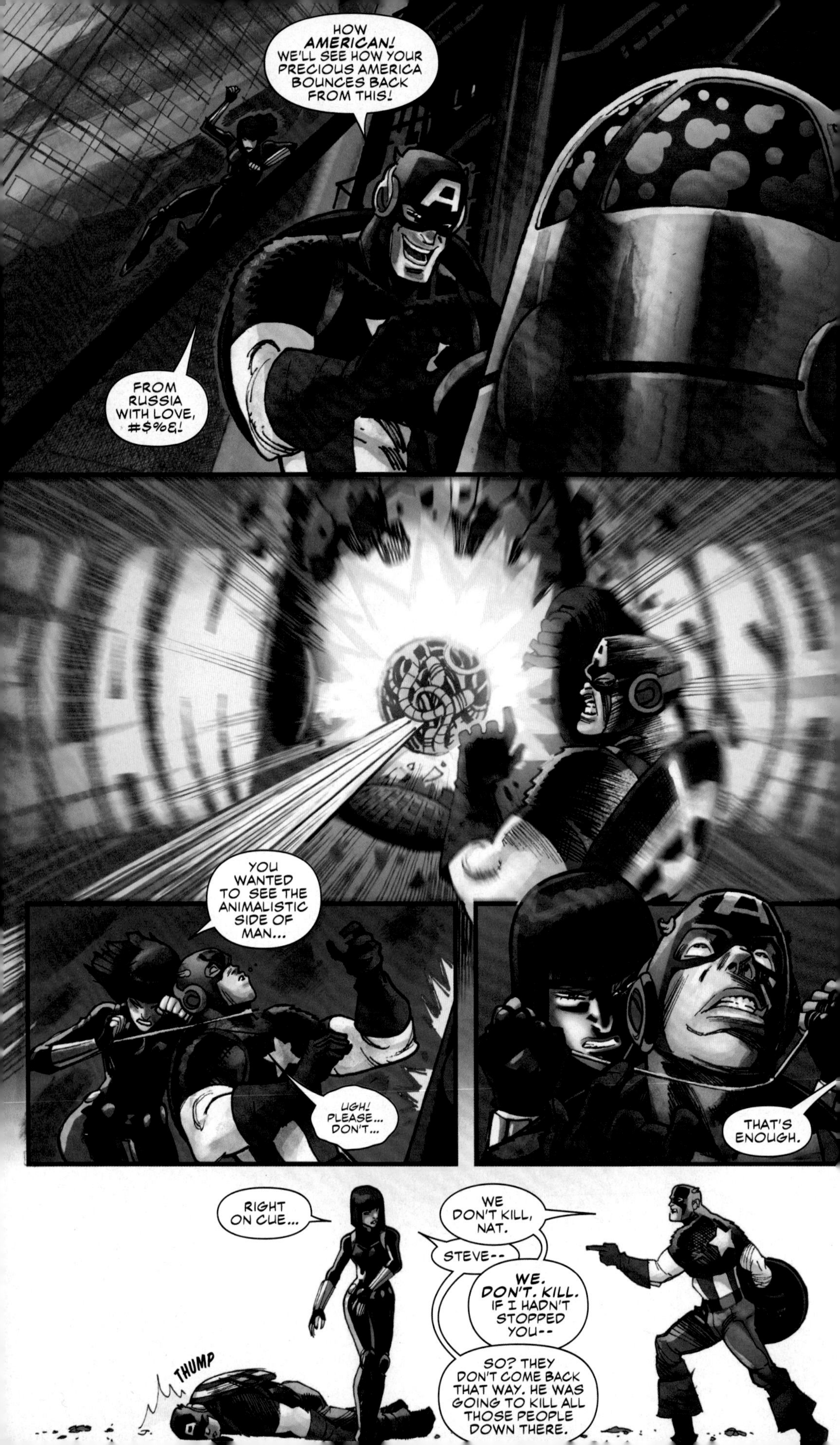
HOW AMERICAN! WE'LL SEE HOW YOUR PRECIOUS AMERICA BOUNCES BACK FROM THIS!
FROM RUSSIA WITH LOVE, #$%&!
YOU WANTED TO SEE THE ANIMALISTIC SIDE OF MAN...
UGH! PLEASE... DON'T...
THAT'S ENOUGH.
RIGHT ON CUE...
WE DON'T KILL, NAT.
STEVE--
WE. DON'T. KILL. IF I HADN'T STOPPED YOU--
SO? THEY DON'T COME BACK THAT WAY. HE WAS GOING TO KILL ALL THOSE PEOPLE DOWN THERE.
THUMP

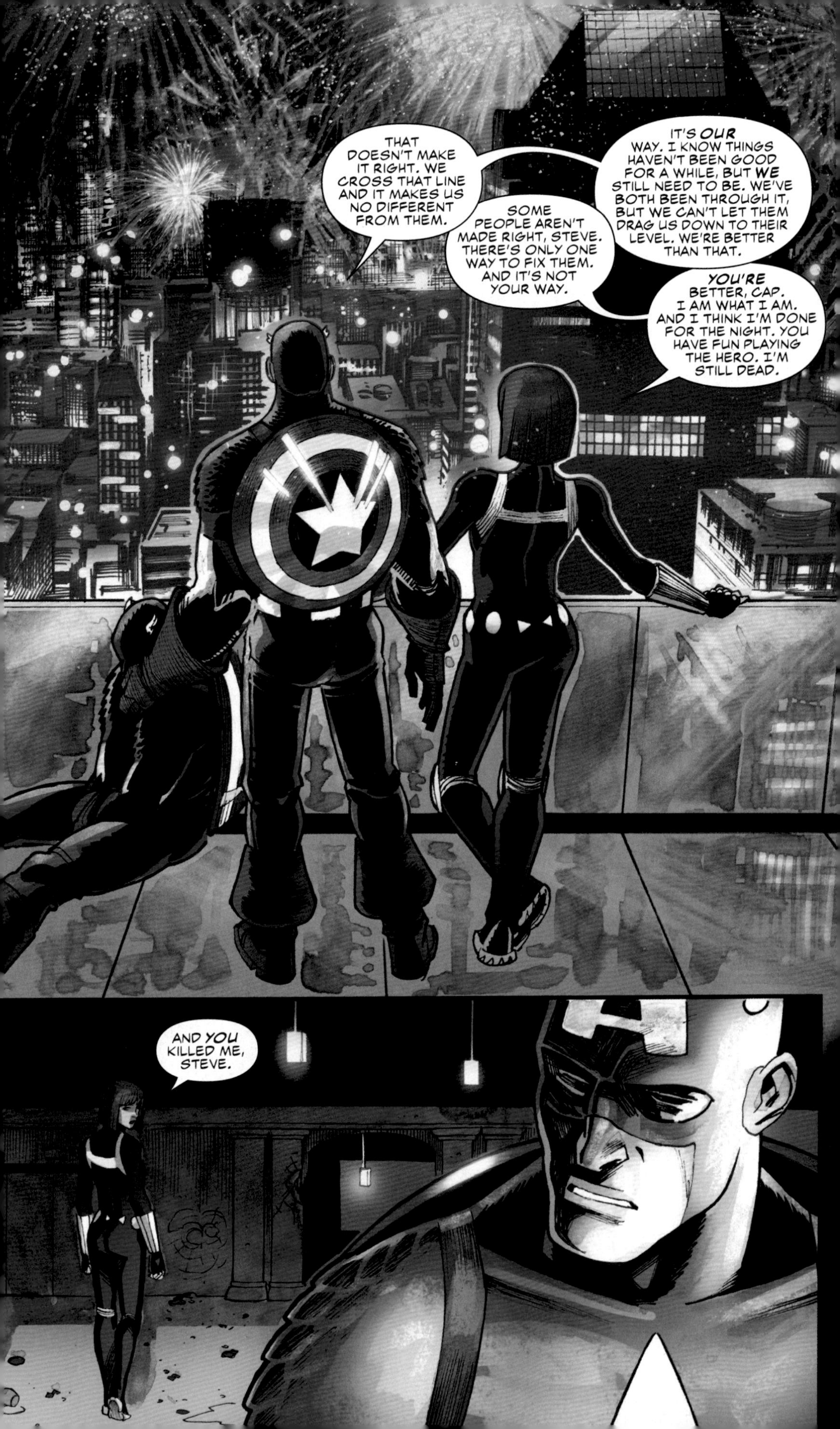

THAT DOESN'T MAKE IT RIGHT. WE CROSS THAT LINE AND IT MAKES US NO DIFFERENT FROM THEM.
SOME PEOPLE AREN'T MADE RIGHT, STEVE. THERE'S ONLY ONE WAY TO FIX THEM. AND IT'S NOT YOUR WAY.
IT'S OUR WAY. I KNOW THINGS HAVEN'T BEEN GOOD FOR A WHILE, BUT WE STILL NEED TO BE. WE'VE BOTH BEEN THROUGH IT, BUT WE CAN'T LET THEM DRAG US DOWN TO THEIR LEVEL. WE'RE BETTER THAN THAT.
YOU'RE BETTER, CAP. I AM WHAT I AM. AND I THINK I'M DONE FOR THE NIGHT. YOU HAVE FUN PLAYING THE HERO. I'M STILL DEAD.
AND YOU KILLED ME, STEVE.

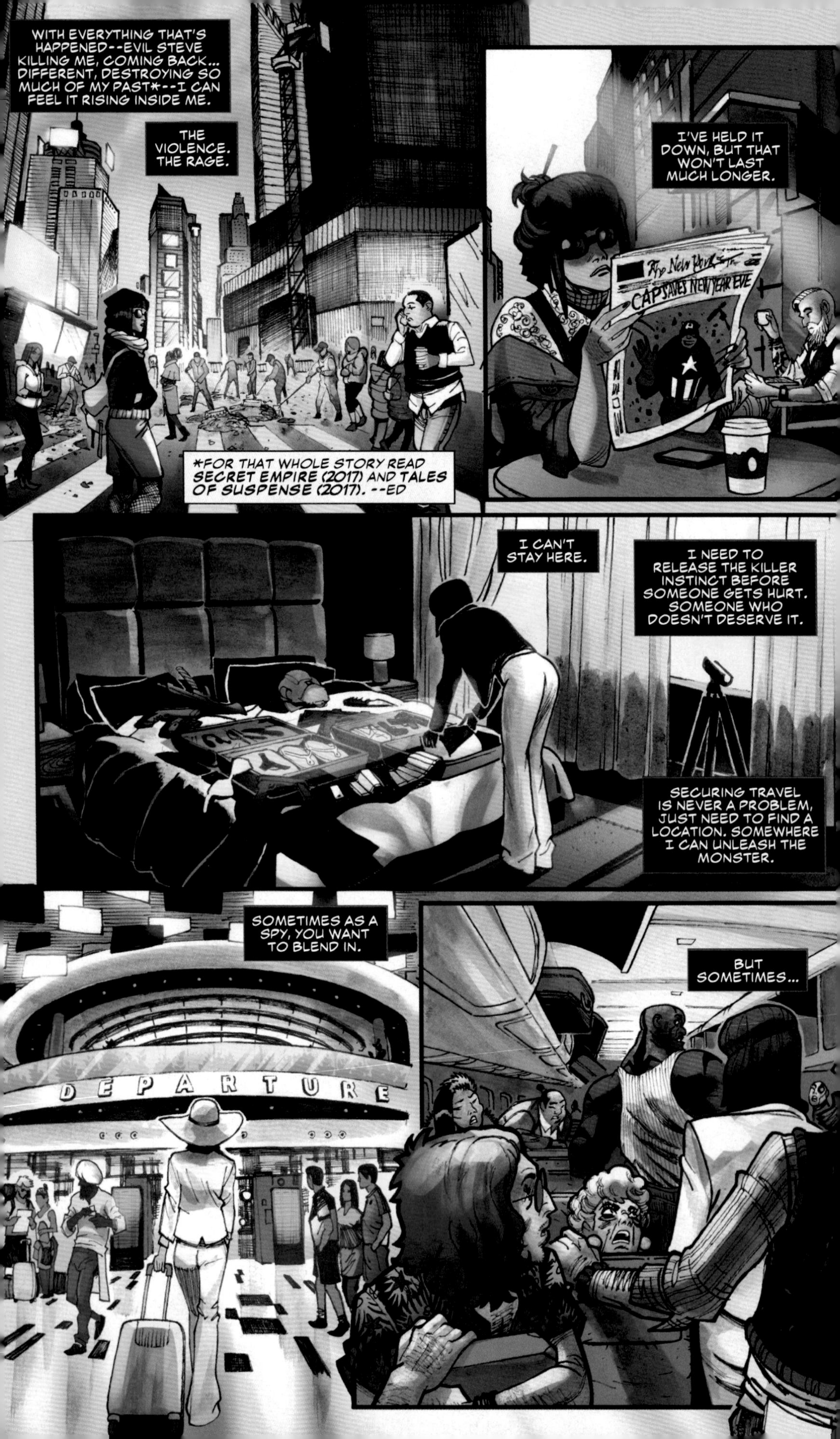
WITH EVERYTHING THAT'S HAPPENED--EVIL STEVE KILLING ME, COMING BACK... DIFFERENT, DESTROYING SO MUCH OF MY PAST*--I CAN FEEL IT RISING INSIDE ME.
THE VIOLENCE. THE RAGE.
*FOR THAT WHOLE STORY READ SECRET EMPIRE (2017) AND TALES OF SUSPENSE (2017). --ED
I'VE HELD IT DOWN, BUT THAT WON'T LAST MUCH LONGER.
CAP SAVES NEW YEAR EVE
I CAN'T STAY HERE.
I NEED TO RELEASE THE KILLER INSTINCT BEFORE SOMEONE GETS HURT. SOMEONE WHO DOESN'T DESERVE IT.
SECURING TRAVEL IS NEVER A PROBLEM, JUST NEED TO FIND A LOCATION. SOMEWHERE I CAN UNLEASH THE MONSTER.
SOMETIMES AS A SPY, YOU WANT TO BLEND IN.
DEPARTURE
BUT SOMETIMES...

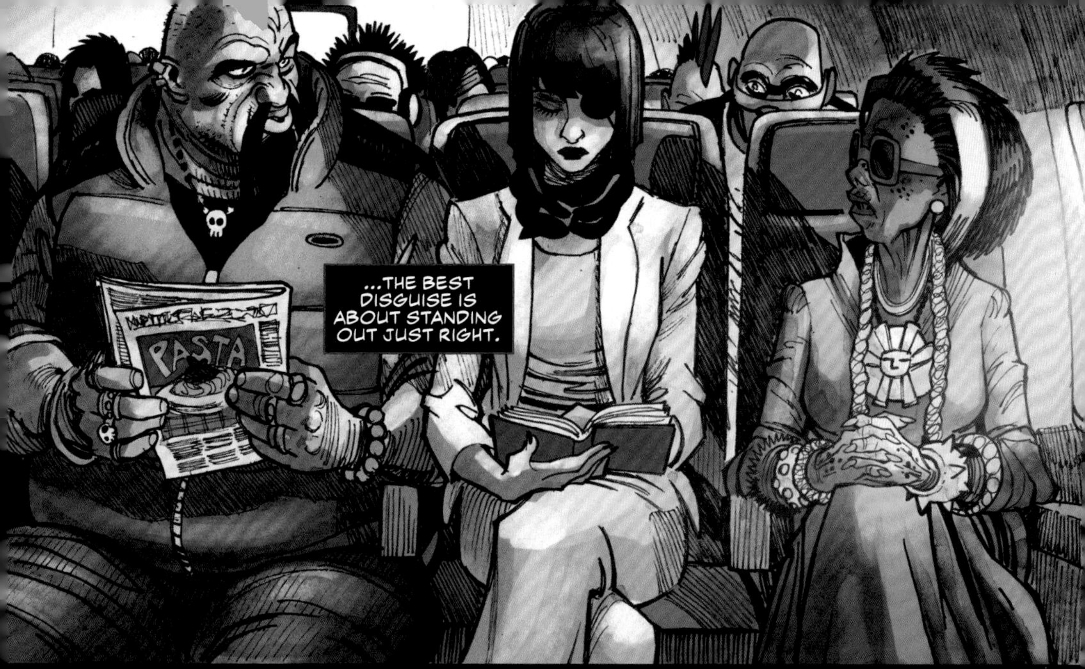
...THE BEST DISGUISE IS ABOUT STANDING OUT JUST RIGHT.
PASTA

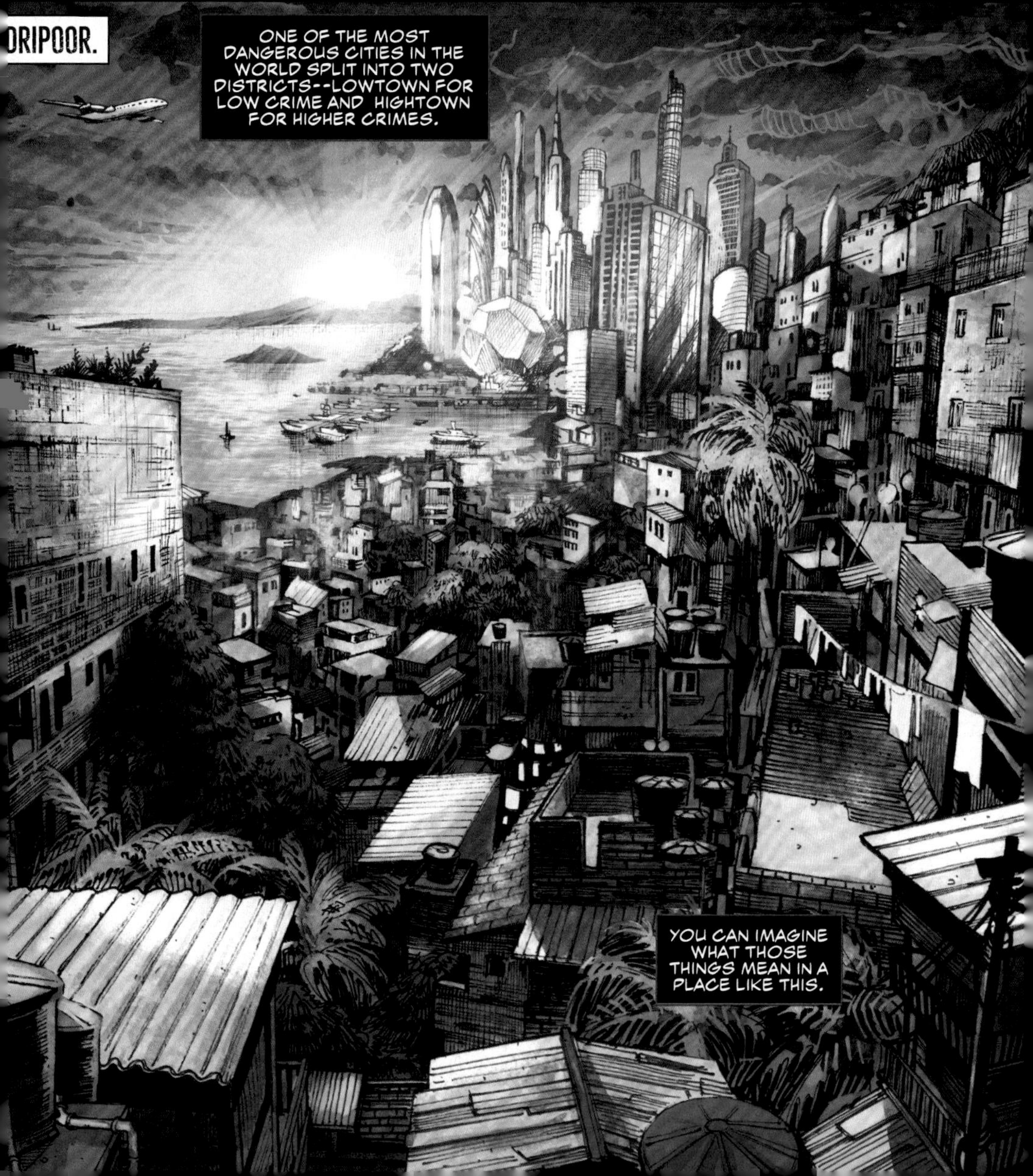
DRIPOOR.
ONE OF THE MOST DANGEROUS CITIES IN THE WORLD SPLIT INTO TWO DISTRICTS--LOWTOWN FOR LOW CRIME AND HIGHTOWN FOR HIGHER CRIMES.
YOU CAN IMAGINE WHAT THOSE THINGS MEAN IN A PLACE LIKE THIS.

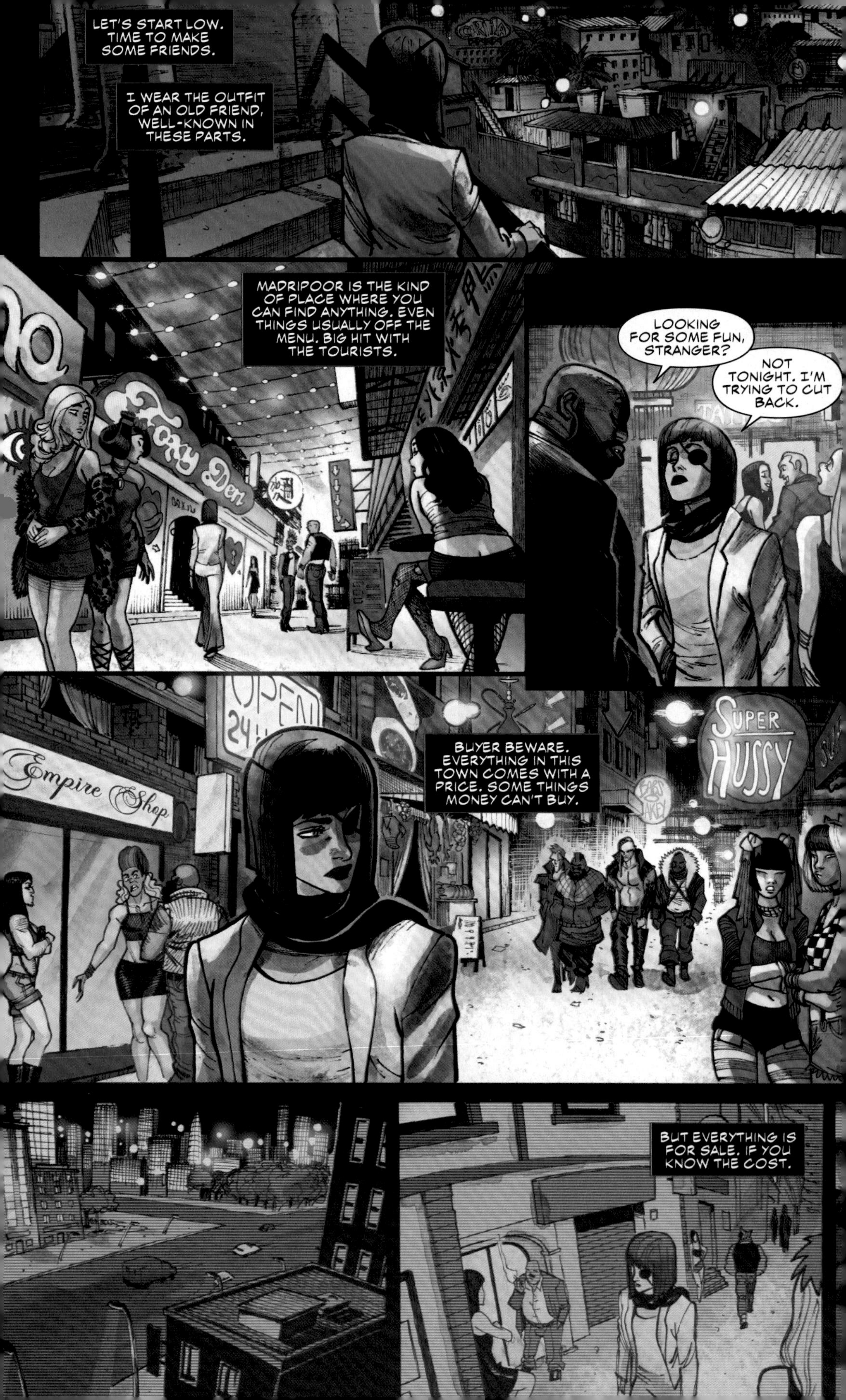
LET'S START LOW. TIME TO MAKE SOME FRIENDS.
I WEAR THE OUTFIT OF AN OLD FRIEND, WELL-KNOWN IN THESE PARTS.
MADRIPOOR IS THE KIND OF PLACE WHERE YOU CAN FIND ANYTHING. EVEN THINGS USUALLY OFF THE MENU. BIG HIT WITH THE TOURISTS.
Foxy Den
LOOKING FOR SOME FUN, STRANGER?
NOT TONIGHT. I'M TRYING TO CUT BACK.
OPEN 24
Empire Shop
BUYER BEWARE. EVERYTHING IN THIS TOWN COMES WITH A PRICE. SOME THINGS MONEY CAN'T BUY.
SUPER HUSSY
BUT EVERYTHING IS FOR SALE. IF YOU KNOW THE COST.

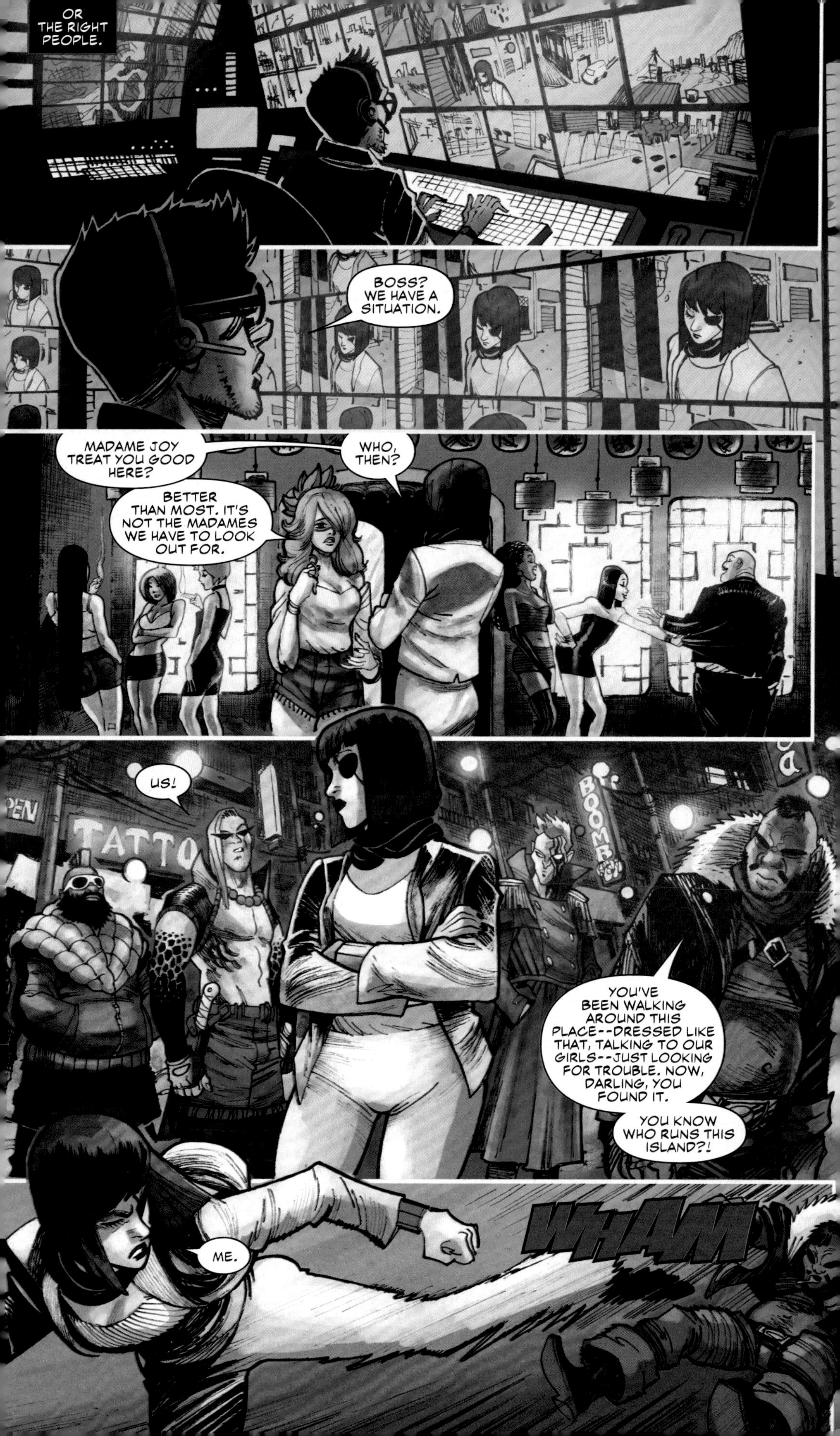

OR THE RIGHT PEOPLE.
BOSS? WE HAVE A SITUATION.
MADAME JOY TREAT YOU GOOD HERE?
WHO, THEN?
BETTER THAN MOST. IT'S NOT THE MADAMES WE HAVE TO LOOK OUT FOR.
US!
TATTO
BOOMB
YOU'VE BEEN WALKING AROUND THIS PLACE--DRESSED LIKE THAT, TALKING TO OUR GIRLS--JUST LOOKING FOR TROUBLE. NOW, DARLING, YOU FOUND IT.
YOU KNOW WHO RUNS THIS ISLAND?!
ME.
WHAM

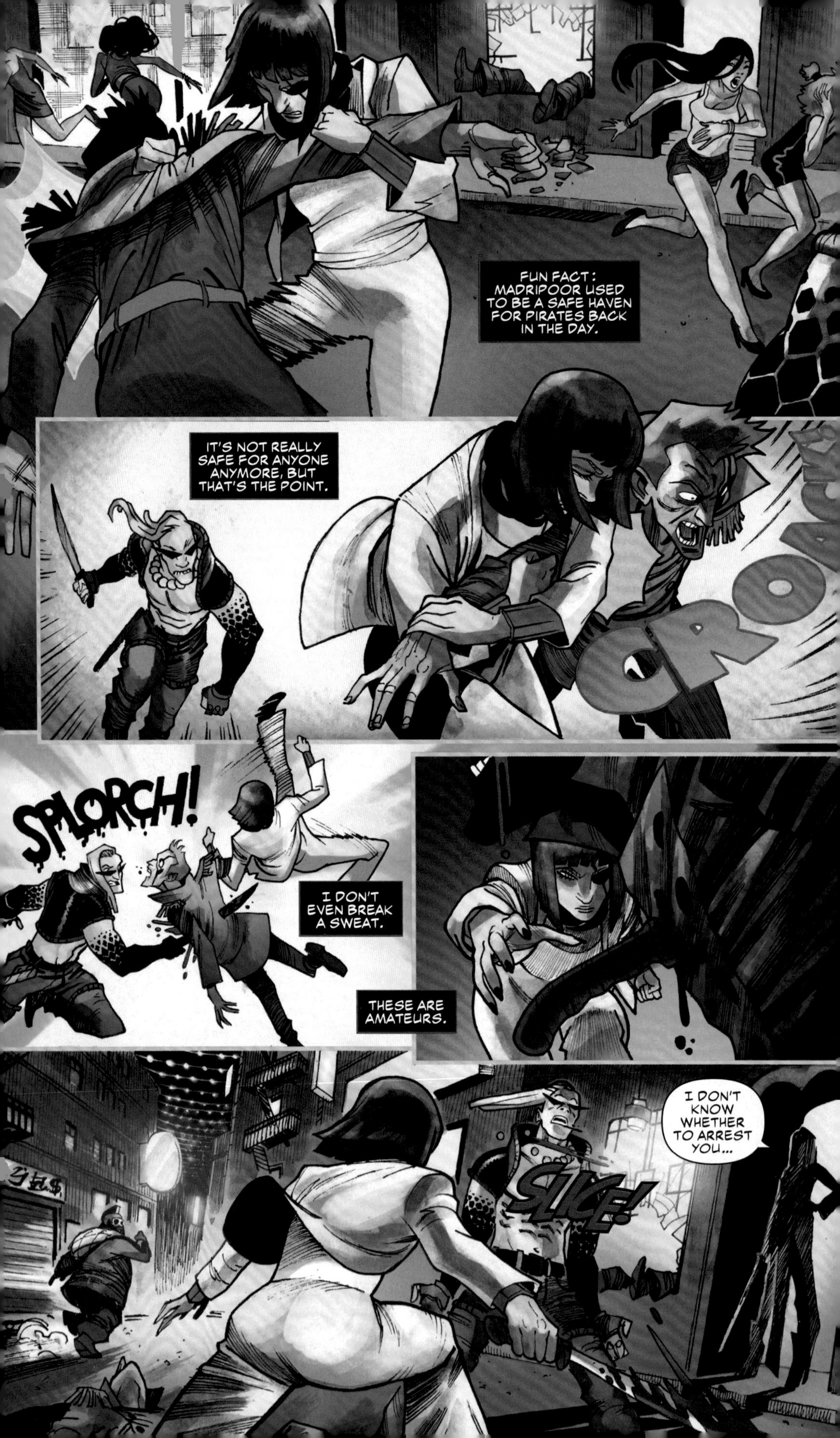
FUN FACT: MADRIPOOR USED TO BE A SAFE HAVEN FOR PIRATES BACK IN THE DAY.
IT'S NOT REALLY SAFE FOR ANYONE ANYMORE, BUT THAT'S THE POINT.
CRONCH!
SPLORCH!
I DON'T EVEN BREAK A SWEAT.
THESE ARE AMATEURS.
SLICE!
I DON'T KNOW WHETHER TO ARREST YOU...

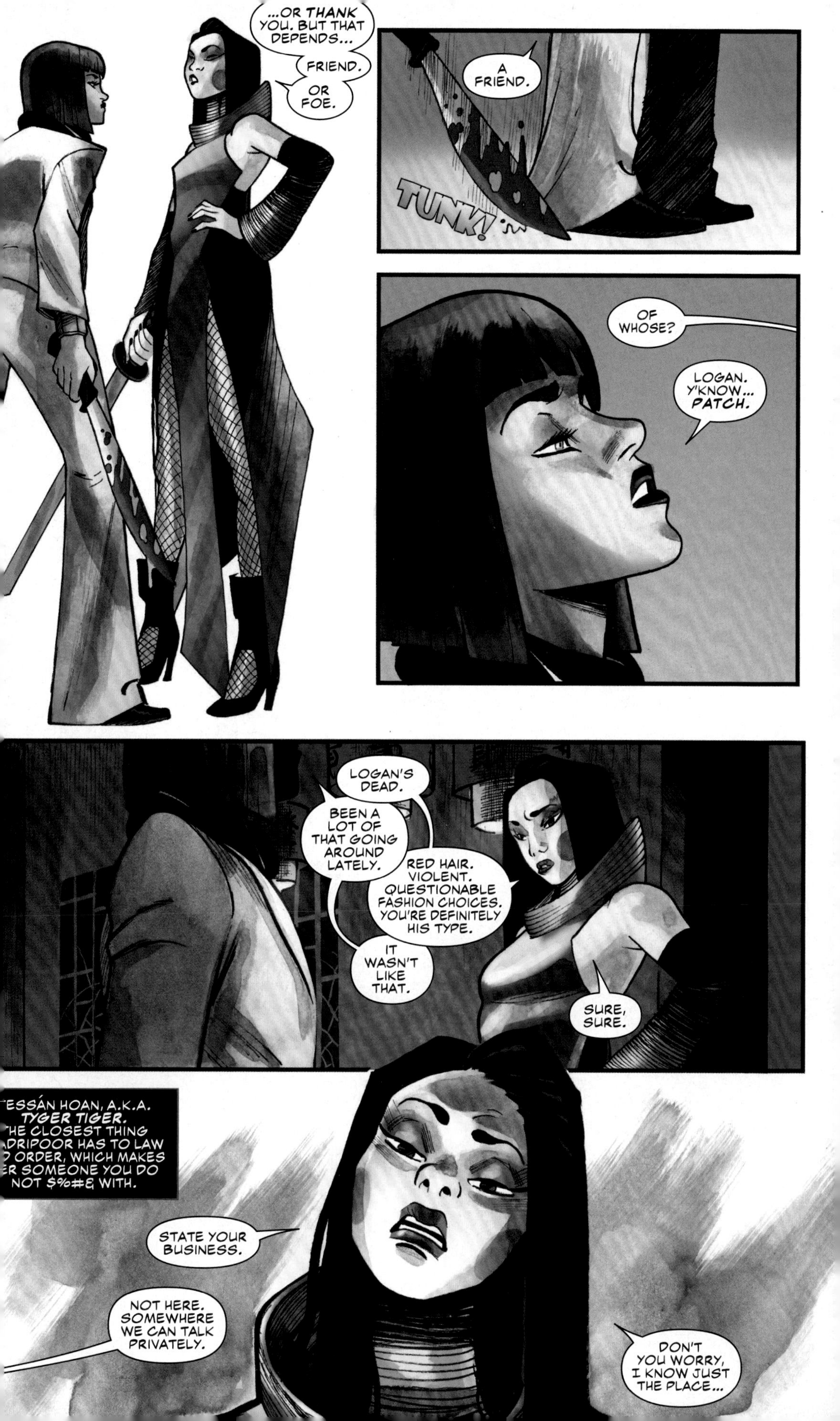
...OR THANK YOU. BUT THAT DEPENDS...
FRIEND.
OR FOE.
A FRIEND.
TUNK!
OF WHOSE?
LOGAN. Y'KNOW... PATCH.
LOGAN'S DEAD.
BEEN A LOT OF THAT GOING AROUND LATELY.
RED HAIR. VIOLENT. QUESTIONABLE FASHION CHOICES. YOU'RE DEFINITELY HIS TYPE.
IT WASN'T LIKE THAT.
SURE, SURE.
TESSÁN HOAN, A.K.A. TYGER TIGER. THE CLOSEST THING MADRIPOOR HAS TO LAW AND ORDER, WHICH MAKES HER SOMEONE YOU DO NOT $%#& WITH.
STATE YOUR BUSINESS.
NOT HERE. SOMEWHERE WE CAN TALK PRIVATELY.
DON'T YOU WORRY, I KNOW JUST THE PLACE...

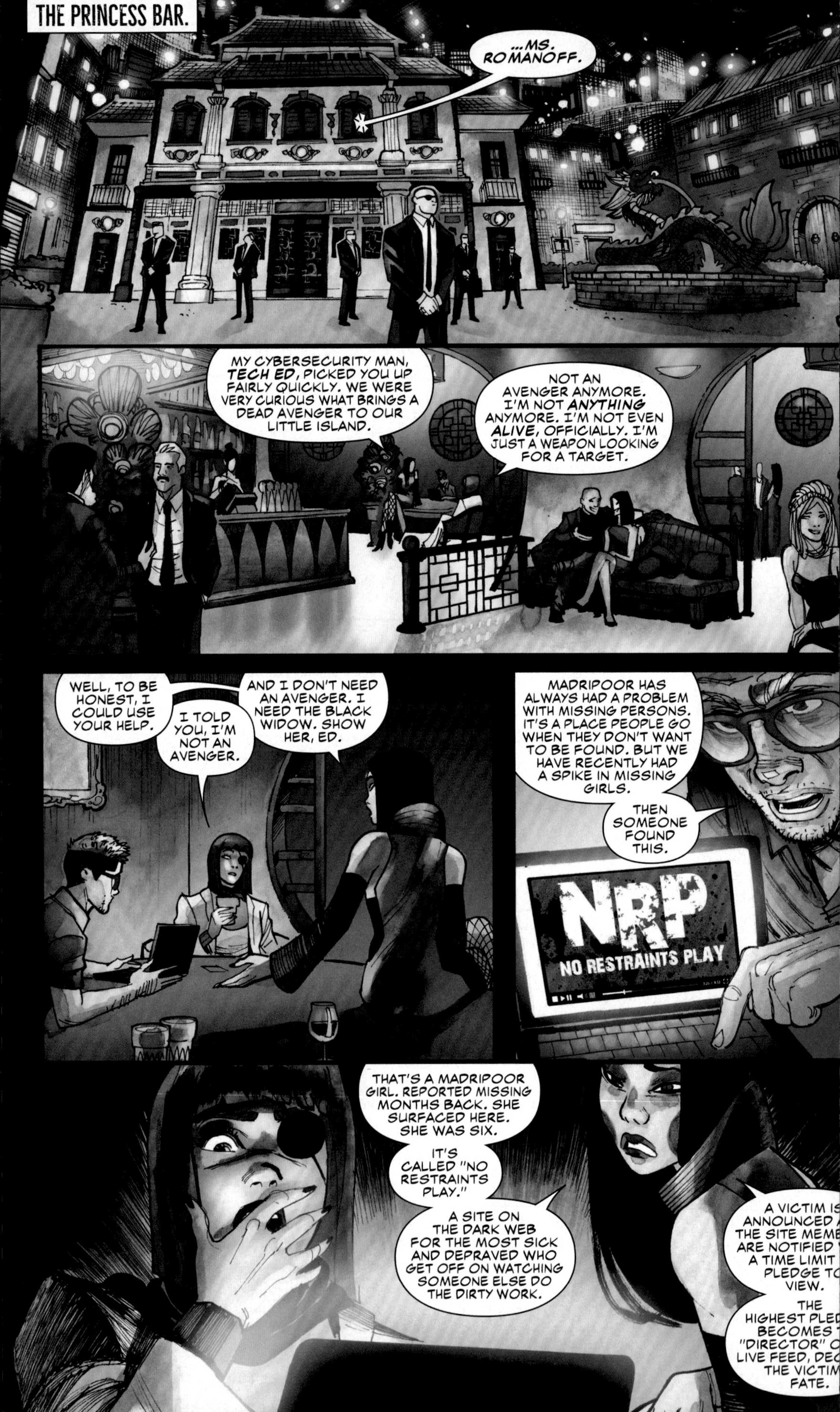
THE PRINCESS BAR.
...MS. ROMANOFF.
MY CYBERSECURITY MAN, TECH ED, PICKED YOU UP FAIRLY QUICKLY. WE WERE VERY CURIOUS WHAT BRINGS A DEAD AVENGER TO OUR LITTLE ISLAND.
NOT AN AVENGER ANYMORE. I'M NOT ANYTHING ANYMORE. I'M NOT EVEN ALIVE, OFFICIALLY. I'M JUST A WEAPON LOOKING FOR A TARGET.
WELL, TO BE HONEST, I COULD USE YOUR HELP.
I TOLD YOU, I'M NOT AN AVENGER.
AND I DON'T NEED AN AVENGER. I NEED THE BLACK WIDOW. SHOW HER, ED.
MADRIPOOR HAS ALWAYS HAD A PROBLEM WITH MISSING PERSONS. IT'S A PLACE PEOPLE GO WHEN THEY DON'T WANT TO BE FOUND. BUT WE HAVE RECENTLY HAD A SPIKE IN MISSING GIRLS.
THEN SOMEONE FOUND THIS.
NRP
NO RESTRAINTS PLAY
THAT'S A MADRIPOOR GIRL. REPORTED MISSING MONTHS BACK. SHE SURFACED HERE. SHE WAS SIX.
IT'S CALLED "NO RESTRAINTS PLAY."
A SITE ON THE DARK WEB FOR THE MOST SICK AND DEPRAVED WHO GET OFF ON WATCHING SOMEONE ELSE DO THE DIRTY WORK.
A VICTIM IS ANNOUNCED A THE SITE MEME ARE NOTIFIED A TIME LIMIT PLEDGE TO VIEW.
THE HIGHEST PLED BECOMES "DIRECTOR" O LIVE FEED, DEC THE VICTIM FATE.

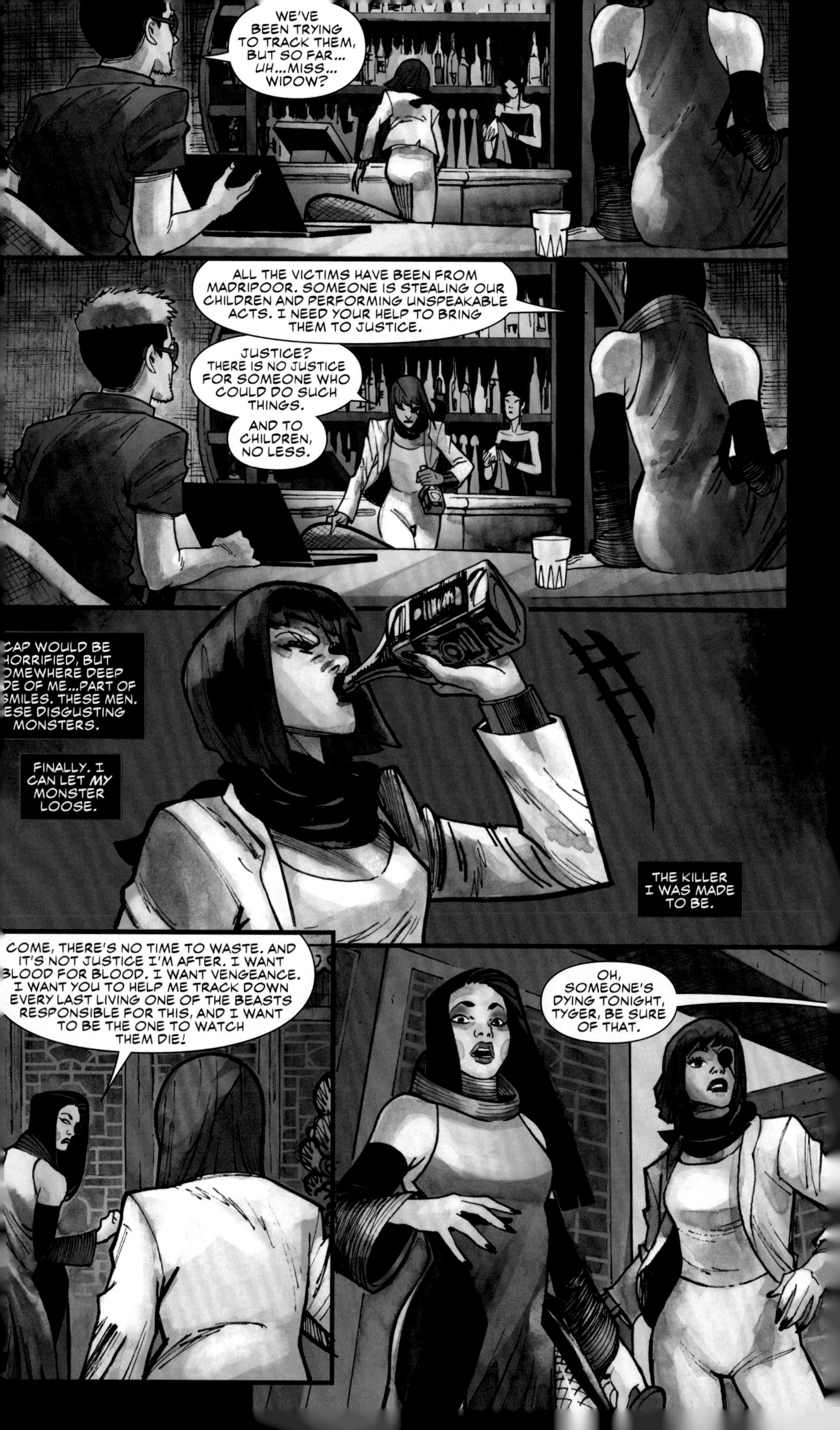

WE'VE BEEN TRYING TO TRACK THEM, BUT SO FAR... UH...MISS... WIDOW?
ALL THE VICTIMS HAVE BEEN FROM MADRIPOOR. SOMEONE IS STEALING OUR CHILDREN AND PERFORMING UNSPEAKABLE ACTS. I NEED YOUR HELP TO BRING THEM TO JUSTICE.
JUSTICE? THERE IS NO JUSTICE FOR SOMEONE WHO COULD DO SUCH THINGS.
AND TO CHILDREN, NO LESS.
CAP WOULD BE HORRIFIED, BUT OMEWHERE DEEP DE OF ME...PART OF SMILES. THESE MEN. ESE DISGUSTING MONSTERS.
FINALLY. I CAN LET *MY* MONSTER LOOSE.
THE KILLER I WAS MADE TO BE.
COME, THERE'S NO TIME TO WASTE. AND IT'S NOT JUSTICE I'M AFTER. I WANT BLOOD FOR BLOOD. I WANT VENGEANCE. I WANT YOU TO HELP ME TRACK DOWN EVERY LAST LIVING ONE OF THE BEASTS RESPONSIBLE FOR THIS, AND I WANT TO BE THE ONE TO WATCH THEM DIE!
OH, SOMEONE'S DYING TONIGHT, TYGER, BE SURE OF THAT.

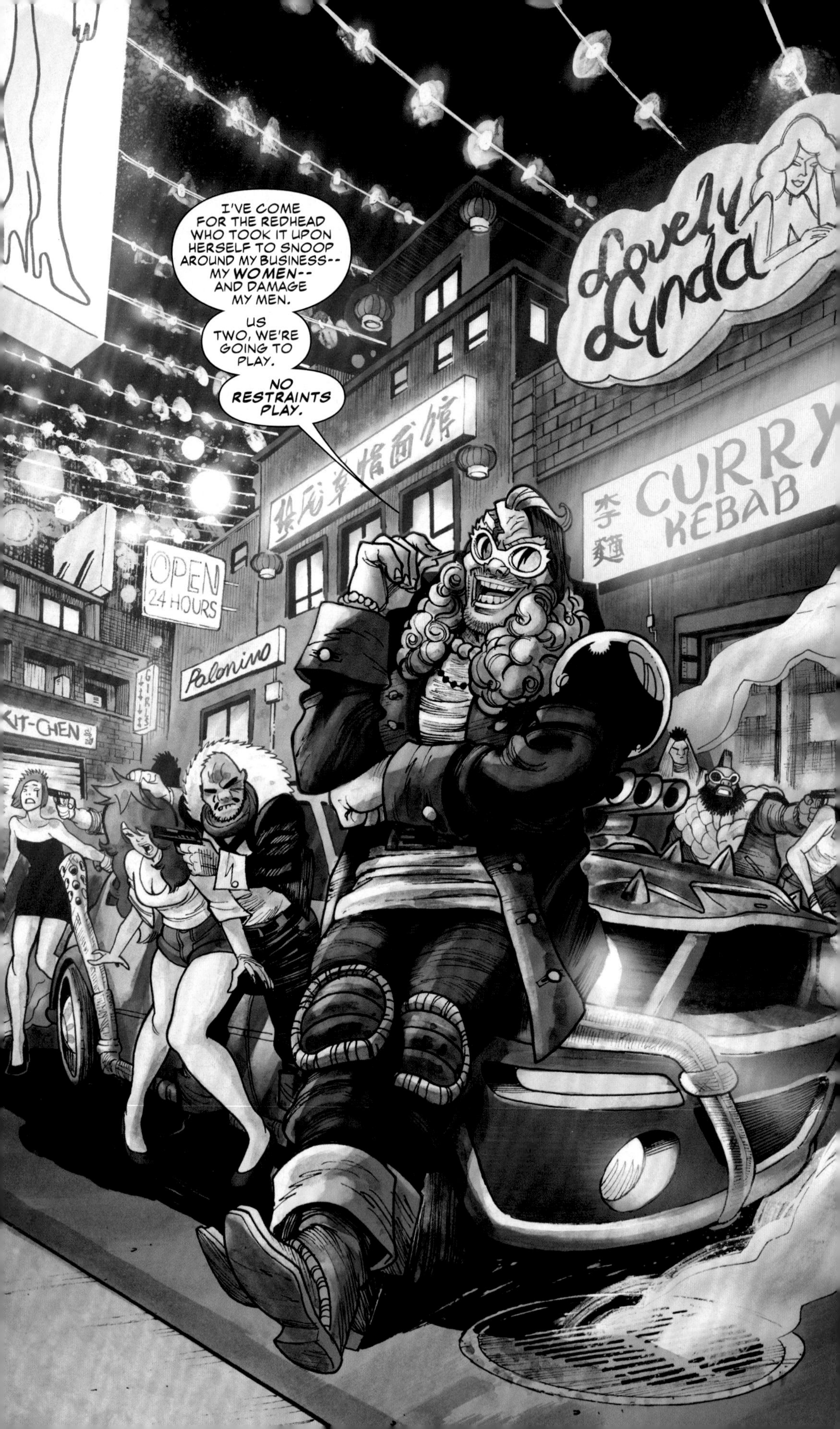
I'VE COME FOR THE REDHEAD WHO TOOK IT UPON HERSELF TO SNOOP AROUND MY BUSINESS-- MY WOMEN-- AND DAMAGE MY MEN.
US TWO, WE'RE GOING TO PLAY.
NO RESTRAINTS PLAY.
Lovely Lynda
CURRY KEBAB
OPEN 24 HOURS
Palomino
GIRLS
KIT-CHEN

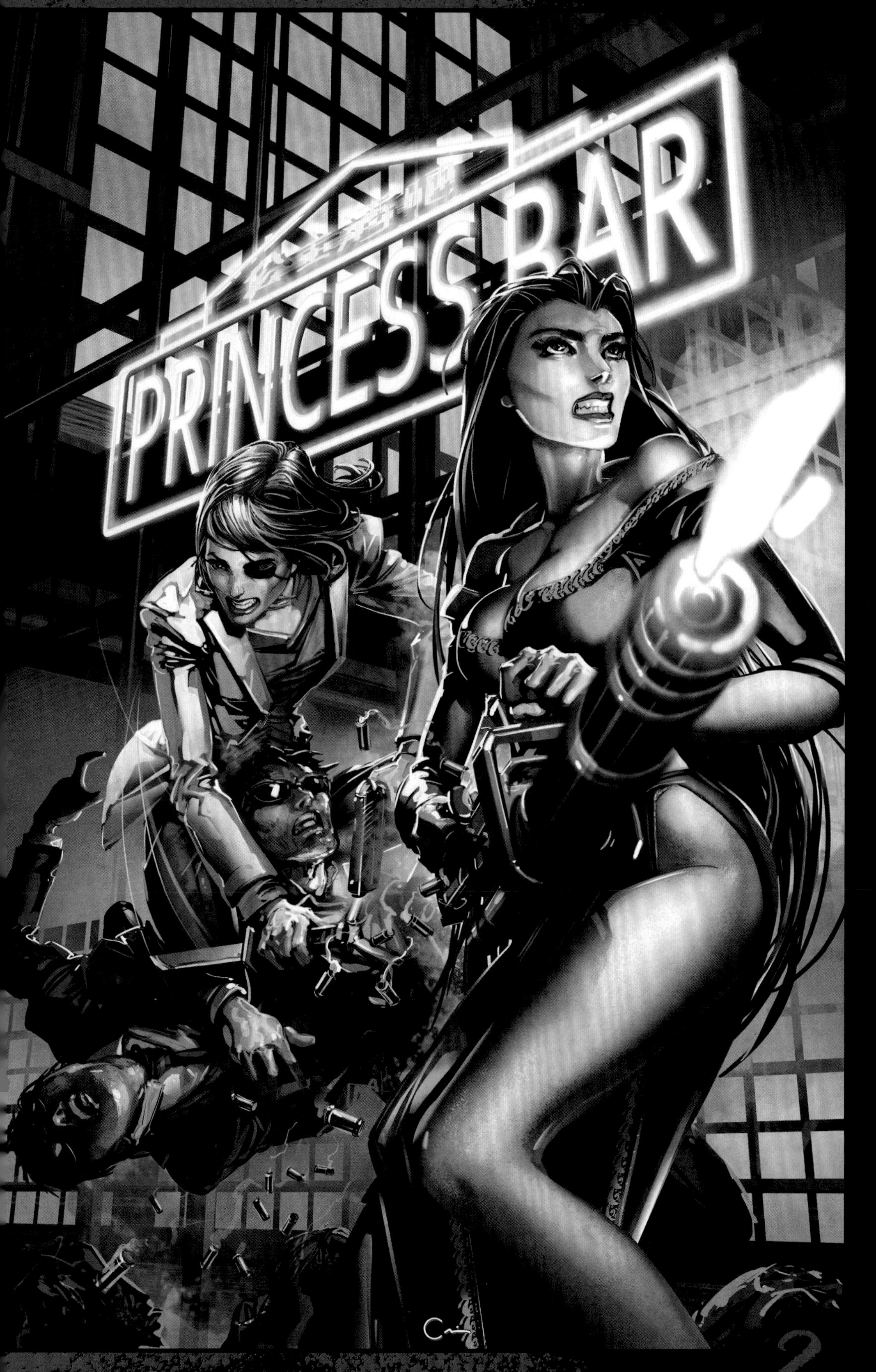
PRINCESS BAR

2

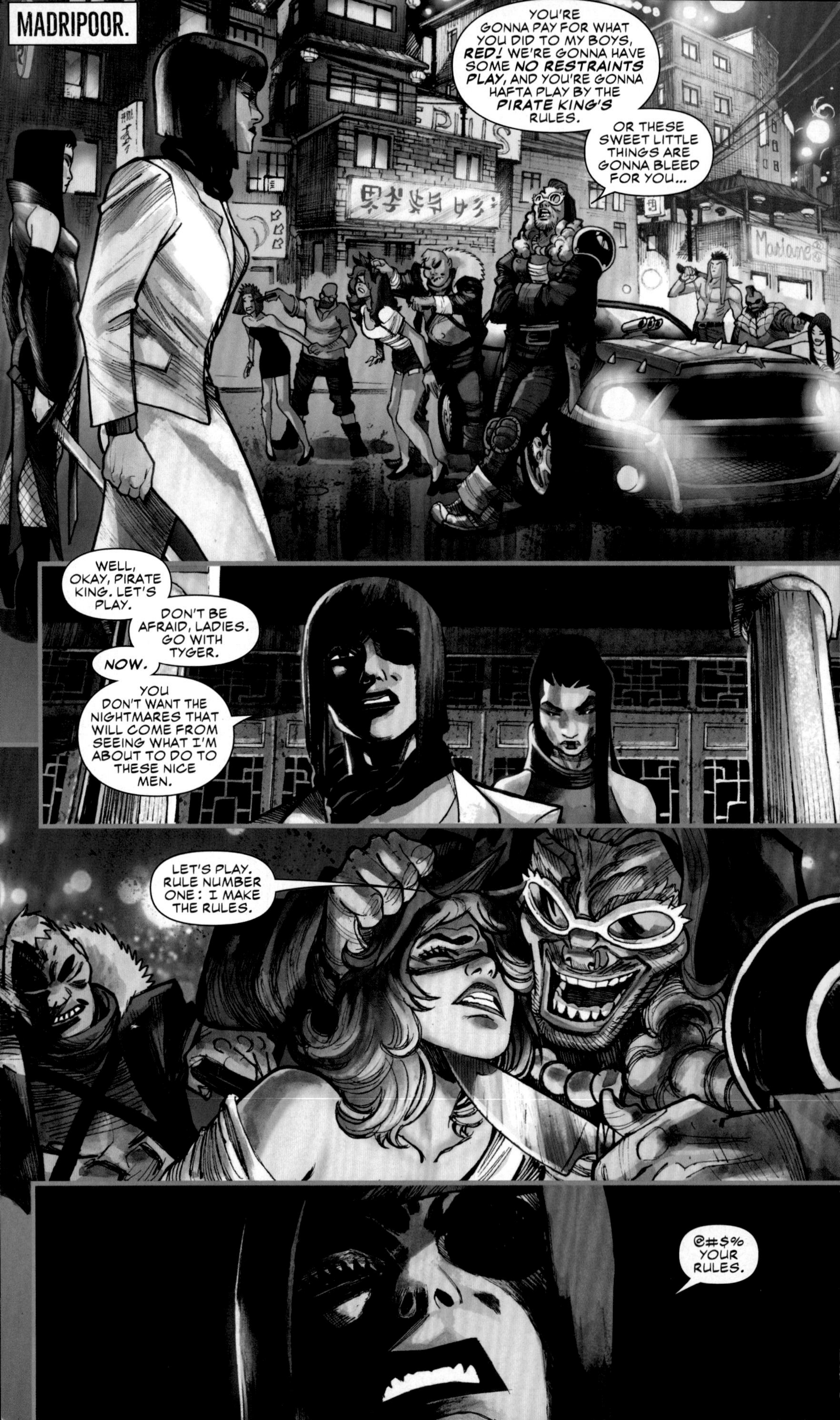
MADRIPOOR.
YOU'RE GONNA PAY FOR WHAT YOU DID TO MY BOYS, RED! WE'RE GONNA HAVE SOME NO RESTRAINTS PLAY, AND YOU'RE GONNA HAFTA PLAY BY THE PIRATE KING'S RULES.
OR THESE SWEET LITTLE THINGS ARE GONNA BLEED FOR YOU...
WELL, OKAY, PIRATE KING. LET'S PLAY.
DON'T BE AFRAID, LADIES. GO WITH TYGER.
NOW.
YOU DON'T WANT THE NIGHTMARES THAT WILL COME FROM SEEING WHAT I'M ABOUT TO DO TO THESE NICE MEN.
LET'S PLAY. RULE NUMBER ONE: I MAKE THE RULES.
@#$% YOUR RULES.

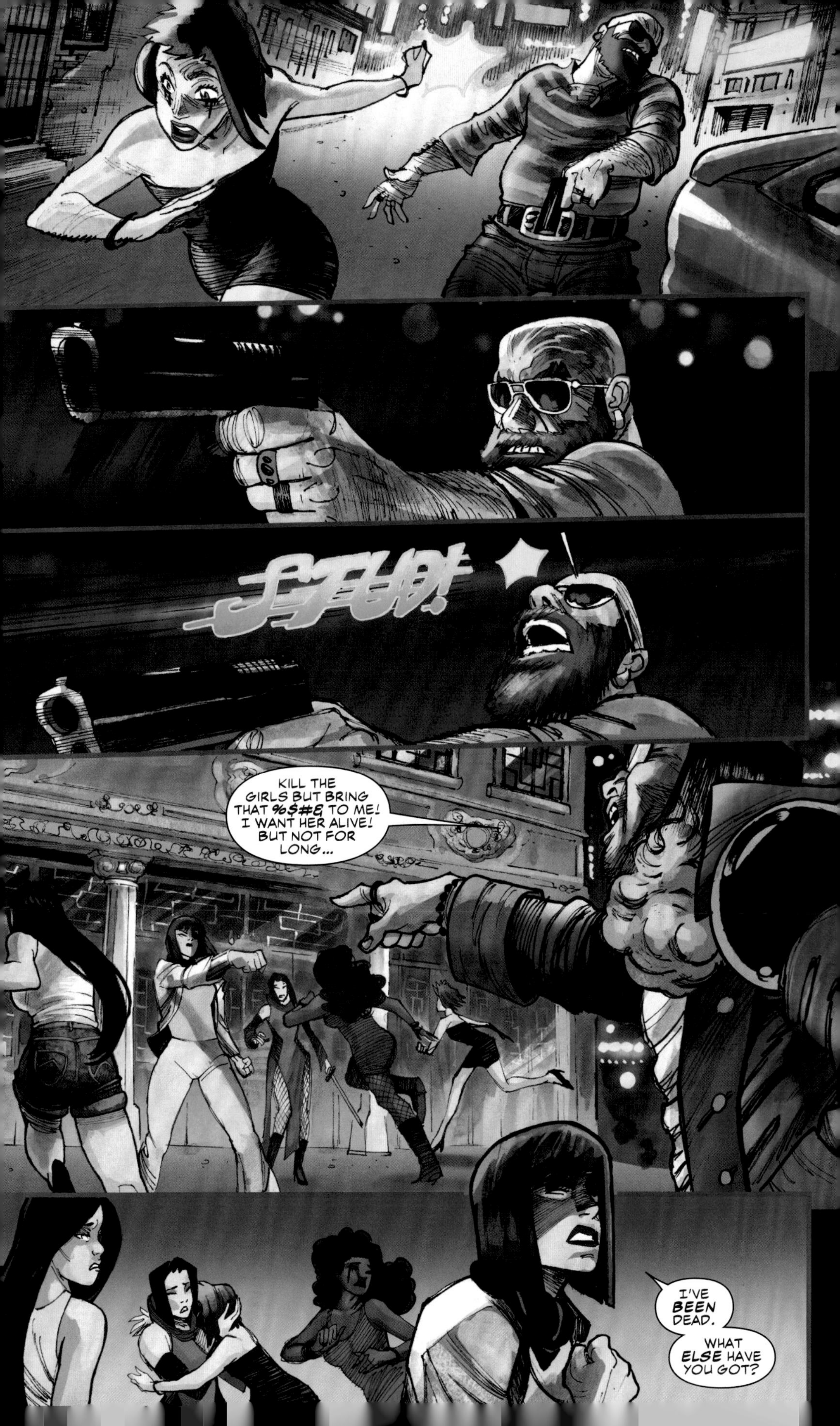
KILL THE GIRLS BUT BRING THAT %$#& TO ME! I WANT HER ALIVE! BUT NOT FOR LONG...
I'VE BEEN DEAD.
WHAT ELSE HAVE YOU GOT?

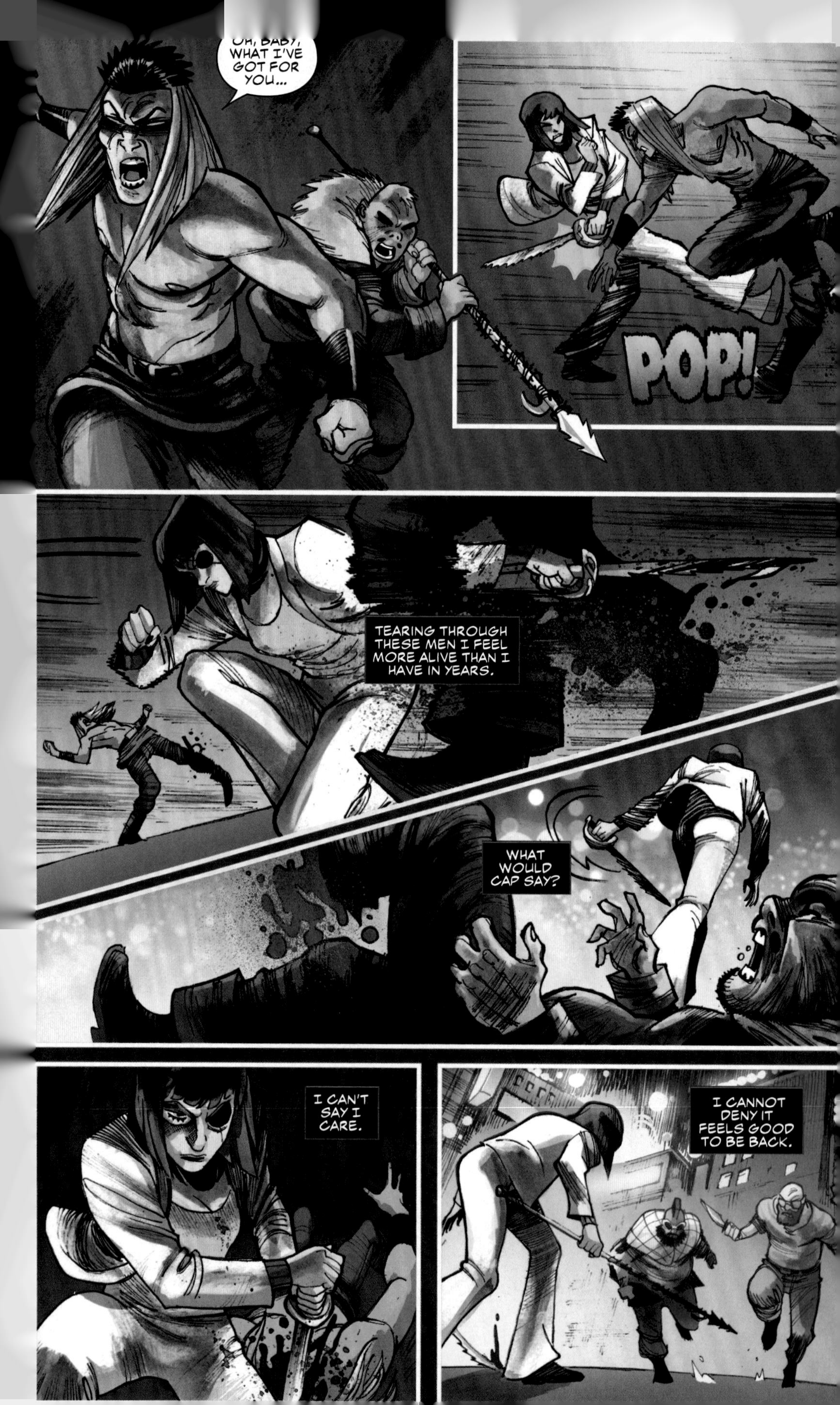
OH, BABY, WHAT I'VE GOT FOR YOU...
POP!
TEARING THROUGH THESE MEN I FEEL MORE ALIVE THAN I HAVE IN YEARS.
WHAT WOULD CAP SAY?
I CAN'T SAY I CARE.
I CANNOT DENY IT FEELS GOOD TO BE BACK.

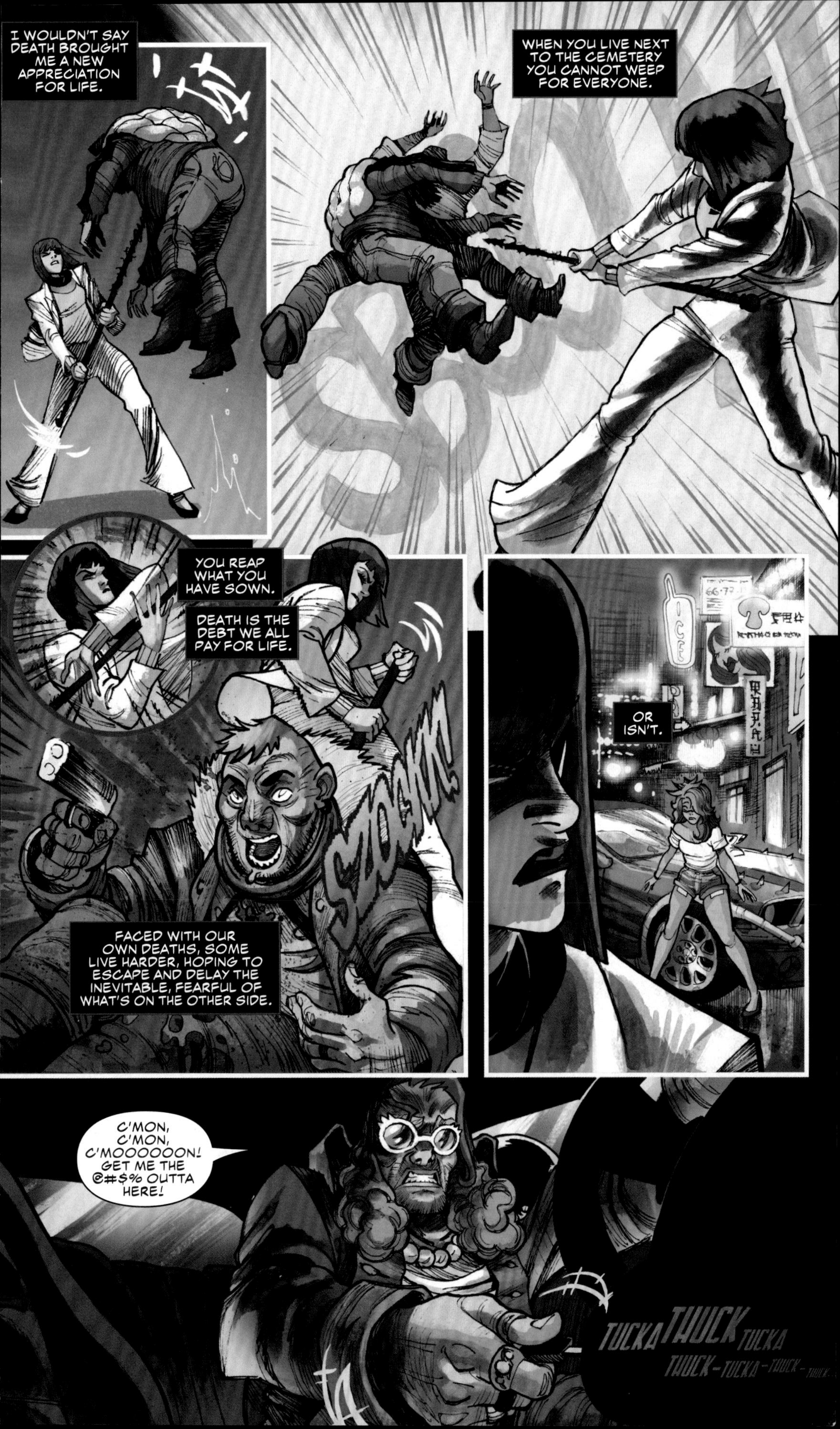
I WOULDN'T SAY DEATH BROUGHT ME A NEW APPRECIATION FOR LIFE.
WHEN YOU LIVE NEXT TO THE CEMETERY YOU CANNOT WEEP FOR EVERYONE.
YOU REAP WHAT YOU HAVE SOWN.
DEATH IS THE DEBT WE ALL PAY FOR LIFE.
STOOKK!
FACED WITH OUR OWN DEATHS, SOME LIVE HARDER, HOPING TO ESCAPE AND DELAY THE INEVITABLE, FEARFUL OF WHAT'S ON THE OTHER SIDE.
OR ISN'T.
ICE
C'MON, C'MON, C'MOOOOOON! GET ME THE @#$% OUTTA HERE!
TUCKA THUCK TUCKA
THUCK-TUCKA-THUCK-THUCK...

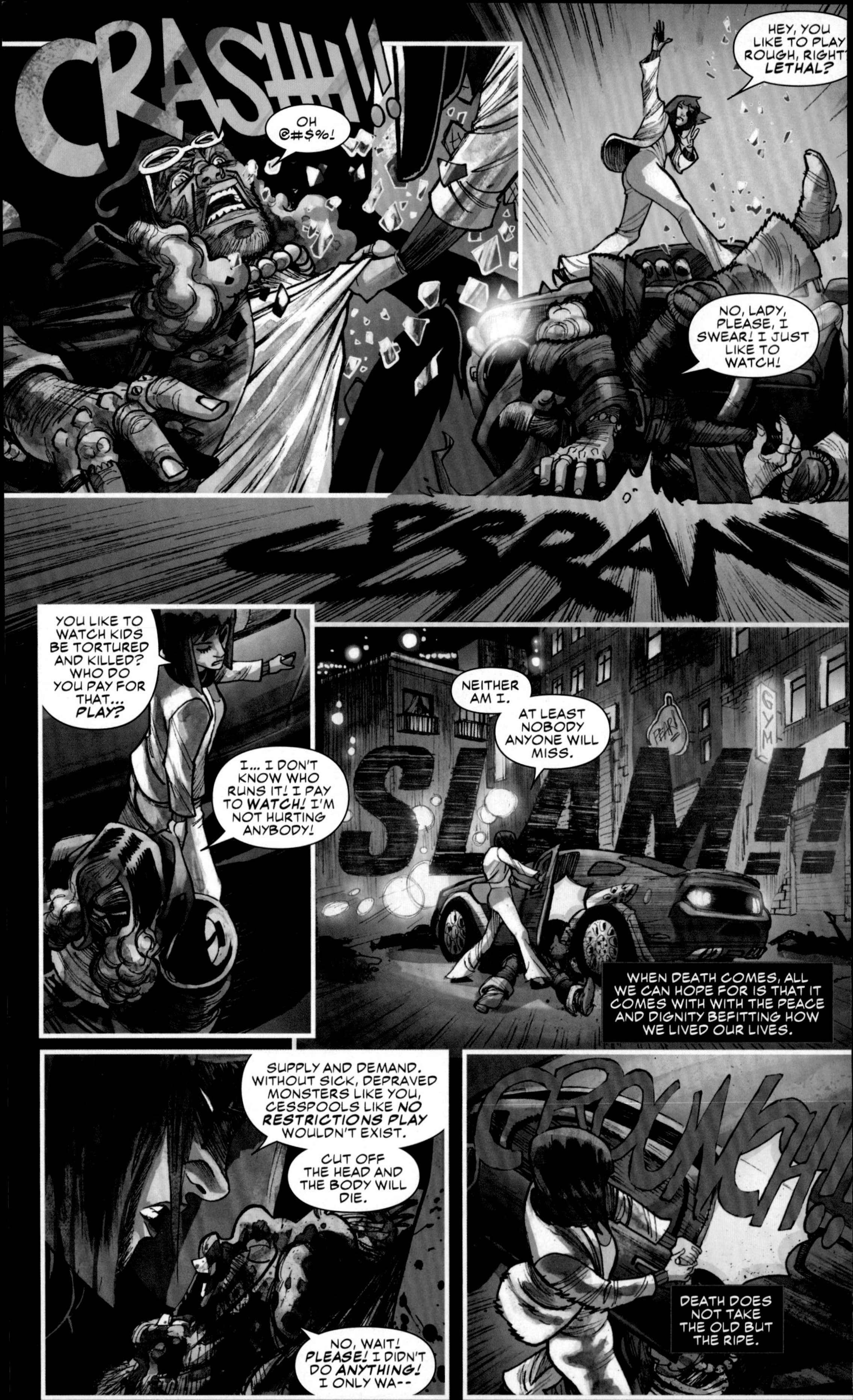
CRASHH!!
OH @#$%!
HEY, YOU LIKE TO PLAY ROUGH, RIGHT LETHAL?
NO, LADY, PLEASE, I SWEAR! I JUST LIKE TO WATCH!
YOU LIKE TO WATCH KIDS BE TORTURED AND KILLED? WHO DO YOU PAY FOR THAT... PLAY?
I... I DON'T KNOW WHO RUNS IT! I PAY TO WATCH! I'M NOT HURTING ANYBODY!
NEITHER AM I.
AT LEAST NOBODY ANYONE WILL MISS.
SLAM!!
WHEN DEATH COMES, ALL WE CAN HOPE FOR IS THAT IT COMES WITH WITH THE PEACE AND DIGNITY BEFITTING HOW WE LIVED OUR LIVES.
SUPPLY AND DEMAND. WITHOUT SICK, DEPRAVED MONSTERS LIKE YOU, CESSPOOLS LIKE NO RESTRICTIONS PLAY WOULDN'T EXIST.
CUT OFF THE HEAD AND THE BODY WILL DIE.
NO, WAIT! PLEASE! I DIDN'T DO ANYTHING! I ONLY WA--
CRUNCH!!
DEATH DOES NOT TAKE THE OLD BUT THE RIPE.

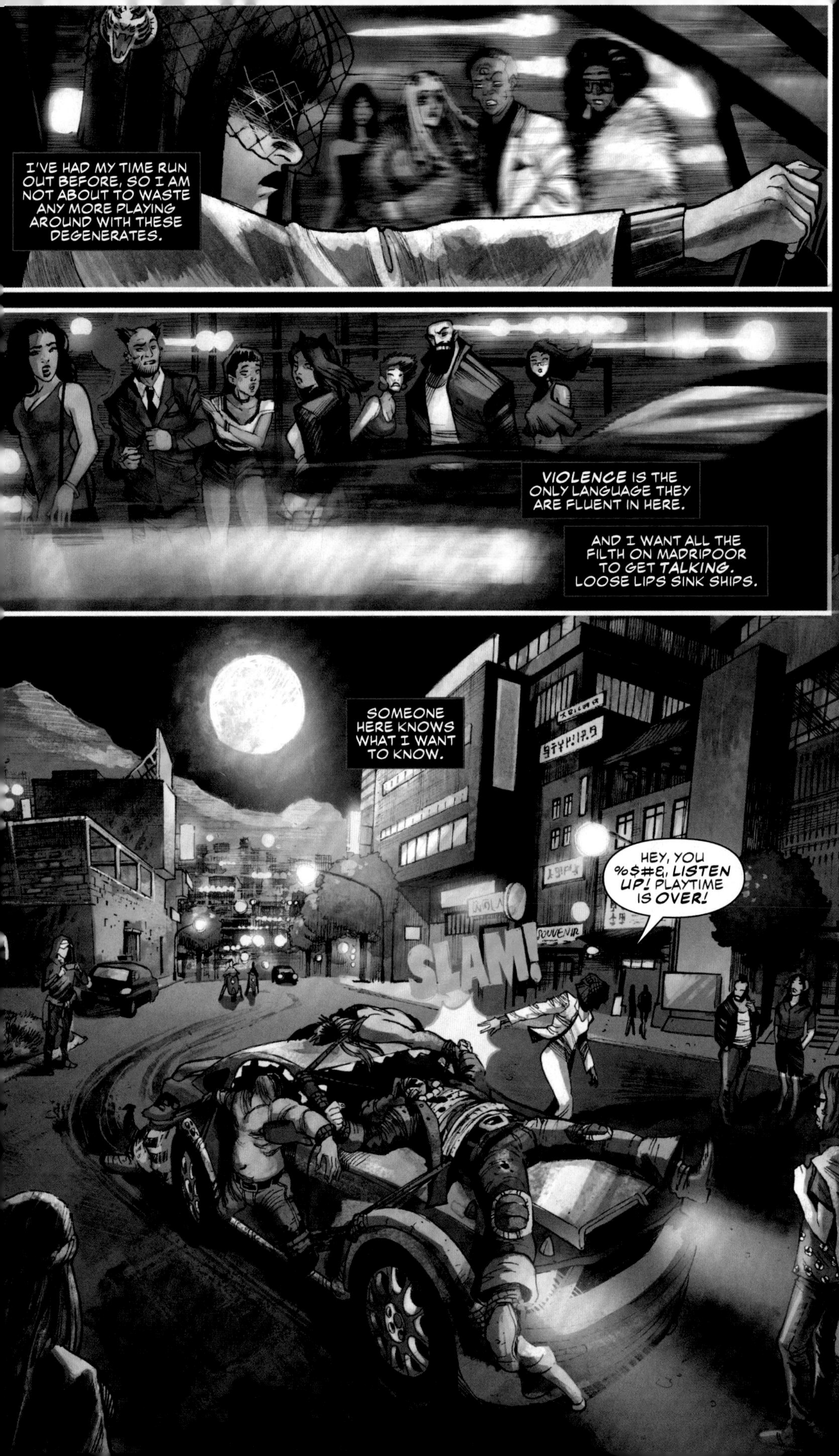
I'VE HAD MY TIME RUN OUT BEFORE, SO I AM NOT ABOUT TO WASTE ANY MORE PLAYING AROUND WITH THESE DEGENERATES.
VIOLENCE IS THE ONLY LANGUAGE THEY ARE FLUENT IN HERE.
AND I WANT ALL THE FILTH ON MADRIPOOR TO GET TALKING. LOOSE LIPS SINK SHIPS.
SOMEONE HERE KNOWS WHAT I WANT TO KNOW.
SLAM!
HEY, YOU %$#&, LISTEN UP! PLAYTIME IS OVER!
SOUVENIR

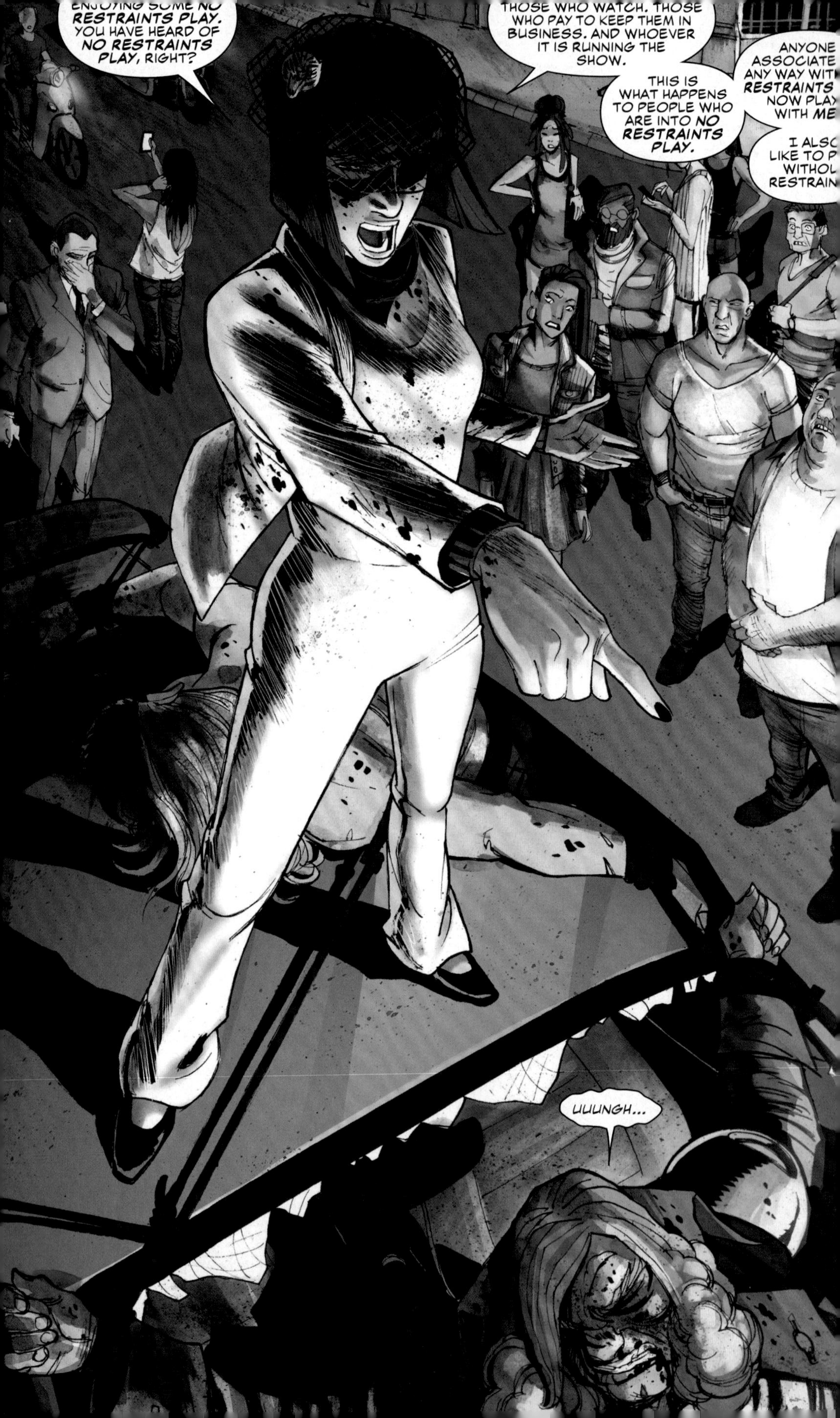
ENJOYING SOME NO RESTRAINTS PLAY. YOU HAVE HEARD OF NO RESTRAINTS PLAY, RIGHT?
THOSE WHO WATCH. THOSE WHO PAY TO KEEP THEM IN BUSINESS. AND WHOEVER IT IS RUNNING THE SHOW.
THIS IS WHAT HAPPENS TO PEOPLE WHO ARE INTO NO RESTRAINTS PLAY.
ANYONE ASSOCIATE ANY WAY WIT RESTRAINTS NOW PLA WITH ME
I ALSO LIKE TO P WITHOU RESTRAIN
UUUNGH...

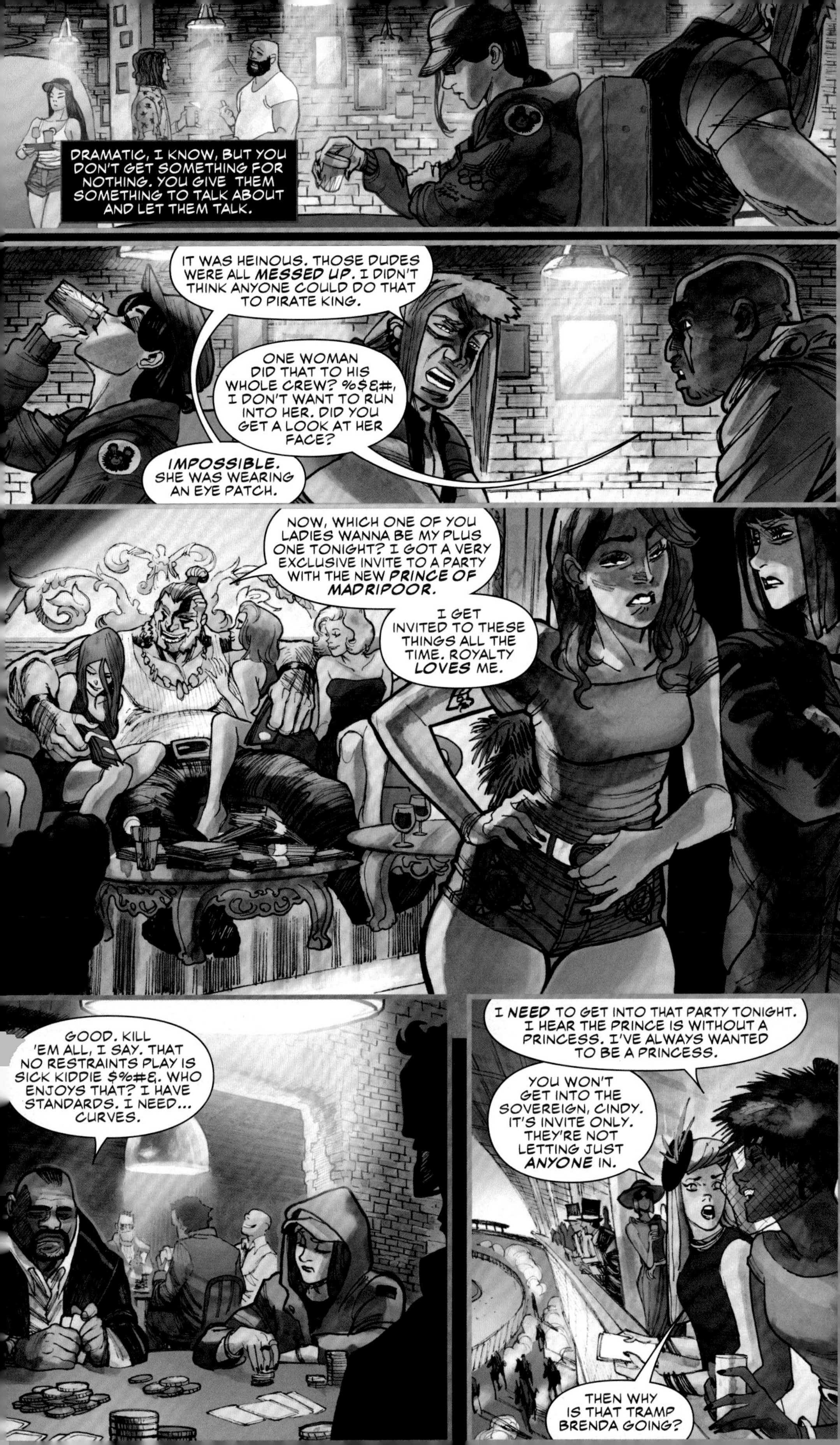
DRAMATIC, I KNOW, BUT YOU DON'T GET SOMETHING FOR NOTHING. YOU GIVE THEM SOMETHING TO TALK ABOUT AND LET THEM TALK.
IT WAS HEINOUS. THOSE DUDES WERE ALL MESSED UP. I DIDN'T THINK ANYONE COULD DO THAT TO PIRATE KING.
ONE WOMAN DID THAT TO HIS WHOLE CREW? %$&#, I DON'T WANT TO RUN INTO HER. DID YOU GET A LOOK AT HER FACE?
IMPOSSIBLE. SHE WAS WEARING AN EYE PATCH.
NOW, WHICH ONE OF YOU LADIES WANNA BE MY PLUS ONE TONIGHT? I GOT A VERY EXCLUSIVE INVITE TO A PARTY WITH THE NEW PRINCE OF MADRIPOOR.
I GET INVITED TO THESE THINGS ALL THE TIME. ROYALTY LOVES ME.
GOOD. KILL 'EM ALL, I SAY. THAT NO RESTRAINTS PLAY IS SICK KIDDIE $%#&. WHO ENJOYS THAT? I HAVE STANDARDS. I NEED... CURVES.
I NEED TO GET INTO THAT PARTY TONIGHT. I HEAR THE PRINCE IS WITHOUT A PRINCESS. I'VE ALWAYS WANTED TO BE A PRINCESS.
YOU WON'T GET INTO THE SOVEREIGN, CINDY. IT'S INVITE ONLY. THEY'RE NOT LETTING JUST ANYONE IN.
THEN WHY IS THAT TRAMP BRENDA GOING?

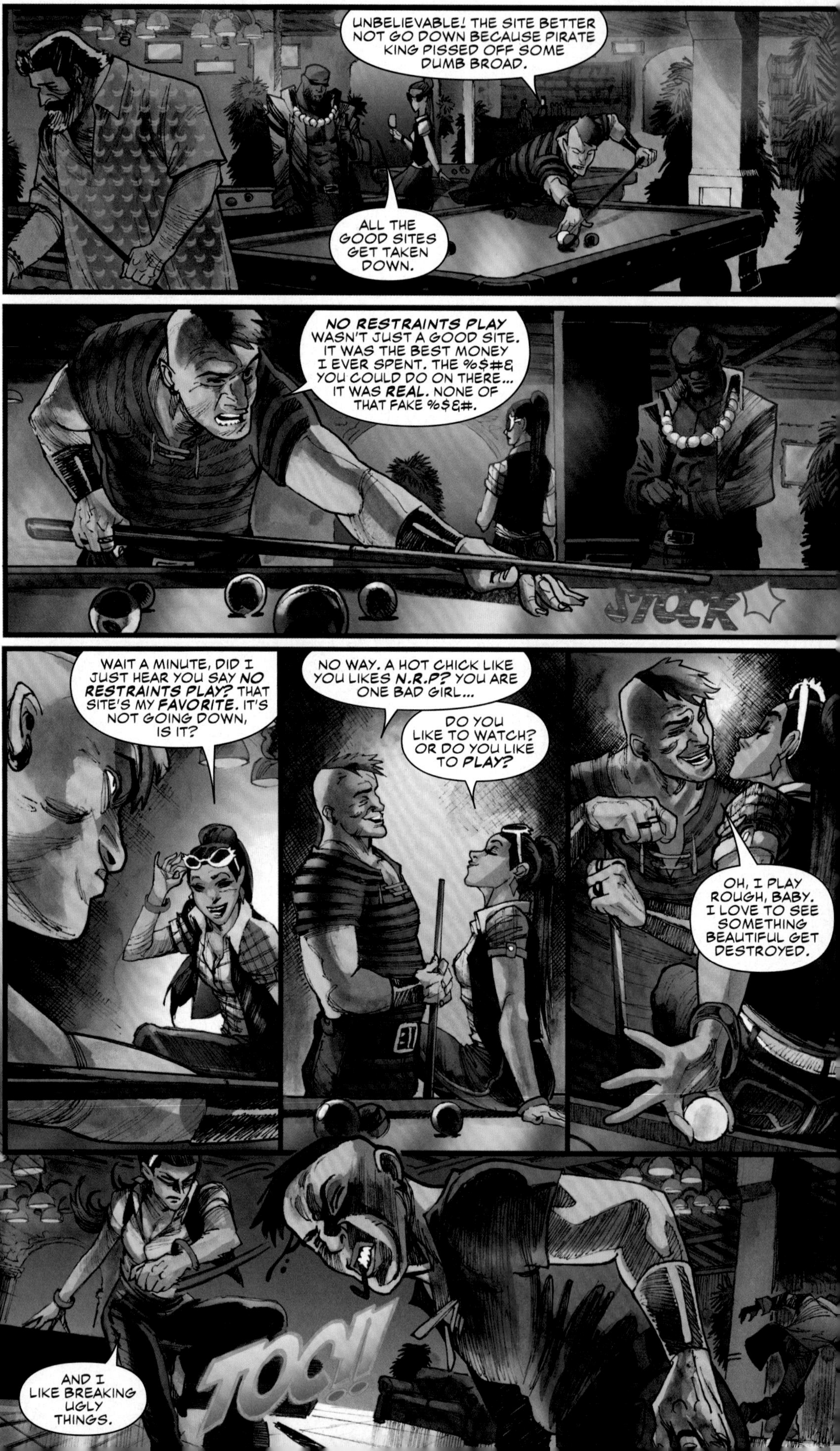

UNBELIEVABLE! THE SITE BETTER NOT GO DOWN BECAUSE PIRATE KING PISSED OFF SOME DUMB BROAD.
ALL THE GOOD SITES GET TAKEN DOWN.
NO RESTRAINTS PLAY WASN'T JUST A GOOD SITE. IT WAS THE BEST MONEY I EVER SPENT. THE %$#& YOU COULD DO ON THERE... IT WAS REAL. NONE OF THAT FAKE %$&#.
STOCK
WAIT A MINUTE, DID I JUST HEAR YOU SAY NO RESTRAINTS PLAY? THAT SITE'S MY FAVORITE. IT'S NOT GOING DOWN, IS IT?
NO WAY. A HOT CHICK LIKE YOU LIKES N.R.P? YOU ARE ONE BAD GIRL...
DO YOU LIKE TO WATCH? OR DO YOU LIKE TO PLAY?
OH, I PLAY ROUGH, BABY. I LOVE TO SEE SOMETHING BEAUTIFUL GET DESTROYED.
AND I LIKE BREAKING UGLY THINGS.
TOC!!

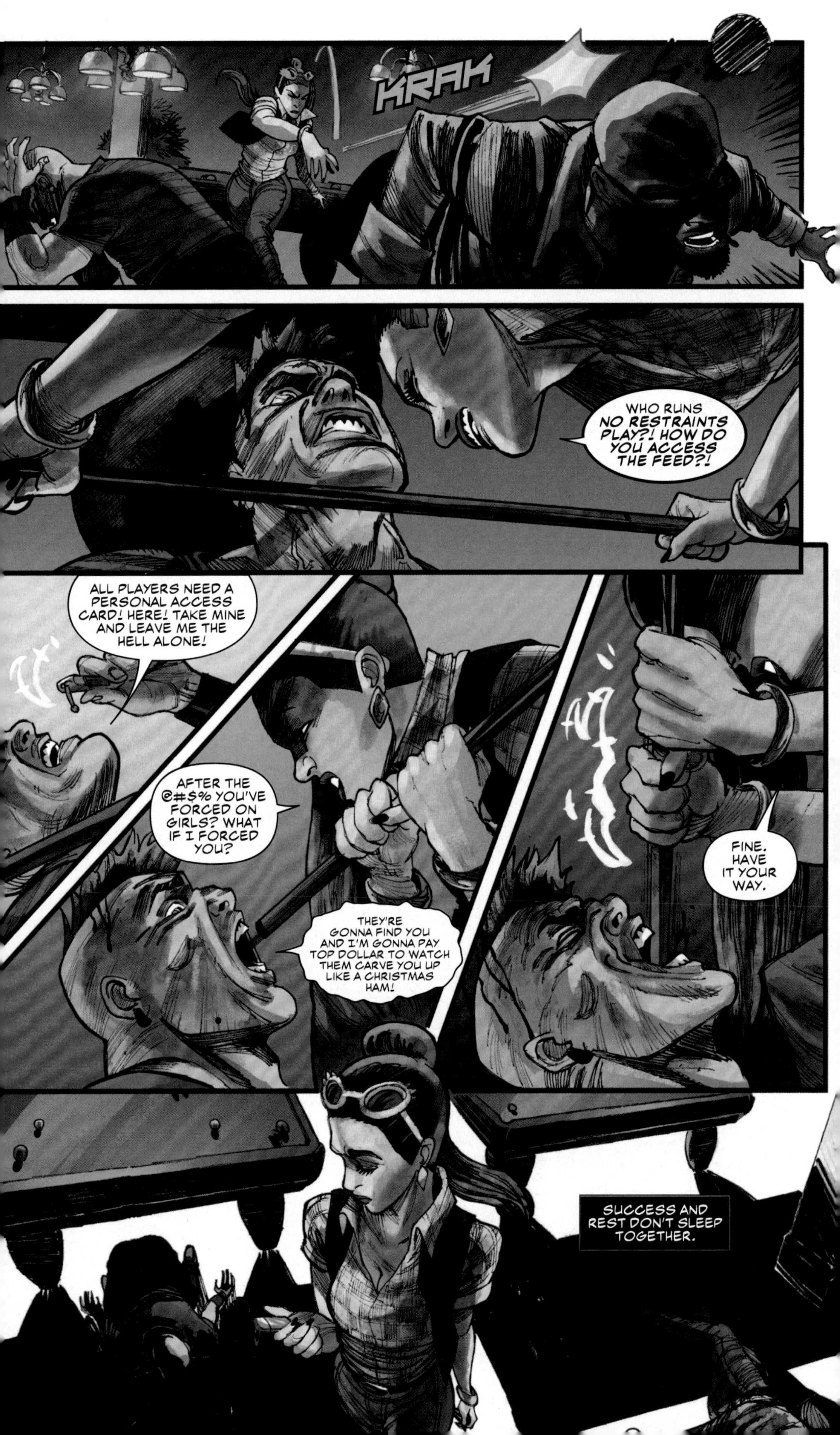
KRAK
WHO RUNS NO RESTRAINTS PLAY?! HOW DO YOU ACCESS THE FEED?!
ALL PLAYERS NEED A PERSONAL ACCESS CARD! HERE! TAKE MINE AND LEAVE ME THE HELL ALONE!
AFTER THE @#$% YOU'VE FORCED ON GIRLS? WHAT IF I FORCED YOU?
THEY'RE GONNA FIND YOU AND I'M GONNA PAY TOP DOLLAR TO WATCH THEM CARVE YOU UP LIKE A CHRISTMAS HAM!
FINE. HAVE IT YOUR WAY.
SUCCESS AND REST DON'T SLEEP TOGETHER.

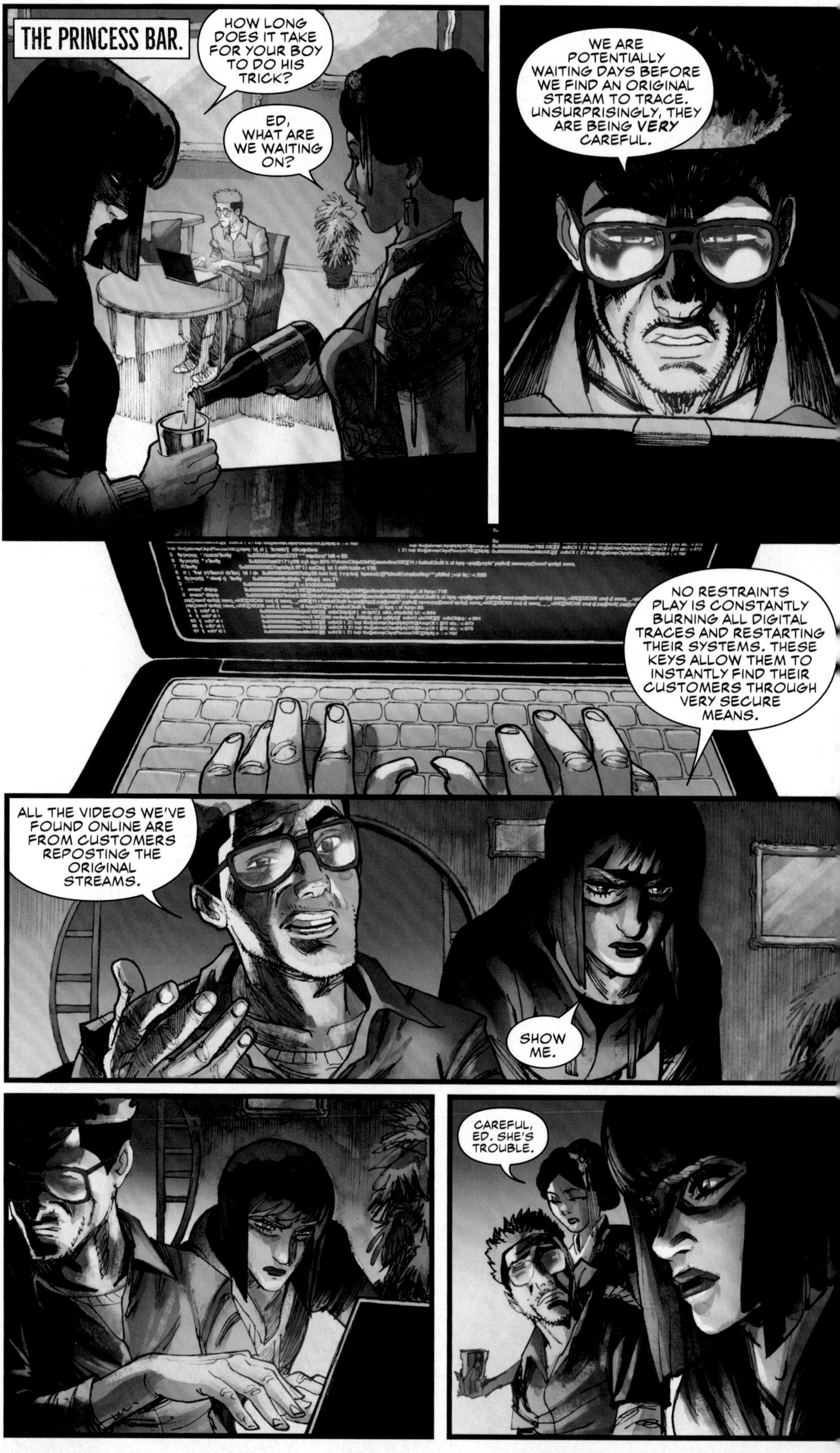
THE PRINCESS BAR.
HOW LONG DOES IT TAKE FOR YOUR BOY TO DO HIS TRICK?
ED, WHAT ARE WE WAITING ON?
WE ARE POTENTIALLY WAITING DAYS BEFORE WE FIND AN ORIGINAL STREAM TO TRACE. UNSURPRISINGLY, THEY ARE BEING VERY CAREFUL.
NO RESTRAINTS PLAY IS CONSTANTLY BURNING ALL DIGITAL TRACES AND RESTARTING THEIR SYSTEMS. THESE KEYS ALLOW THEM TO INSTANTLY FIND THEIR CUSTOMERS THROUGH VERY SECURE MEANS.
ALL THE VIDEOS WE'VE FOUND ONLINE ARE FROM CUSTOMERS REPOSTING THE ORIGINAL STREAMS.
SHOW ME.
CAREFUL, ED. SHE'S TROUBLE.

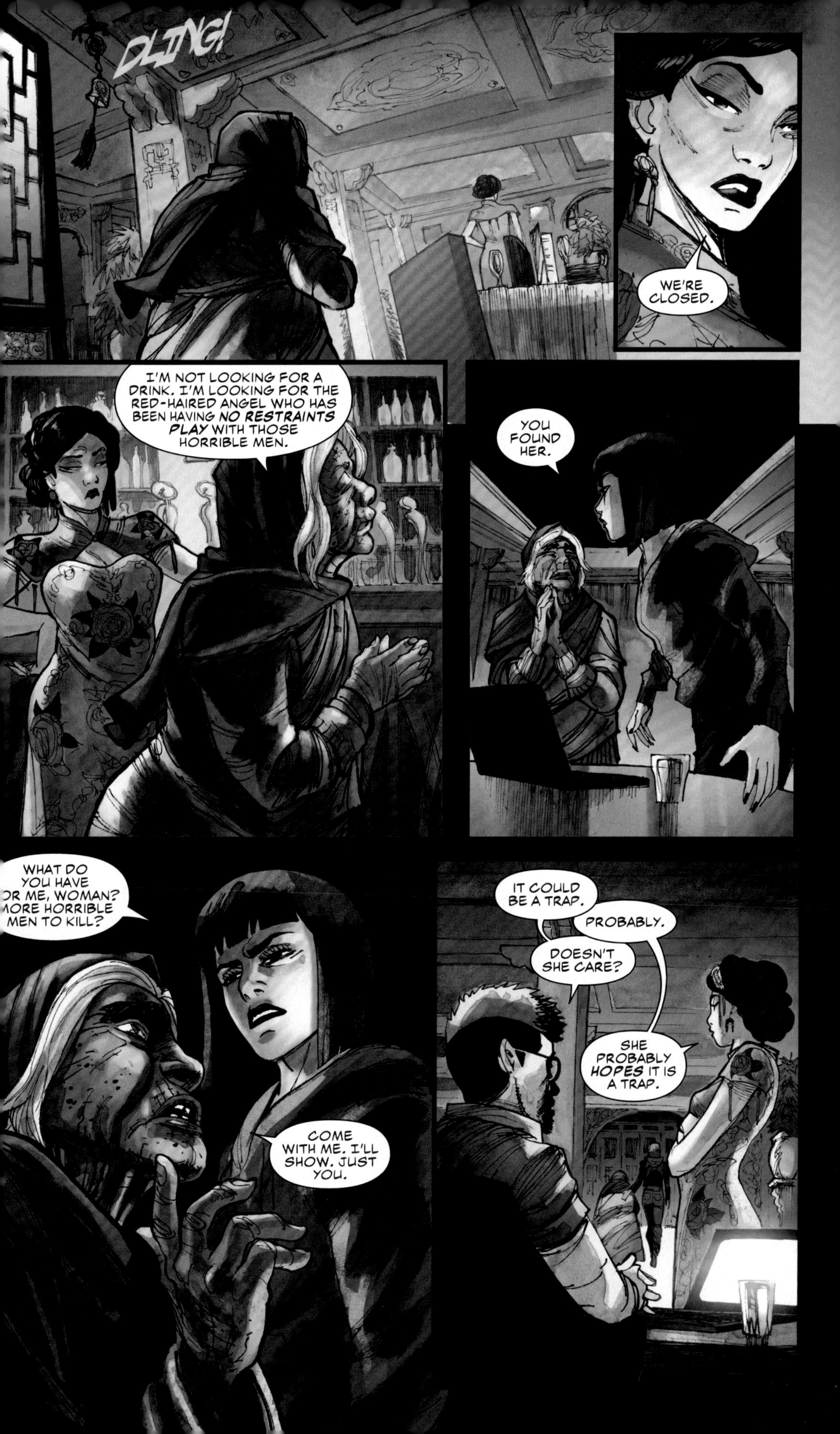
DLING!
WE'RE CLOSED.
I'M NOT LOOKING FOR A DRINK. I'M LOOKING FOR THE RED-HAIRED ANGEL WHO HAS BEEN HAVING NO RESTRAINTS PLAY WITH THOSE HORRIBLE MEN.
YOU FOUND HER.
WHAT DO YOU HAVE OR ME, WOMAN? MORE HORRIBLE MEN TO KILL?
COME WITH ME. I'LL SHOW. JUST YOU.
IT COULD BE A TRAP.
PROBABLY.
DOESN'T SHE CARE?
SHE PROBABLY HOPES IT IS A TRAP.

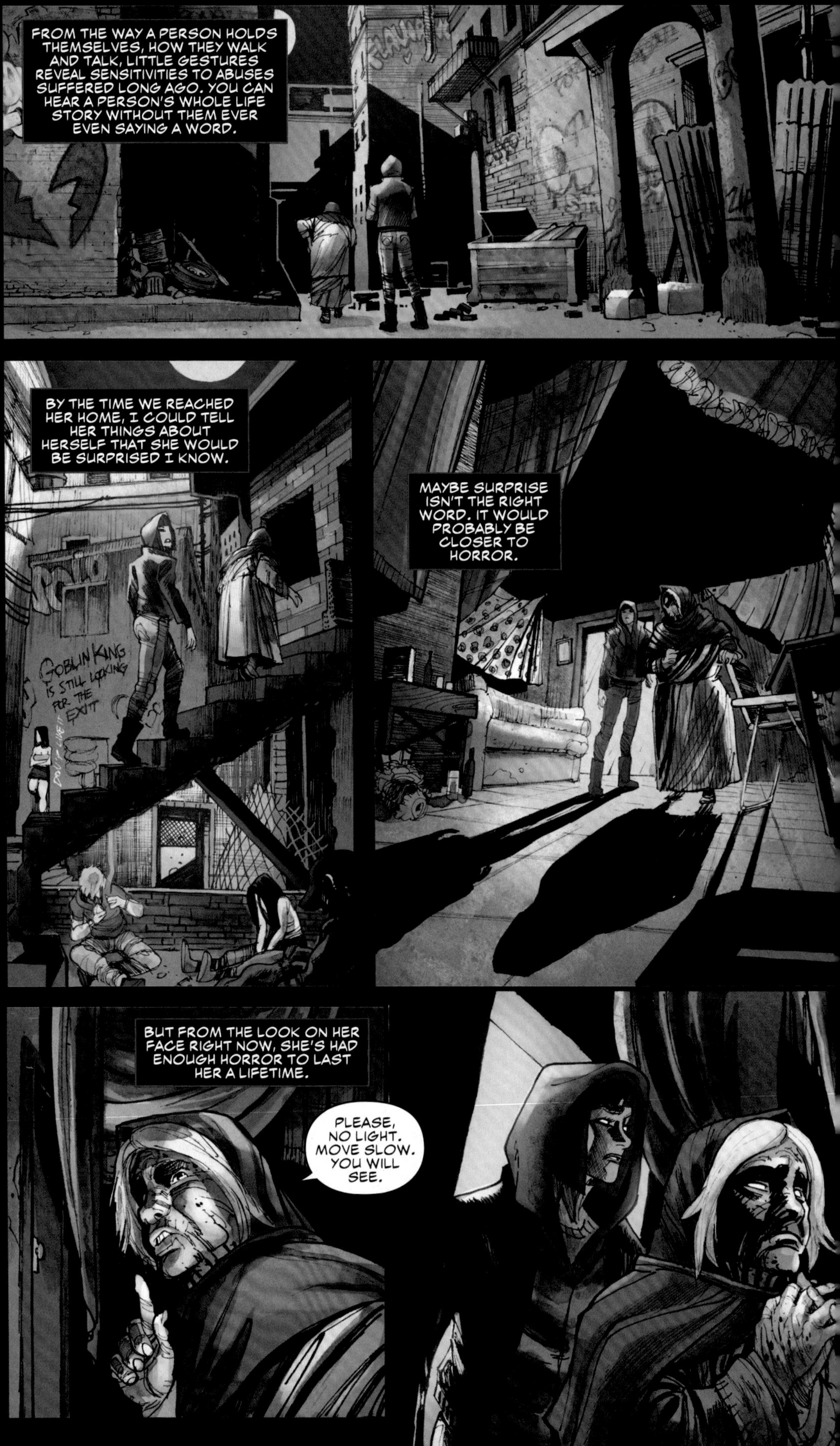
FROM THE WAY A PERSON HOLDS THEMSELVES, HOW THEY WALK AND TALK, LITTLE GESTURES REVEAL SENSITIVITIES TO ABUSES SUFFERED LONG AGO. YOU CAN HEAR A PERSON'S WHOLE LIFE STORY WITHOUT THEM EVER EVEN SAYING A WORD.
BY THE TIME WE REACHED HER HOME, I COULD TELL HER THINGS ABOUT HERSELF THAT SHE WOULD BE SURPRISED I KNOW.
GOBLIN KING IS STILL LOOKING FOR THE EXIT
MAYBE SURPRISE ISN'T THE RIGHT WORD. IT WOULD PROBABLY BE CLOSER TO HORROR.
BUT FROM THE LOOK ON HER FACE RIGHT NOW, SHE'S HAD ENOUGH HORROR TO LAST HER A LIFETIME.
PLEASE, NO LIGHT. MOVE SLOW. YOU WILL SEE.

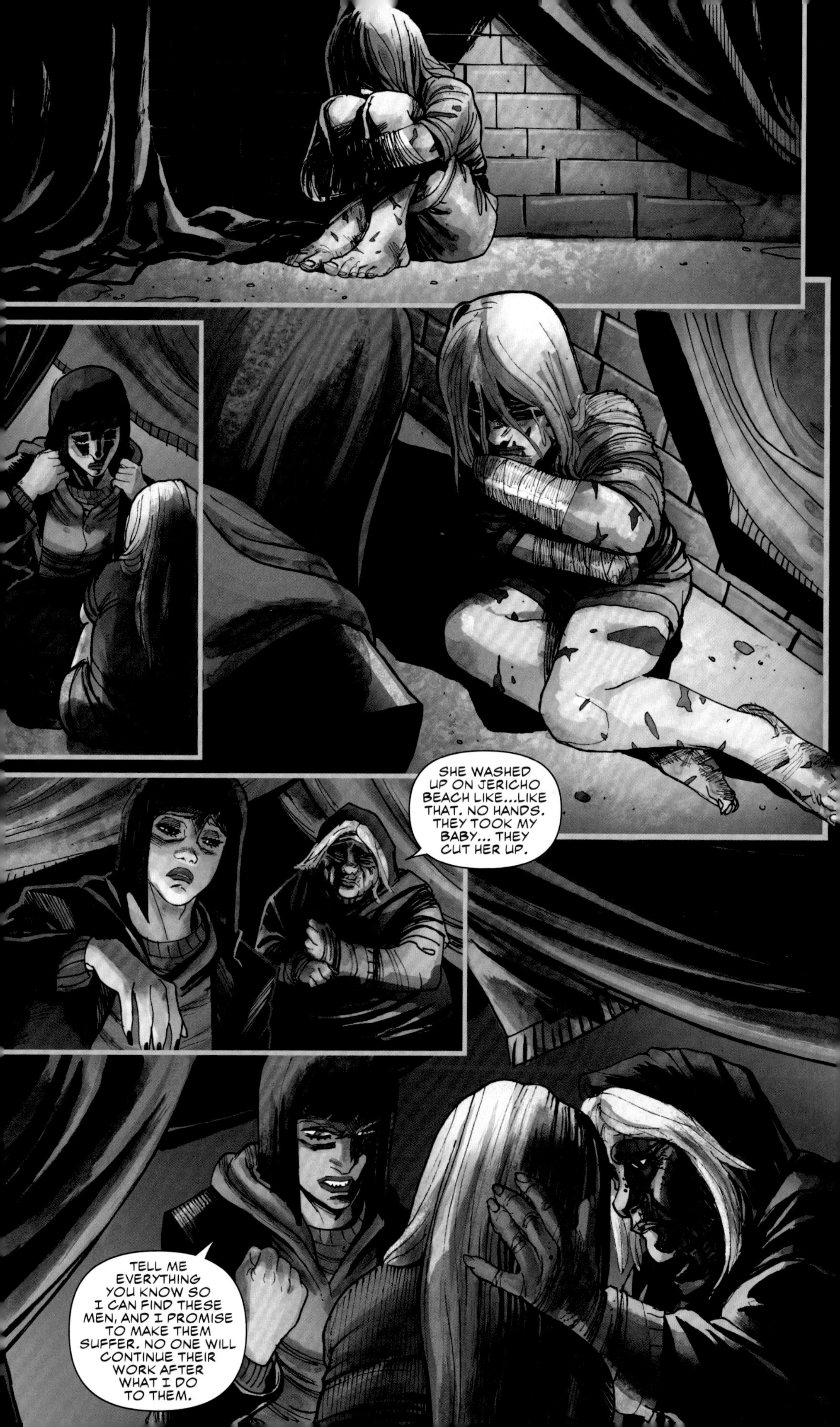
SHE WASHED UP ON JERICHO BEACH LIKE...LIKE THAT. NO HANDS. THEY TOOK MY BABY... THEY CUT HER UP.
TELL ME EVERYTHING YOU KNOW SO I CAN FIND THESE MEN, AND I PROMISE TO MAKE THEM SUFFER. NO ONE WILL CONTINUE THEIR WORK AFTER WHAT I DO TO THEM.

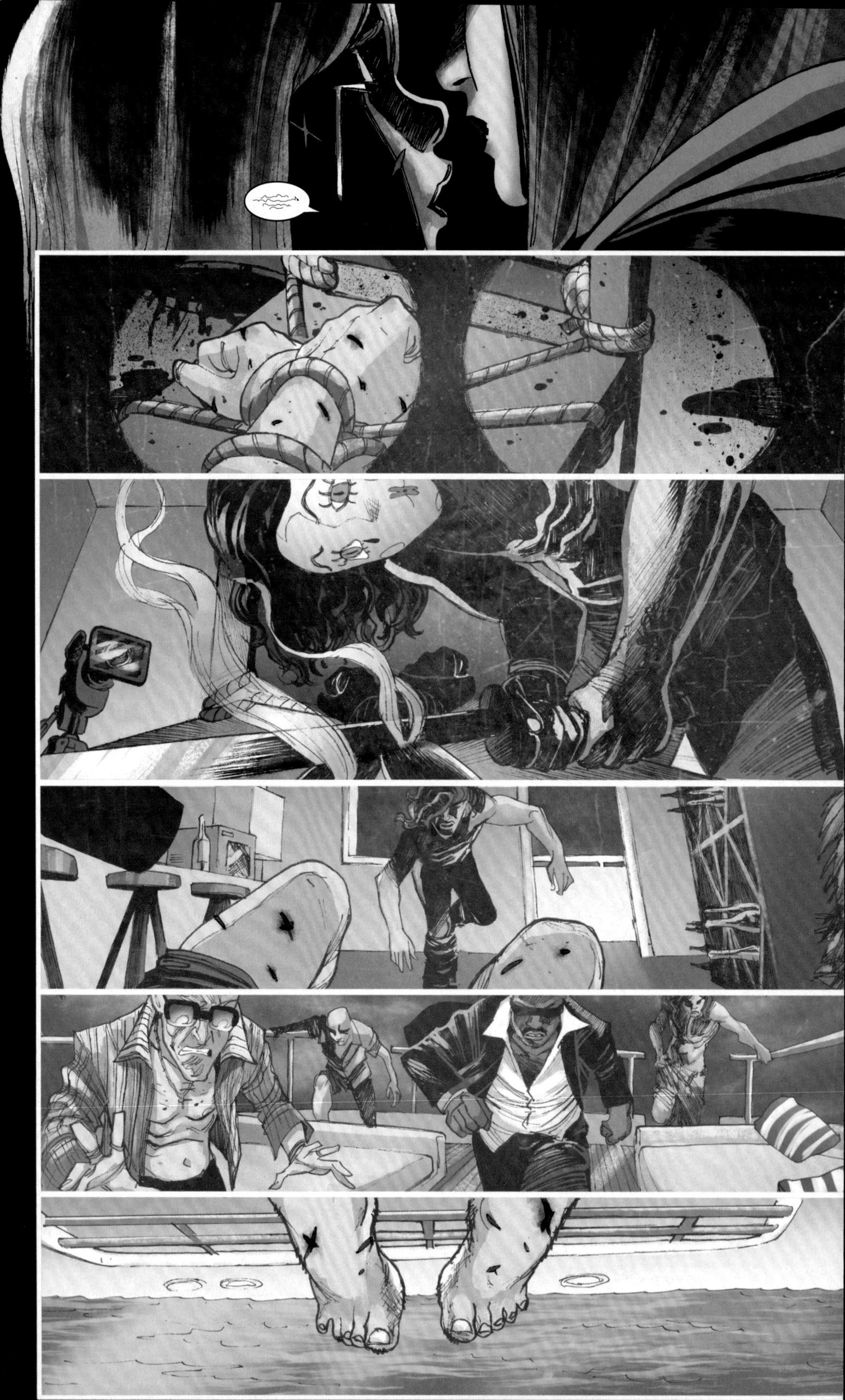

I KNOW THIS IS PAINFUL, BUT IS THERE ANYTHING YOU REMEMBER ABOUT THE MEN THAT COULD HELP ME IDENTIFY THEM?

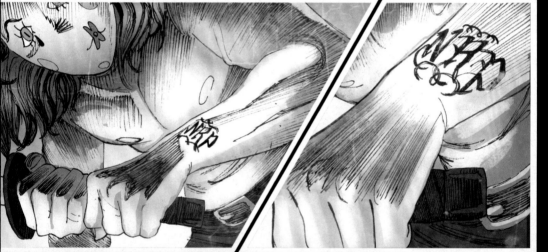

I HAVE TO GET TO WORK NOW, BUT I HAVE A FRIEND WHO WILL BE GETTING IN TOUCH ABOUT SOME PROSTHETICS FOR YOUR DAUGHTER.

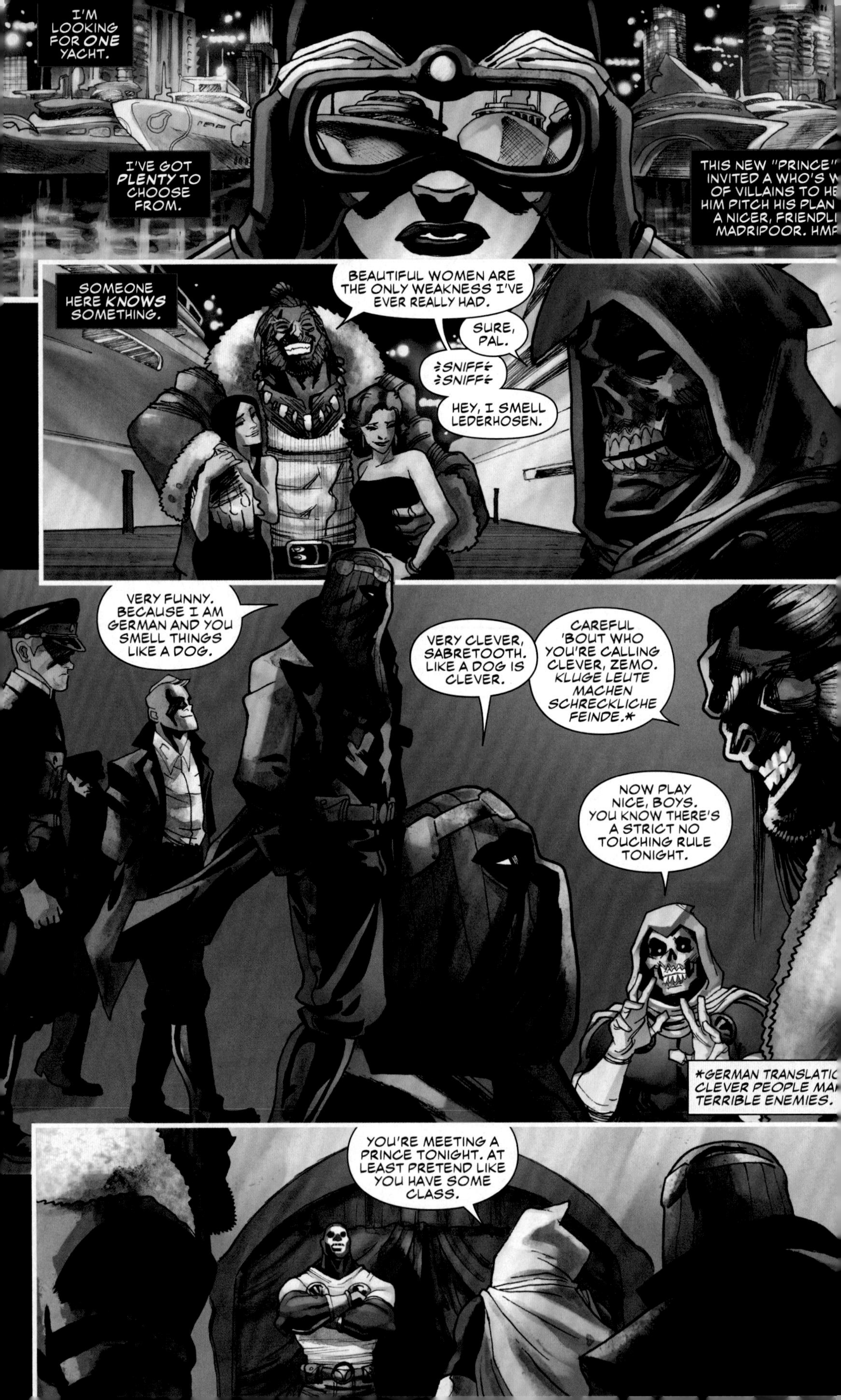

I'M LOOKING FOR ONE YACHT.
I'VE GOT PLENTY TO CHOOSE FROM.
THIS NEW "PRINCE" INVITED A WHO'S W
OF VILLAINS TO HE
HIM PITCH HIS PLAN
A NICER, FRIENDLI
MADRIPOOR. HMP
SOMEONE HERE KNOWS SOMETHING.
BEAUTIFUL WOMEN ARE THE ONLY WEAKNESS I'VE EVER REALLY HAD.
SURE, PAL.
SNIFF SNIFF
HEY, I SMELL LEDERHOSEN.
VERY FUNNY. BECAUSE I AM GERMAN AND YOU SMELL THINGS LIKE A DOG.
VERY CLEVER, SABRETOOTH. LIKE A DOG IS CLEVER.
CAREFUL 'BOUT WHO YOU'RE CALLING CLEVER, ZEMO. KLUGE LEUTE MACHEN SCHRECKLICHE FEINDE.*
NOW PLAY NICE, BOYS. YOU KNOW THERE'S A STRICT NO TOUCHING RULE TONIGHT.
*GERMAN TRANSLATIC
CLEVER PEOPLE MA
TERRIBLE ENEMIES.
YOU'RE MEETING A PRINCE TONIGHT. AT LEAST PRETEND LIKE YOU HAVE SOME CLASS.

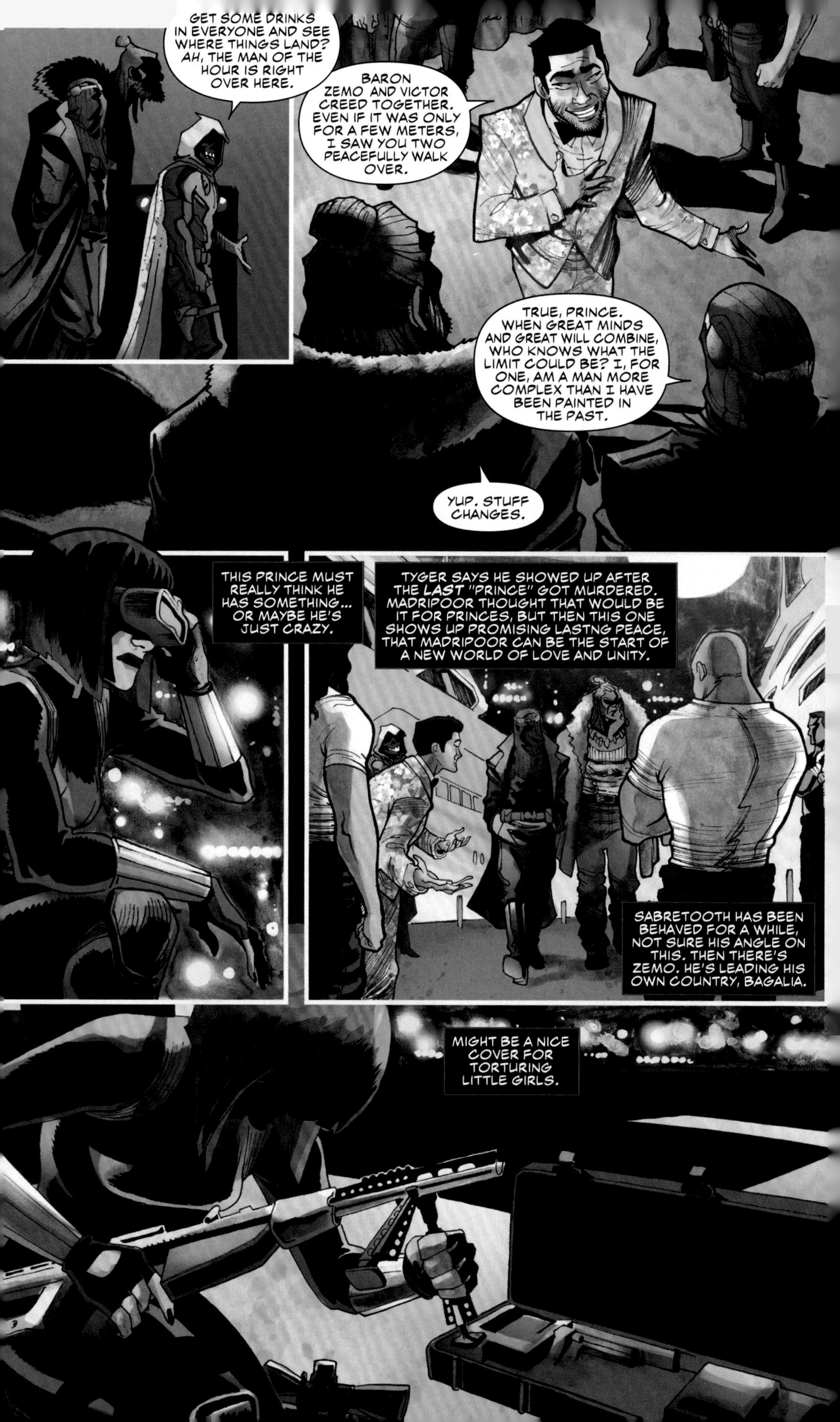
GET SOME DRINKS IN EVERYONE AND SEE WHERE THINGS LAND? AH, THE MAN OF THE HOUR IS RIGHT OVER HERE.
BARON ZEMO AND VICTOR CREED TOGETHER. EVEN IF IT WAS ONLY FOR A FEW METERS, I SAW YOU TWO PEACEFULLY WALK OVER.
TRUE, PRINCE. WHEN GREAT MINDS AND GREAT WILL COMBINE, WHO KNOWS WHAT THE LIMIT COULD BE? I, FOR ONE, AM A MAN MORE COMPLEX THAN I HAVE BEEN PAINTED IN THE PAST.
YUP. STUFF CHANGES.
THIS PRINCE MUST REALLY THINK HE HAS SOMETHING... OR MAYBE HE'S JUST CRAZY.
TYGER SAYS HE SHOWED UP AFTER THE LAST "PRINCE" GOT MURDERED. MADRIPOOR THOUGHT THAT WOULD BE IT FOR PRINCES, BUT THEN THIS ONE SHOWS UP PROMISING LASTNG PEACE, THAT MADRIPOOR CAN BE THE START OF A NEW WORLD OF LOVE AND UNITY.
SABRETOOTH HAS BEEN BEHAVED FOR A WHILE, NOT SURE HIS ANGLE ON THIS. THEN THERE'S ZEMO. HE'S LEADING HIS OWN COUNTRY, BAGALIA.
MIGHT BE A NICE COVER FOR TORTURING LITTLE GIRLS.

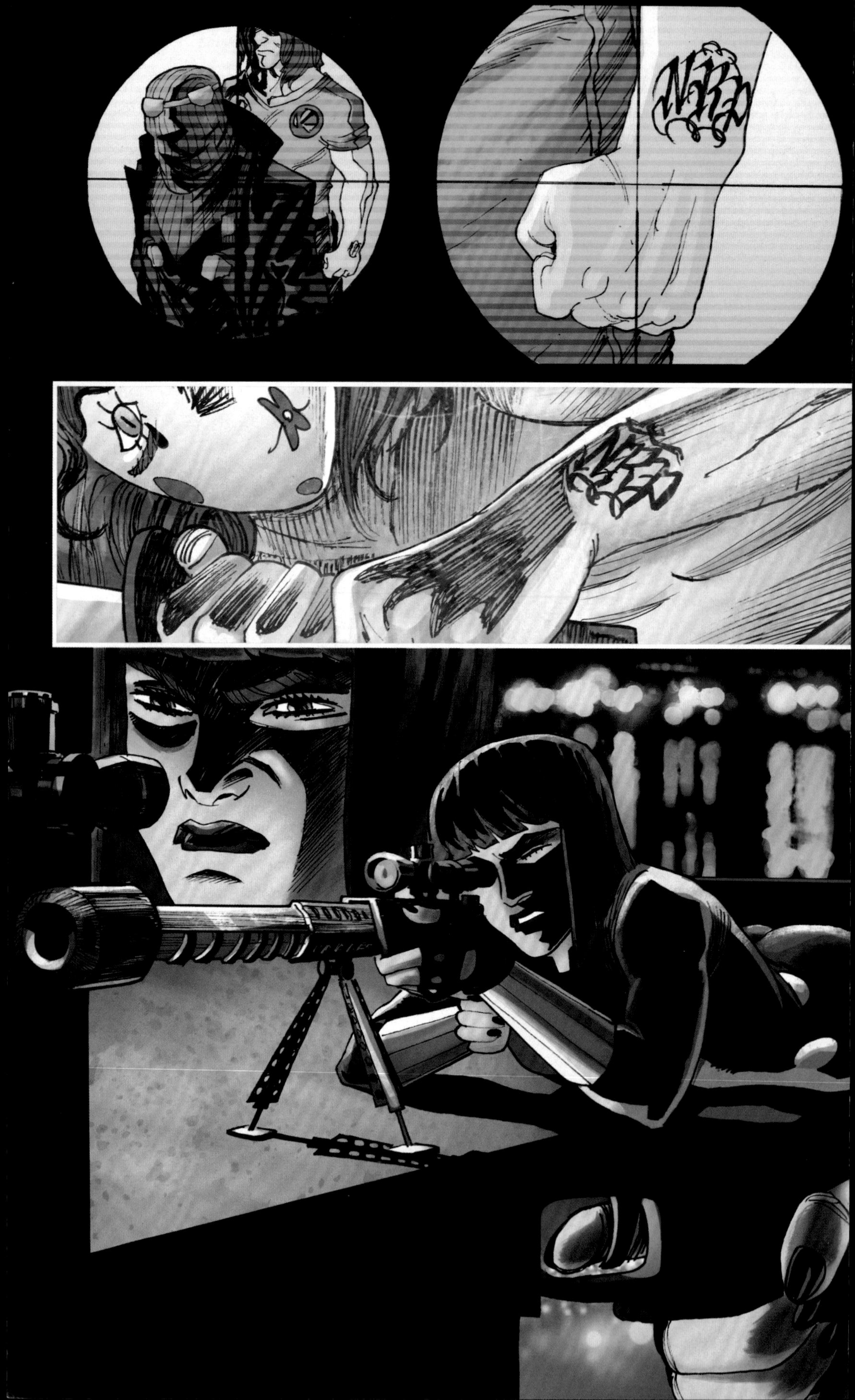

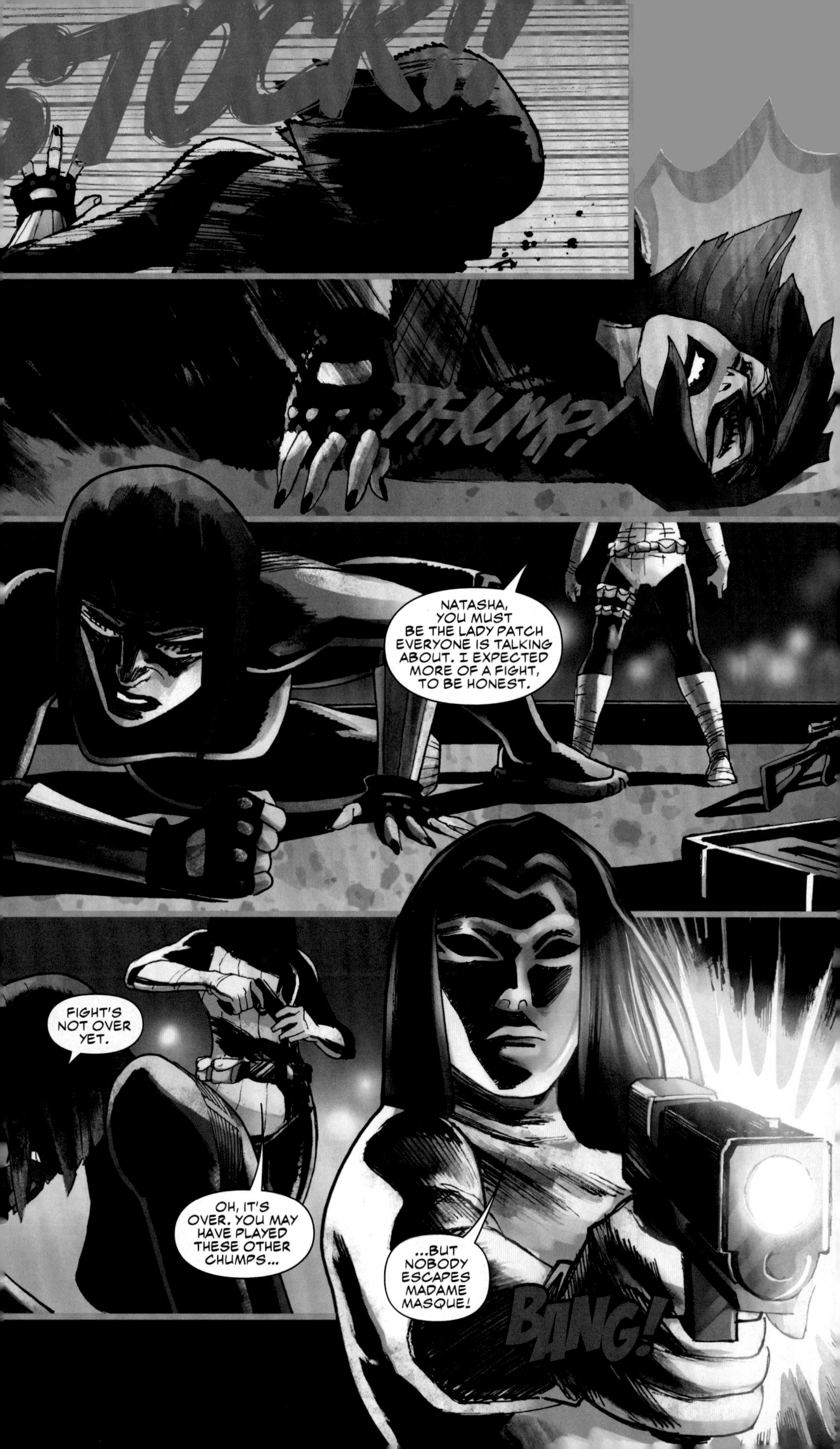
STOCK!!
THUMP!
NATASHA, YOU MUST BE THE LADY PATCH EVERYONE IS TALKING ABOUT. I EXPECTED MORE OF A FIGHT, TO BE HONEST.
FIGHT'S NOT OVER YET.
OH, IT'S OVER. YOU MAY HAVE PLAYED THESE OTHER CHUMPS...
...BUT NOBODY ESCAPES MADAME MASQUE!
BANG!

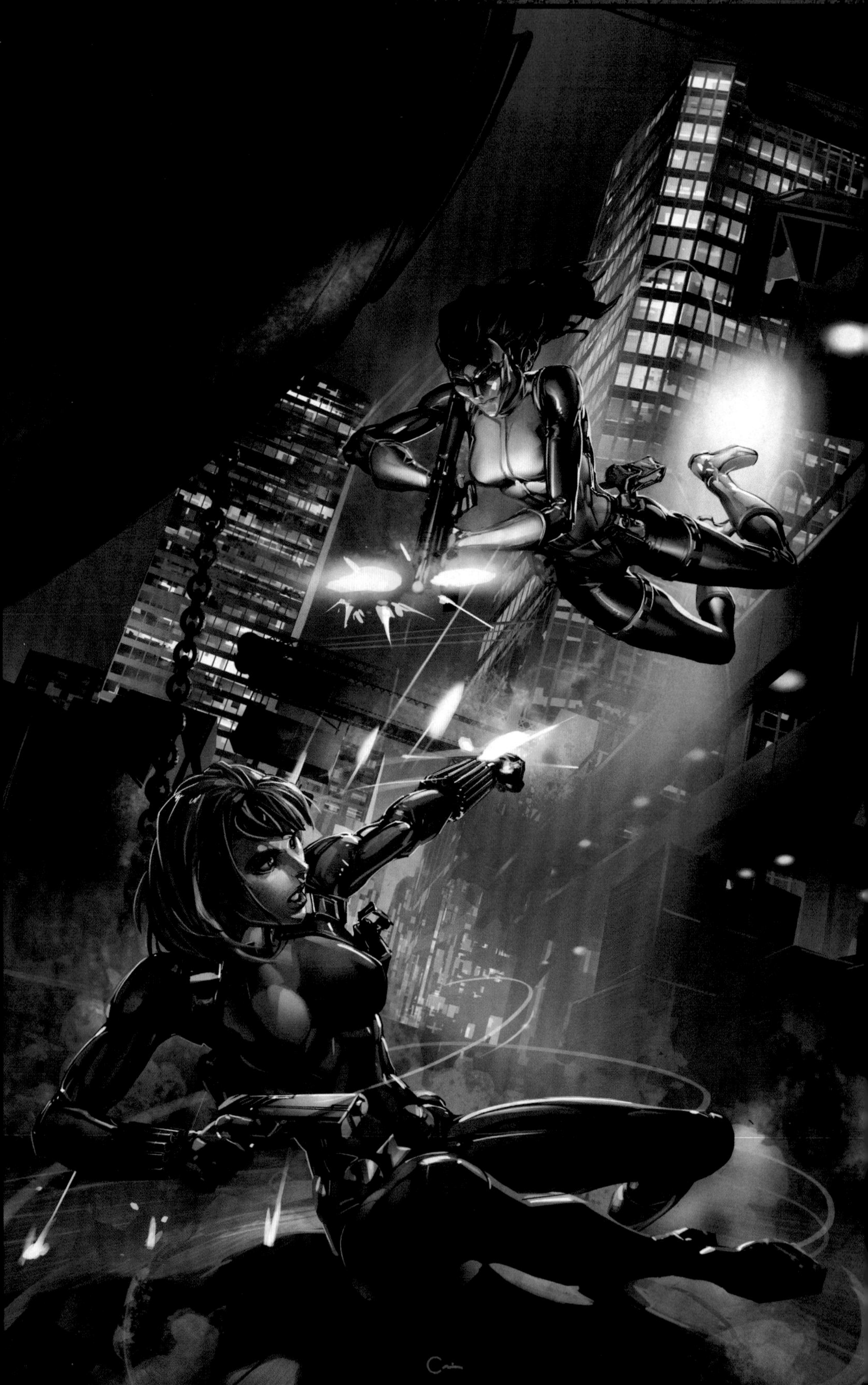

3

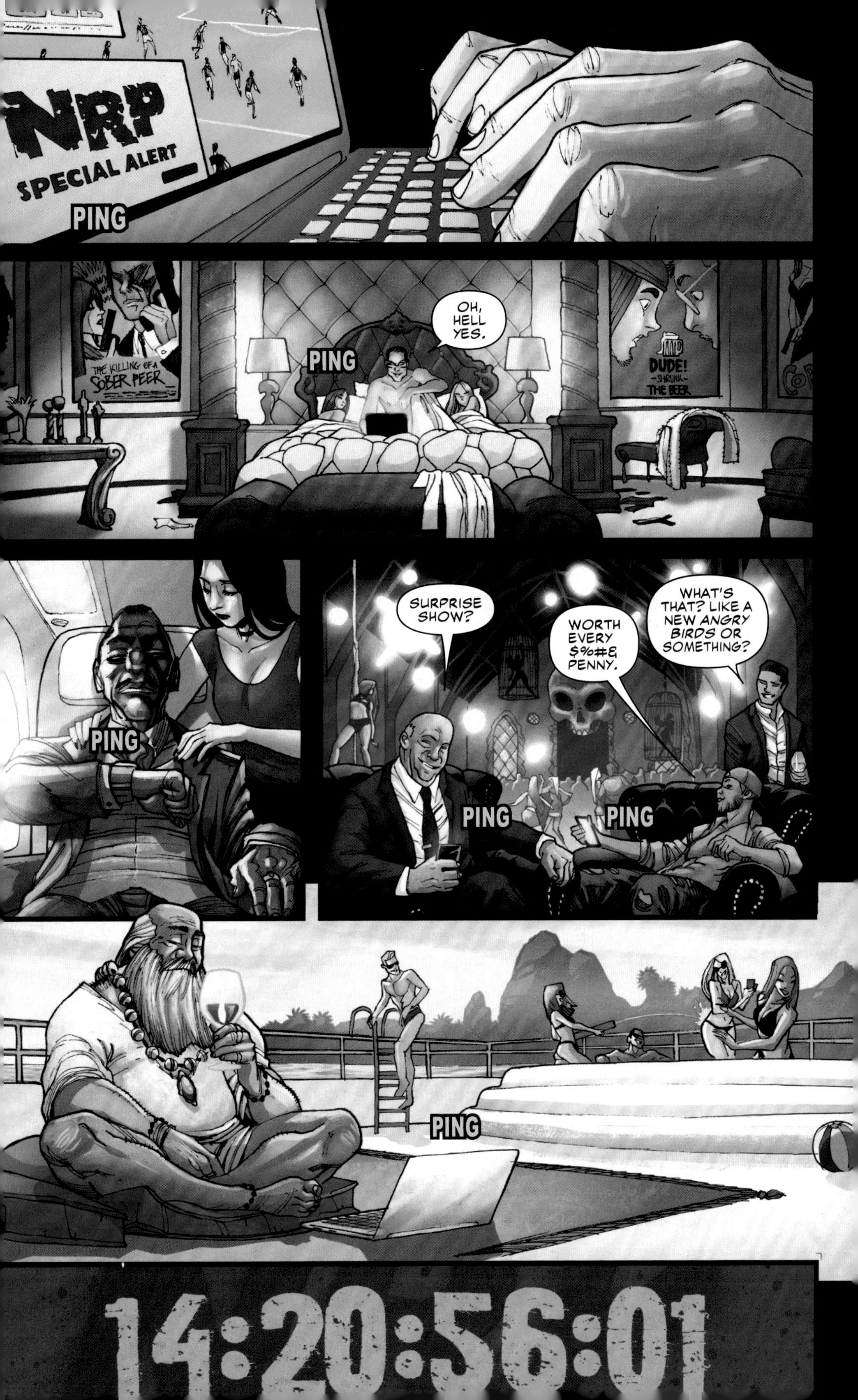
NRP
SPECIAL ALERT
PING
THE KILLING OF A SOBER PEER
PING
OH, HELL YES.
DUDE!
THE BEER
PING
SURPRISE SHOW?
WORTH EVERY $%#& PENNY.
WHAT'S THAT? LIKE A NEW ANGRY BIRDS OR SOMETHING?
PING
PING
PING
14:20:56:01

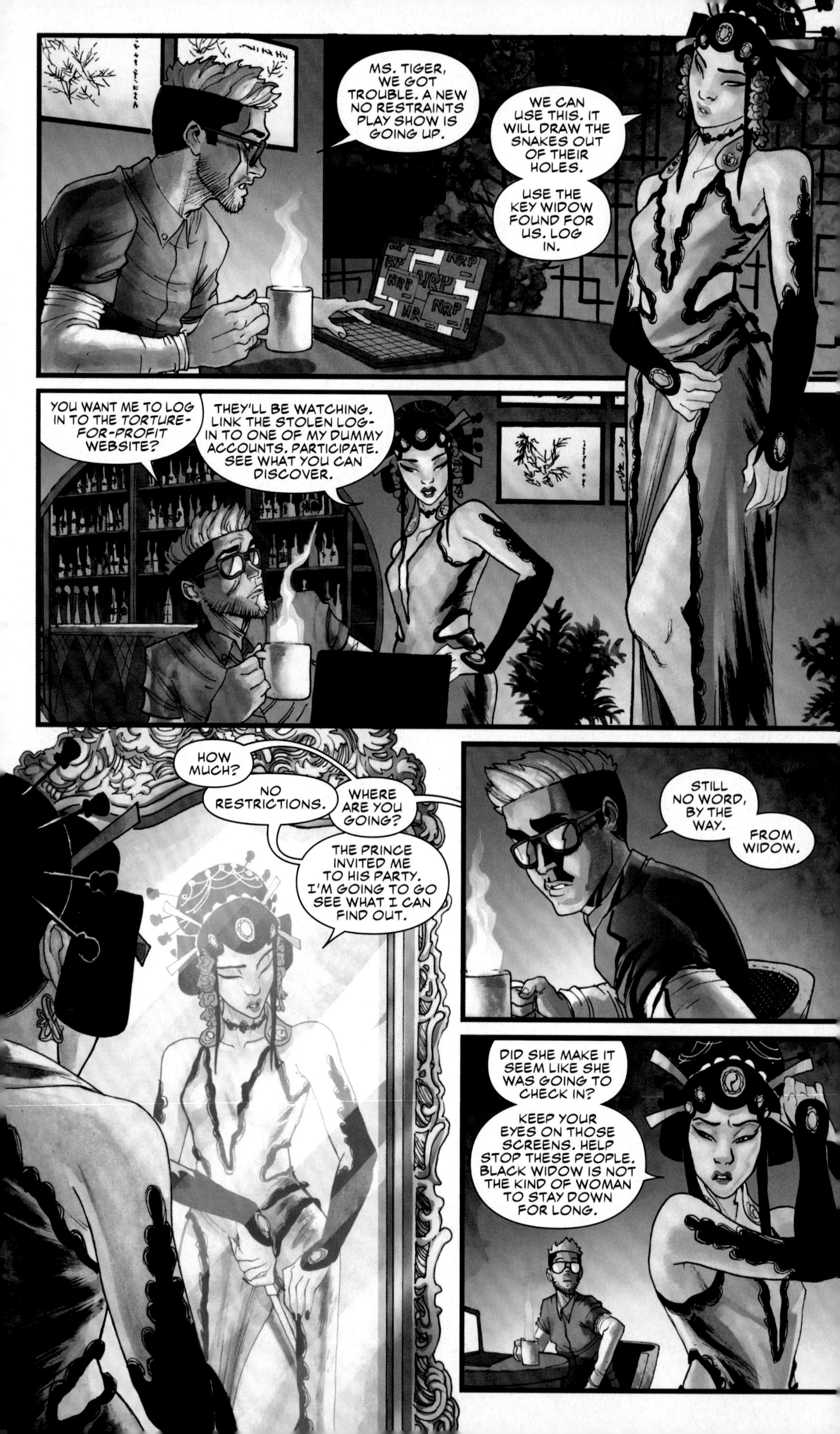
MS. TIGER, WE GOT TROUBLE. A NEW NO RESTRAINTS PLAY SHOW IS GOING UP.
WE CAN USE THIS. IT WILL DRAW THE SNAKES OUT OF THEIR HOLES.
USE THE KEY WIDOW FOUND FOR US. LOG IN.
YOU WANT ME TO LOG IN TO THE *TORTURE-FOR-PROFIT* WEBSITE?
THEY'LL BE WATCHING. LINK THE STOLEN LOG-IN TO ONE OF MY DUMMY ACCOUNTS. PARTICIPATE. SEE WHAT YOU CAN DISCOVER.
HOW MUCH?
NO RESTRICTIONS.
WHERE ARE YOU GOING?
THE PRINCE INVITED ME TO HIS PARTY. I'M GOING TO GO SEE WHAT I CAN FIND OUT.
STILL NO WORD, BY THE WAY.
FROM WIDOW.
DID SHE MAKE IT SEEM LIKE SHE WAS GOING TO CHECK IN?
KEEP YOUR EYES ON THOSE SCREENS. HELP STOP THESE PEOPLE. BLACK WIDOW IS NOT THE KIND OF WOMAN TO STAY DOWN FOR LONG.

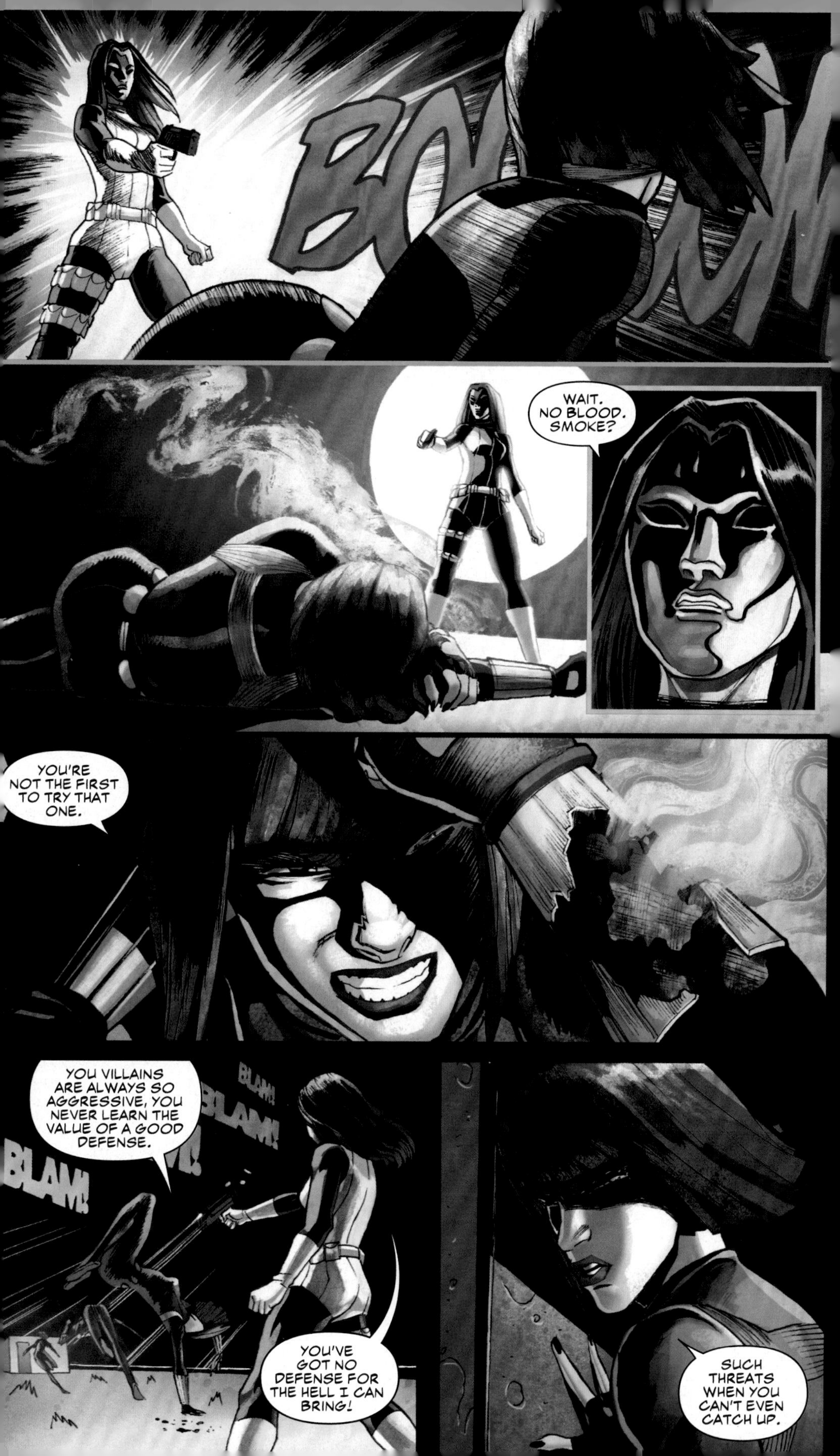
BOOM
WAIT. NO BLOOD. SMOKE?
YOU'RE NOT THE FIRST TO TRY THAT ONE.
YOU VILLAINS ARE ALWAYS SO AGGRESSIVE, YOU NEVER LEARN THE VALUE OF A GOOD DEFENSE.
BLAM!
BLAM!
BLAM!
YOU'VE GOT NO DEFENSE FOR THE HELL I CAN BRING!
SUCH THREATS WHEN YOU CAN'T EVEN CATCH UP.

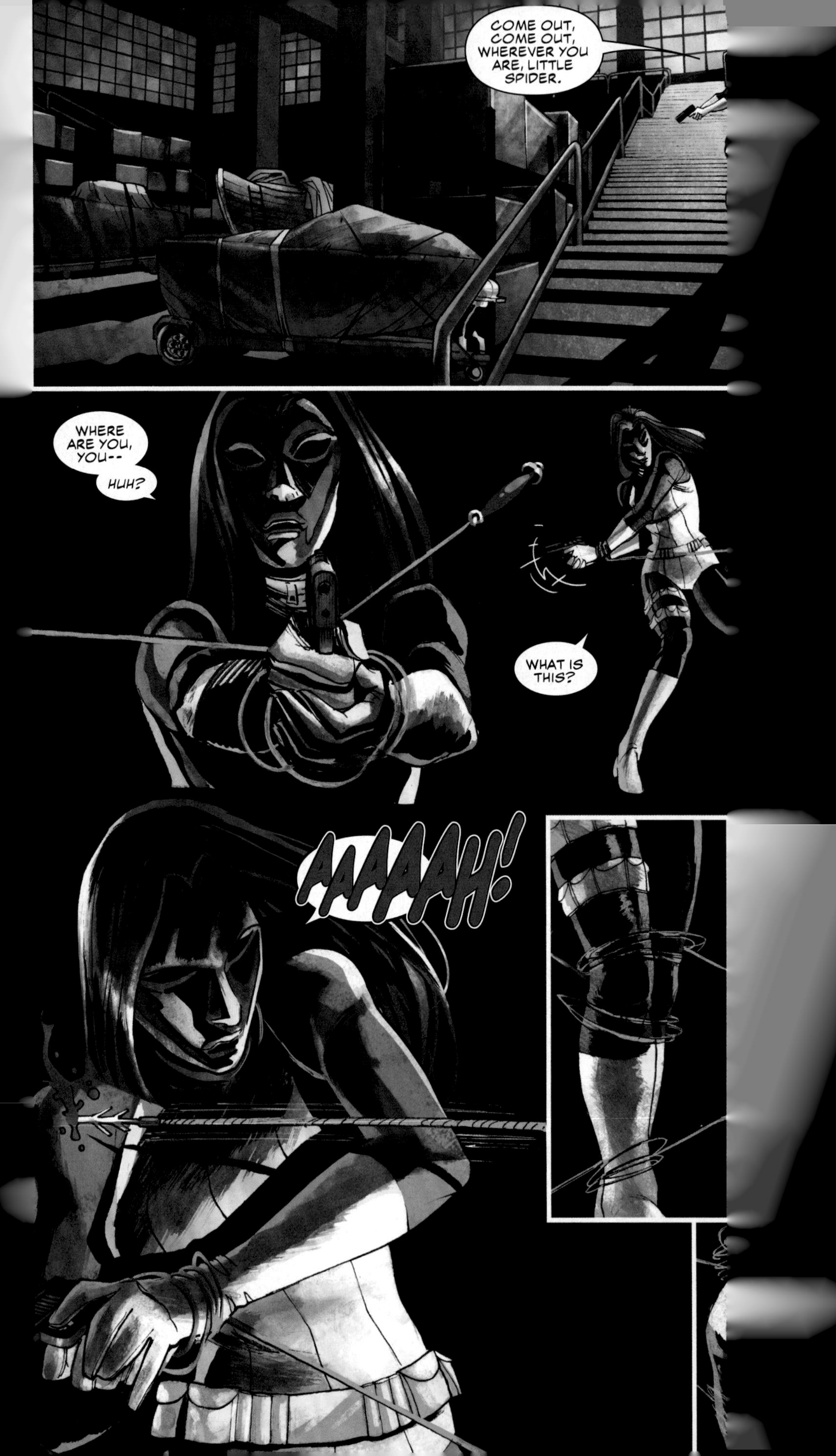
COME OUT, COME OUT, WHEREVER YOU ARE, LITTLE SPIDER.
WHERE ARE YOU, YOU--
HUH?
WHAT IS THIS?
AAAAAH!

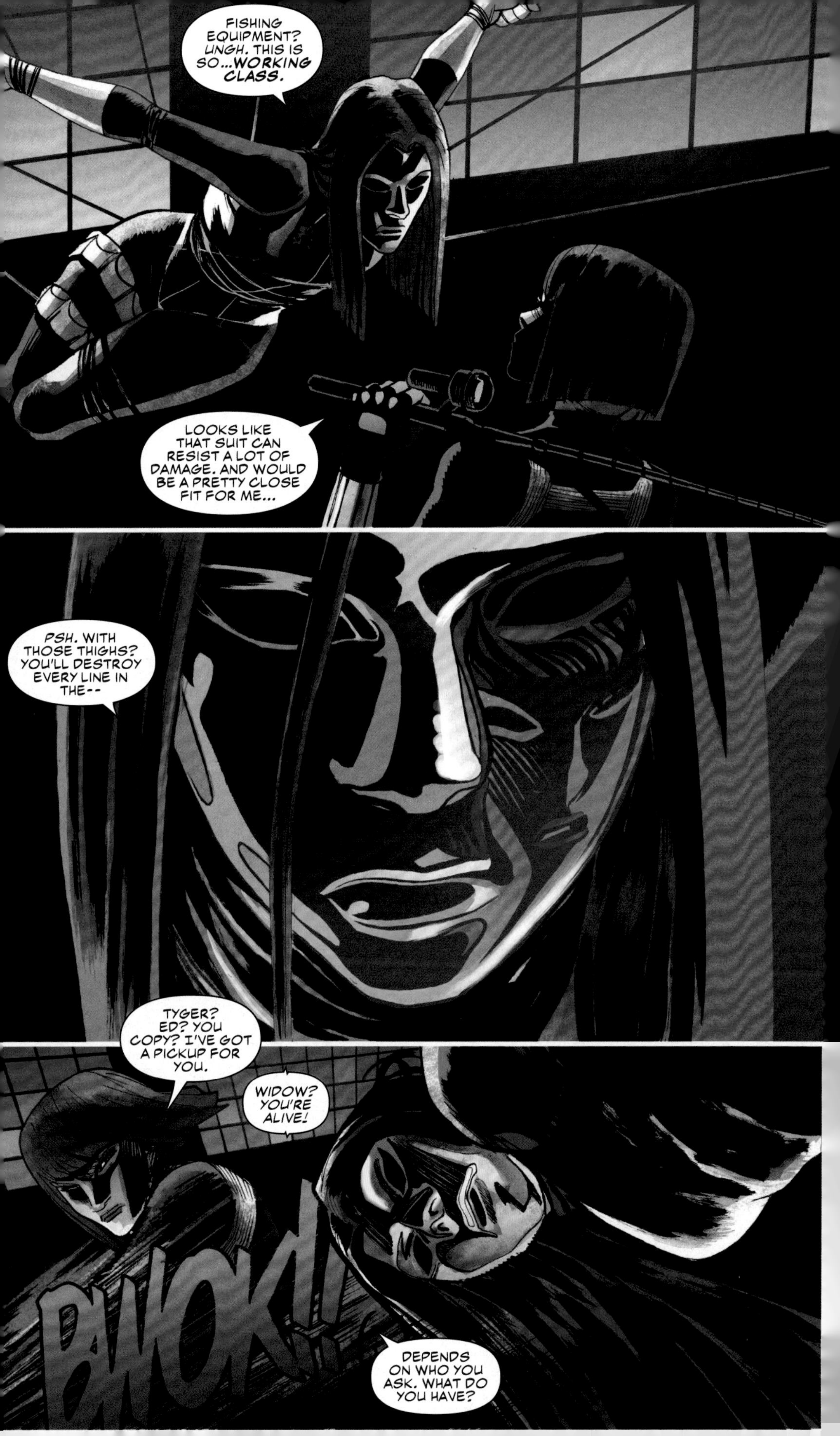
FISHING EQUIPMENT? UNGH. THIS IS SO...**WORKING CLASS.**
LOOKS LIKE THAT SUIT CAN RESIST A LOT OF DAMAGE. AND WOULD BE A PRETTY CLOSE FIT FOR ME...
PSH. WITH THOSE THIGHS? YOU'LL DESTROY EVERY LINE IN THE--
TYGER? ED? YOU COPY? I'VE GOT A PICKUP FOR YOU.
WIDOW? YOU'RE ALIVE!
BWOK!!
DEPENDS ON WHO YOU ASK. WHAT DO YOU HAVE?

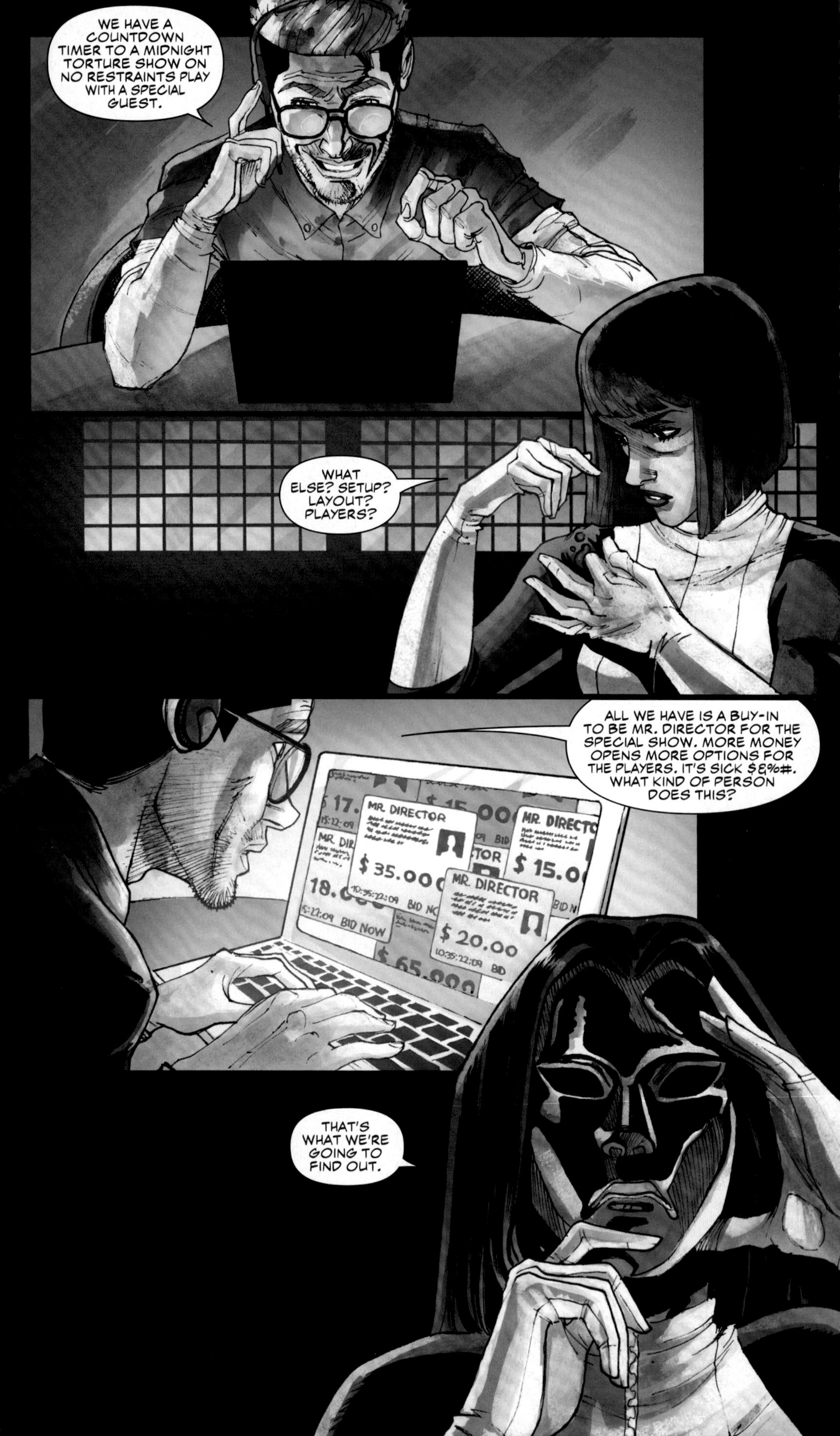
WE HAVE A COUNTDOWN TIMER TO A MIDNIGHT TORTURE SHOW ON NO RESTRAINTS PLAY WITH A SPECIAL GUEST.
WHAT ELSE? SETUP? LAYOUT? PLAYERS?
ALL WE HAVE IS A BUY-IN TO BE MR. DIRECTOR FOR THE SPECIAL SHOW. MORE MONEY OPENS MORE OPTIONS FOR THE PLAYERS. IT'S SICK $&%#. WHAT KIND OF PERSON DOES THIS?
MR. DIRECTOR
$ 35.00
MR. DIRECTOR
$ 20.00
MR. DIRECTO
$ 15.0
BID NOW
THAT'S WHAT WE'RE GOING TO FIND OUT.

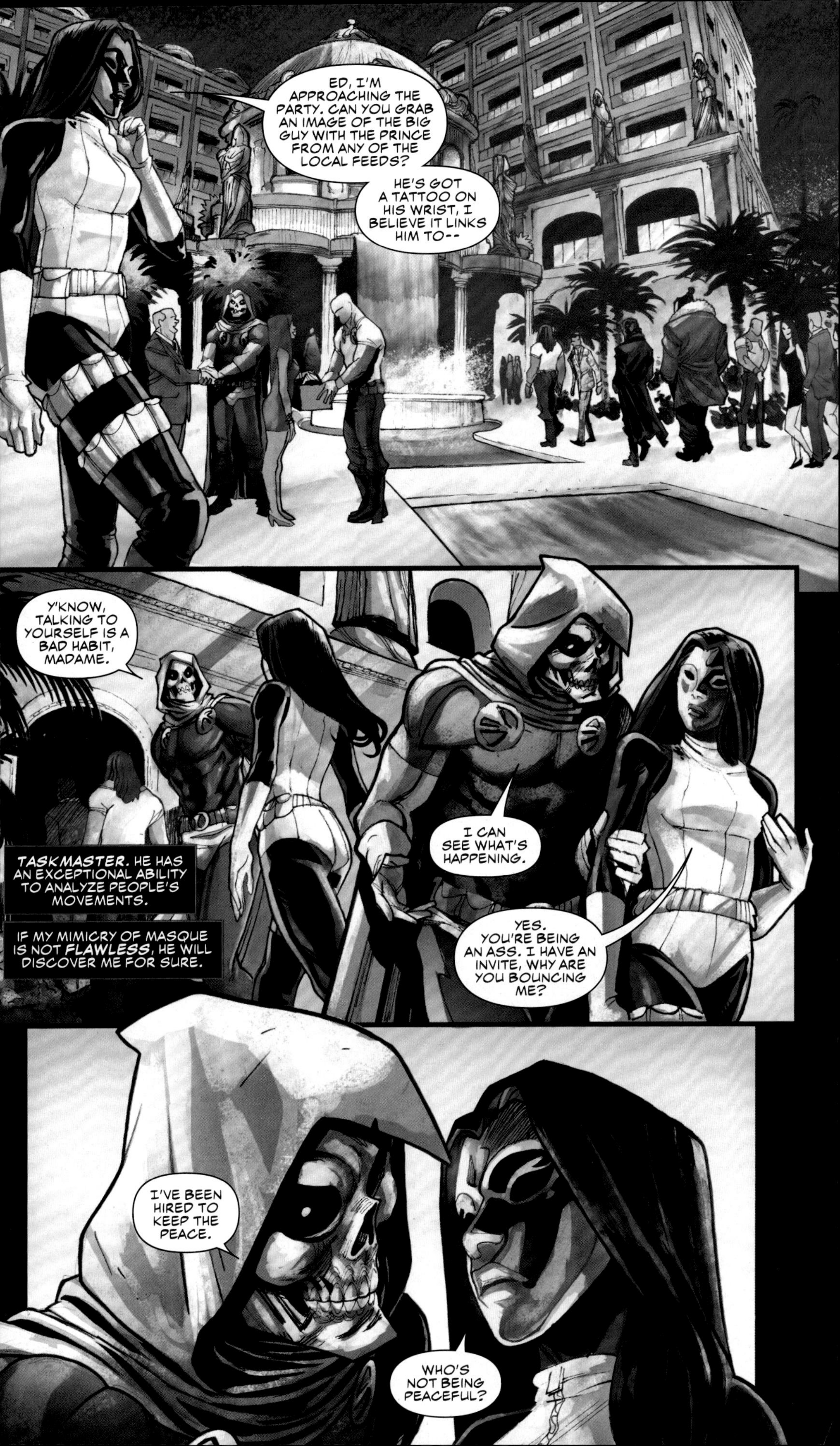
ED, I'M APPROACHING THE PARTY. CAN YOU GRAB AN IMAGE OF THE BIG GUY WITH THE PRINCE FROM ANY OF THE LOCAL FEEDS?
HE'S GOT A TATTOO ON HIS WRIST, I BELIEVE IT LINKS HIM TO--
Y'KNOW, TALKING TO YOURSELF IS A BAD HABIT, MADAME.
TASKMASTER. HE HAS AN EXCEPTIONAL ABILITY TO ANALYZE PEOPLE'S MOVEMENTS.
IF MY MIMICRY OF MASQUE IS NOT FLAWLESS, HE WILL DISCOVER ME FOR SURE.
I CAN SEE WHAT'S HAPPENING.
YES. YOU'RE BEING AN ASS. I HAVE AN INVITE, WHY ARE YOU BOUNCING ME?
I'VE BEEN HIRED TO KEEP THE PEACE.
WHO'S NOT BEING PEACEFUL?

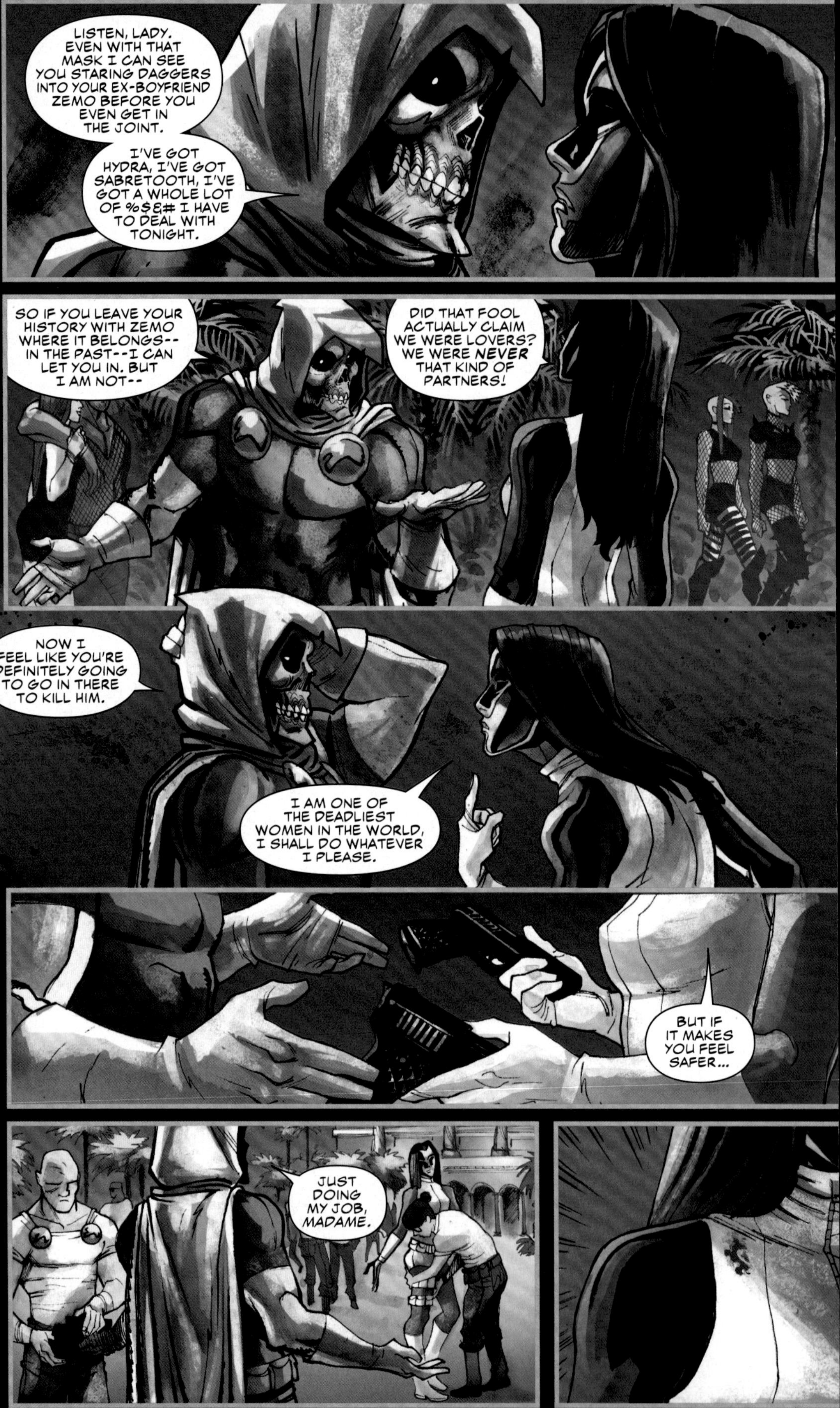
LISTEN, LADY. EVEN WITH THAT MASK I CAN SEE YOU STARING DAGGERS INTO YOUR EX-BOYFRIEND ZEMO BEFORE YOU EVEN GET IN THE JOINT.
I'VE GOT HYDRA, I'VE GOT SABRETOOTH, I'VE GOT A WHOLE LOT OF %$&# I HAVE TO DEAL WITH TONIGHT.
SO IF YOU LEAVE YOUR HISTORY WITH ZEMO WHERE IT BELONGS-- IN THE PAST--I CAN LET YOU IN. BUT I AM NOT--
DID THAT FOOL ACTUALLY CLAIM WE WERE LOVERS? WE WERE NEVER THAT KIND OF PARTNERS!
NOW I FEEL LIKE YOU'RE DEFINITELY GOING TO GO IN THERE TO KILL HIM.
I AM ONE OF THE DEADLIEST WOMEN IN THE WORLD, I SHALL DO WHATEVER I PLEASE.
BUT IF IT MAKES YOU FEEL SAFER...
JUST DOING MY JOB, MADAME.

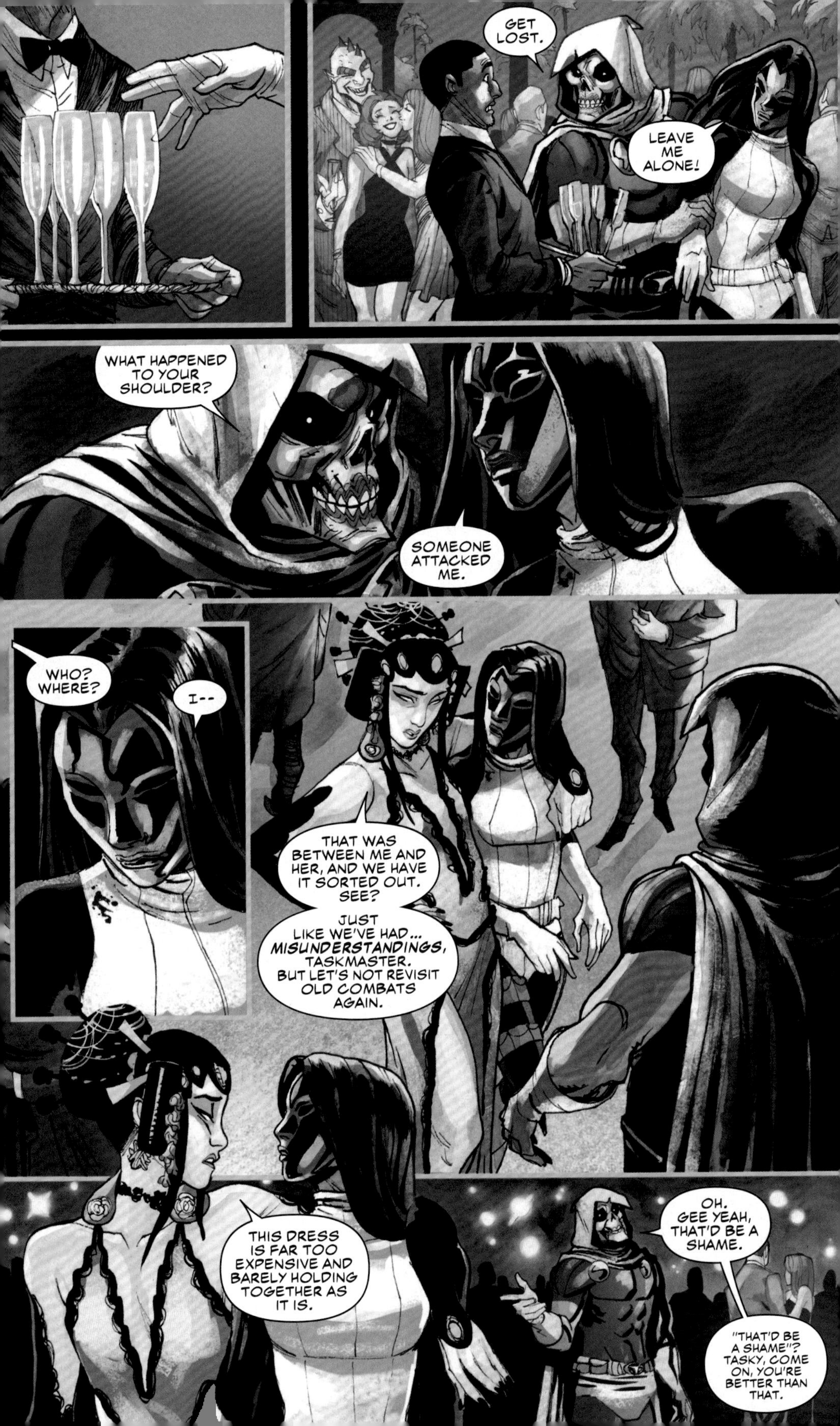
GET LOST.
LEAVE ME ALONE!
WHAT HAPPENED TO YOUR SHOULDER?
SOMEONE ATTACKED ME.
WHO? WHERE?
I--
THAT WAS BETWEEN ME AND HER, AND WE HAVE IT SORTED OUT. SEE?
JUST LIKE WE'VE HAD... MISUNDERSTANDINGS, TASKMASTER. BUT LET'S NOT REVISIT OLD COMBATS AGAIN.
THIS DRESS IS FAR TOO EXPENSIVE AND BARELY HOLDING TOGETHER AS IT IS.
OH. GEE YEAH, THAT'D BE A SHAME.
"THAT'D BE A SHAME"? TASKY, COME ON, YOU'RE BETTER THAN THAT.

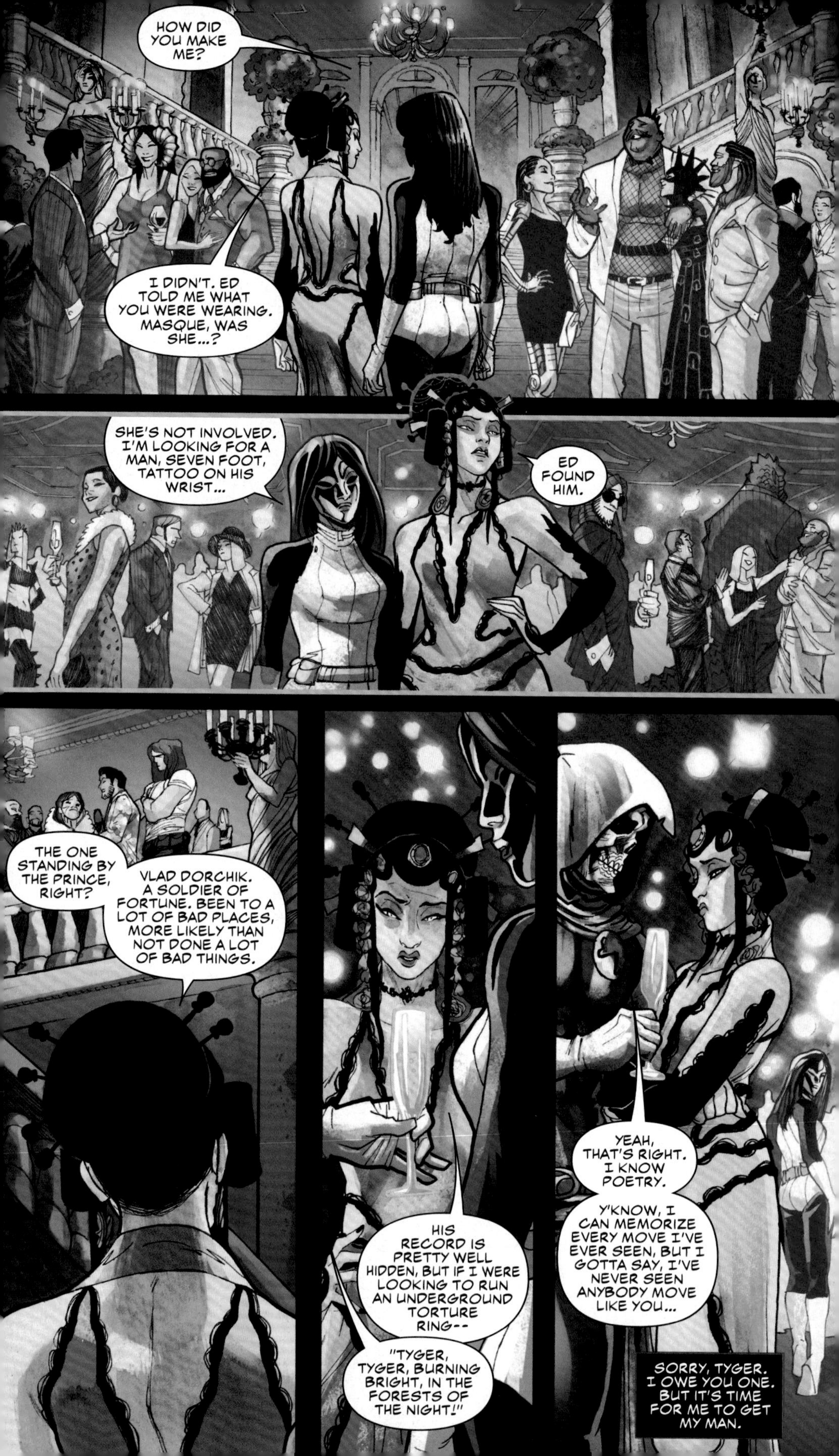
HOW DID YOU MAKE ME?
I DIDN'T. ED TOLD ME WHAT YOU WERE WEARING. MASQUE, WAS SHE...?
SHE'S NOT INVOLVED. I'M LOOKING FOR A MAN, SEVEN FOOT, TATTOO ON HIS WRIST...
ED FOUND HIM.
THE ONE STANDING BY THE PRINCE, RIGHT?
VLAD DORCHIK. A SOLDIER OF FORTUNE. BEEN TO A LOT OF BAD PLACES, MORE LIKELY THAN NOT DONE A LOT OF BAD THINGS.
HIS RECORD IS PRETTY WELL HIDDEN, BUT IF I WERE LOOKING TO RUN AN UNDERGROUND TORTURE RING--
"TYGER, TYGER, BURNING BRIGHT, IN THE FORESTS OF THE NIGHT!"
YEAH, THAT'S RIGHT. I KNOW POETRY.
Y'KNOW, I CAN MEMORIZE EVERY MOVE I'VE EVER SEEN, BUT I GOTTA SAY, I'VE NEVER SEEN ANYBODY MOVE LIKE YOU...
SORRY, TYGER. I OWE YOU ONE. BUT IT'S TIME FOR ME TO GET MY MAN.

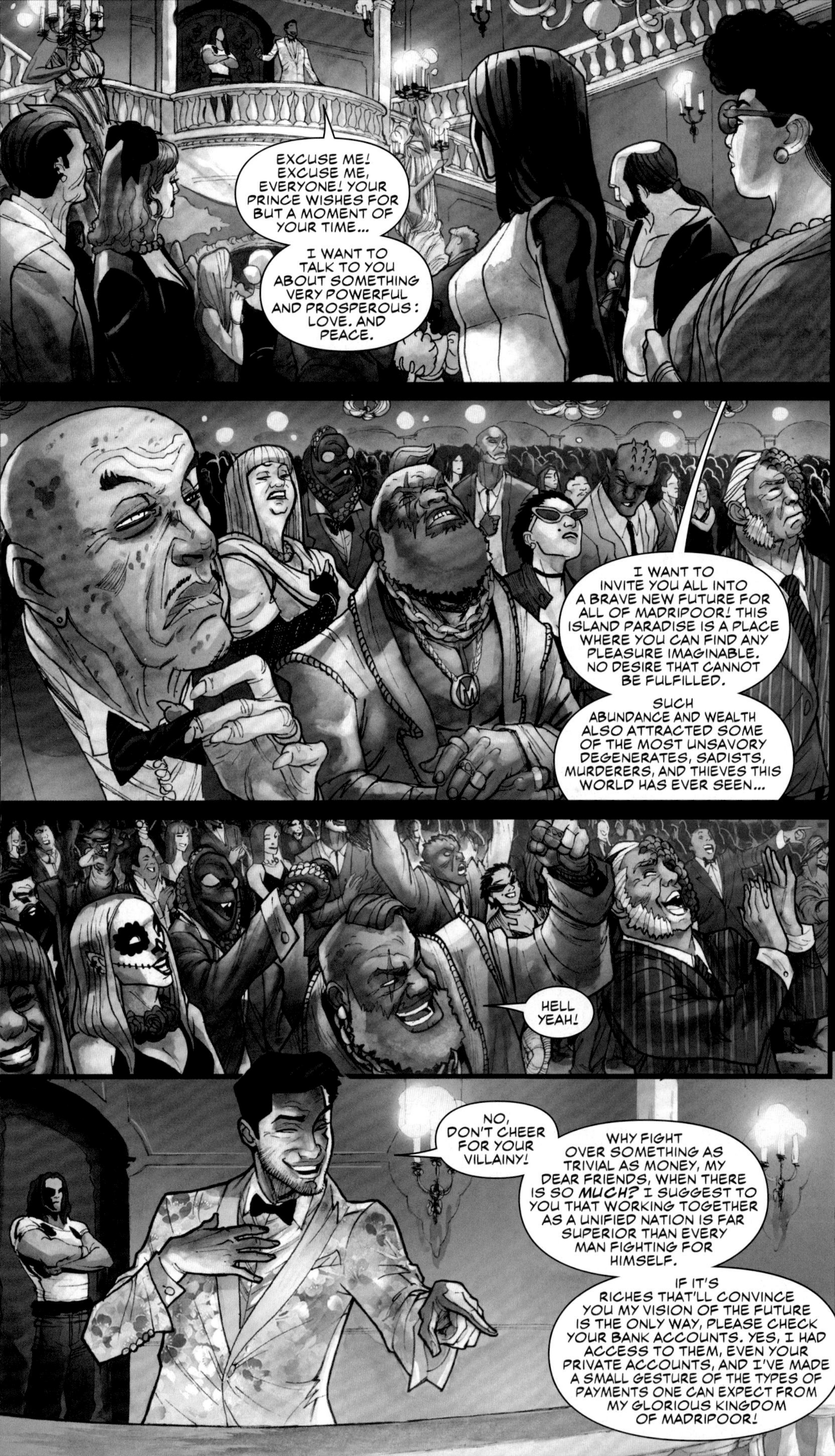
EXCUSE ME! EXCUSE ME, EVERYONE! YOUR PRINCE WISHES FOR BUT A MOMENT OF YOUR TIME...
I WANT TO TALK TO YOU ABOUT SOMETHING VERY POWERFUL AND PROSPEROUS: LOVE. AND PEACE.
I WANT TO INVITE YOU ALL INTO A BRAVE NEW FUTURE FOR ALL OF MADRIPOOR! THIS ISLAND PARADISE IS A PLACE WHERE YOU CAN FIND ANY PLEASURE IMAGINABLE. NO DESIRE THAT CANNOT BE FULFILLED.
SUCH ABUNDANCE AND WEALTH ALSO ATTRACTED SOME OF THE MOST UNSAVORY DEGENERATES, SADISTS, MURDERERS, AND THIEVES THIS WORLD HAS EVER SEEN...
HELL YEAH!
NO, DON'T CHEER FOR YOUR VILLAINY!
WHY FIGHT OVER SOMETHING AS TRIVIAL AS MONEY, MY DEAR FRIENDS, WHEN THERE IS SO *MUCH*? I SUGGEST TO YOU THAT WORKING TOGETHER AS A UNIFIED NATION IS FAR SUPERIOR THAN EVERY MAN FIGHTING FOR HIMSELF.
IF IT'S RICHES THAT'LL CONVINCE YOU MY VISION OF THE FUTURE IS THE ONLY WAY, PLEASE CHECK YOUR BANK ACCOUNTS. YES, I HAD ACCESS TO THEM, EVEN YOUR PRIVATE ACCOUNTS, AND I'VE MADE A SMALL GESTURE OF THE TYPES OF PAYMENTS ONE CAN EXPECT FROM MY GLORIOUS KINGDOM OF MADRIPOOR!

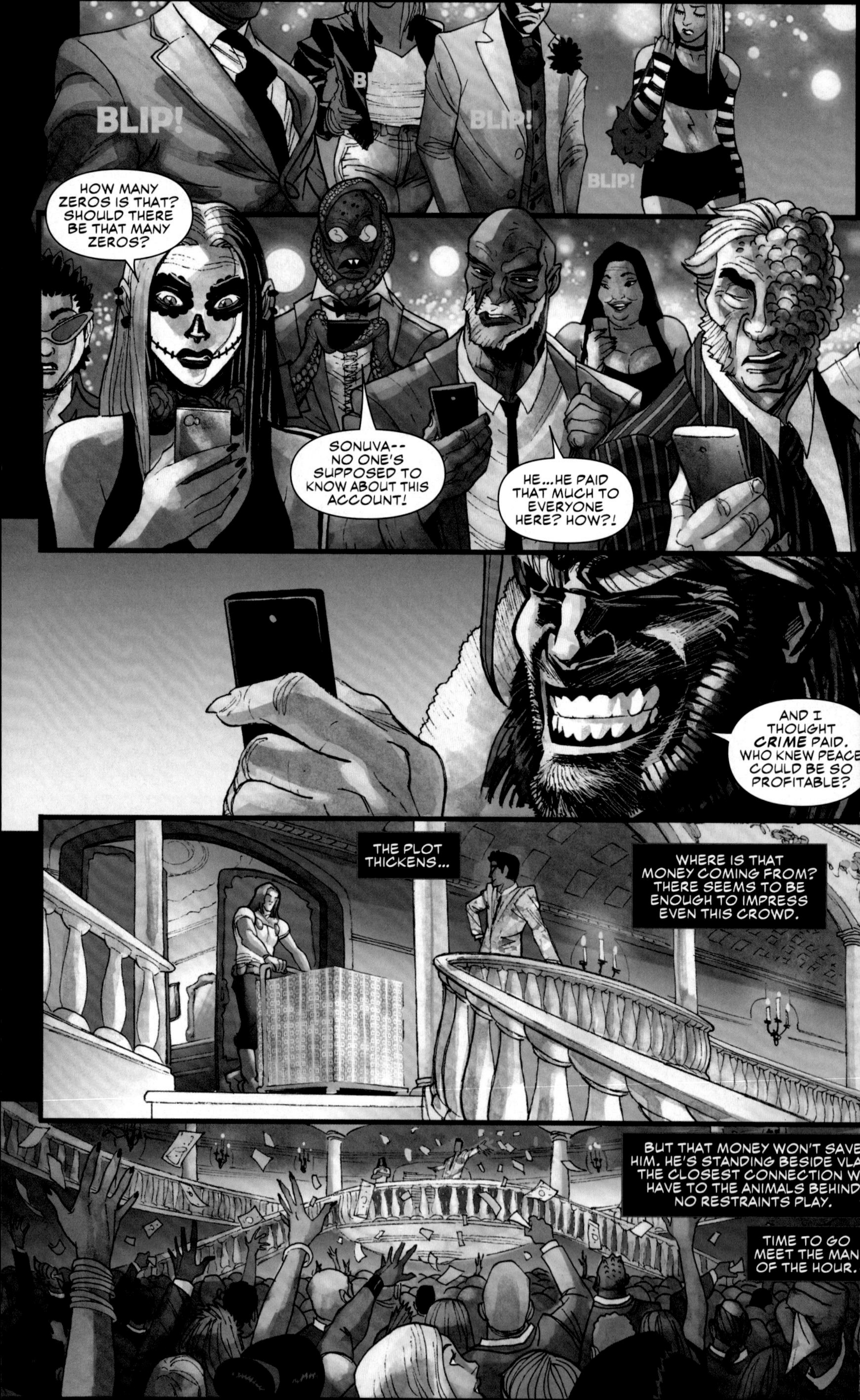
BLIP!
BLIP!
BLIP!
BLIP!
HOW MANY ZEROS IS THAT? SHOULD THERE BE THAT MANY ZEROS?
SONUVA-- NO ONE'S SUPPOSED TO KNOW ABOUT THIS ACCOUNT!
HE...HE PAID THAT MUCH TO EVERYONE HERE? HOW?!
AND I THOUGHT CRIME PAID. WHO KNEW PEACE COULD BE SO PROFITABLE?
THE PLOT THICKENS...
WHERE IS THAT MONEY COMING FROM? THERE SEEMS TO BE ENOUGH TO IMPRESS EVEN THIS CROWD.
BUT THAT MONEY WON'T SAVE HIM. HE'S STANDING BESIDE VLA THE CLOSEST CONNECTION W HAVE TO THE ANIMALS BEHIND NO RESTRAINTS PLAY.
TIME TO GO MEET THE MAN OF THE HOUR.

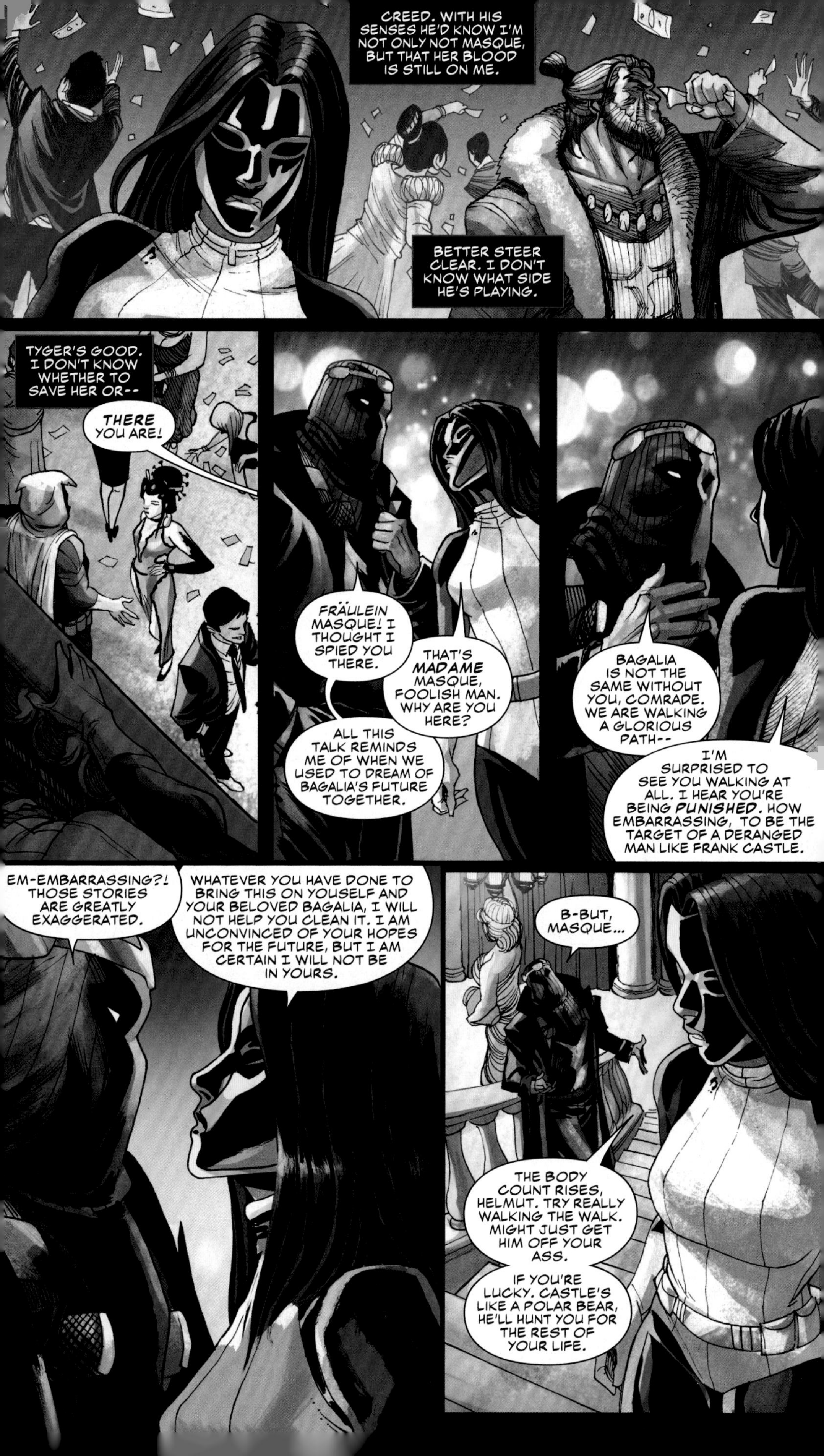
CREED. WITH HIS SENSES HE'D KNOW I'M NOT ONLY NOT MASQUE, BUT THAT HER BLOOD IS STILL ON ME.
BETTER STEER CLEAR. I DON'T KNOW WHAT SIDE HE'S PLAYING.
TYGER'S GOOD. I DON'T KNOW WHETHER TO SAVE HER OR--
THERE YOU ARE!
FRÄULEIN MASQUE! I THOUGHT I SPIED YOU THERE.
THAT'S MADAME MASQUE, FOOLISH MAN. WHY ARE YOU HERE?
ALL THIS TALK REMINDS ME OF WHEN WE USED TO DREAM OF BAGALIA'S FUTURE TOGETHER.
BAGALIA IS NOT THE SAME WITHOUT YOU, COMRADE. WE ARE WALKING A GLORIOUS PATH--
I'M SURPRISED TO SEE YOU WALKING AT ALL. I HEAR YOU'RE BEING PUNISHED. HOW EMBARRASSING, TO BE THE TARGET OF A DERANGED MAN LIKE FRANK CASTLE.
EM-EMBARRASSING?! THOSE STORIES ARE GREATLY EXAGGERATED.
WHATEVER YOU HAVE DONE TO BRING THIS ON YOUSELF AND YOUR BELOVED BAGALIA, I WILL NOT HELP YOU CLEAN IT. I AM UNCONVINCED OF YOUR HOPES FOR THE FUTURE, BUT I AM CERTAIN I WILL NOT BE IN YOURS.
B-BUT, MASQUE...
THE BODY COUNT RISES, HELMUT. TRY REALLY WALKING THE WALK. MIGHT JUST GET HIM OFF YOUR ASS.
IF YOU'RE LUCKY. CASTLE'S LIKE A POLAR BEAR, HE'LL HUNT YOU FOR THE REST OF YOUR LIFE.

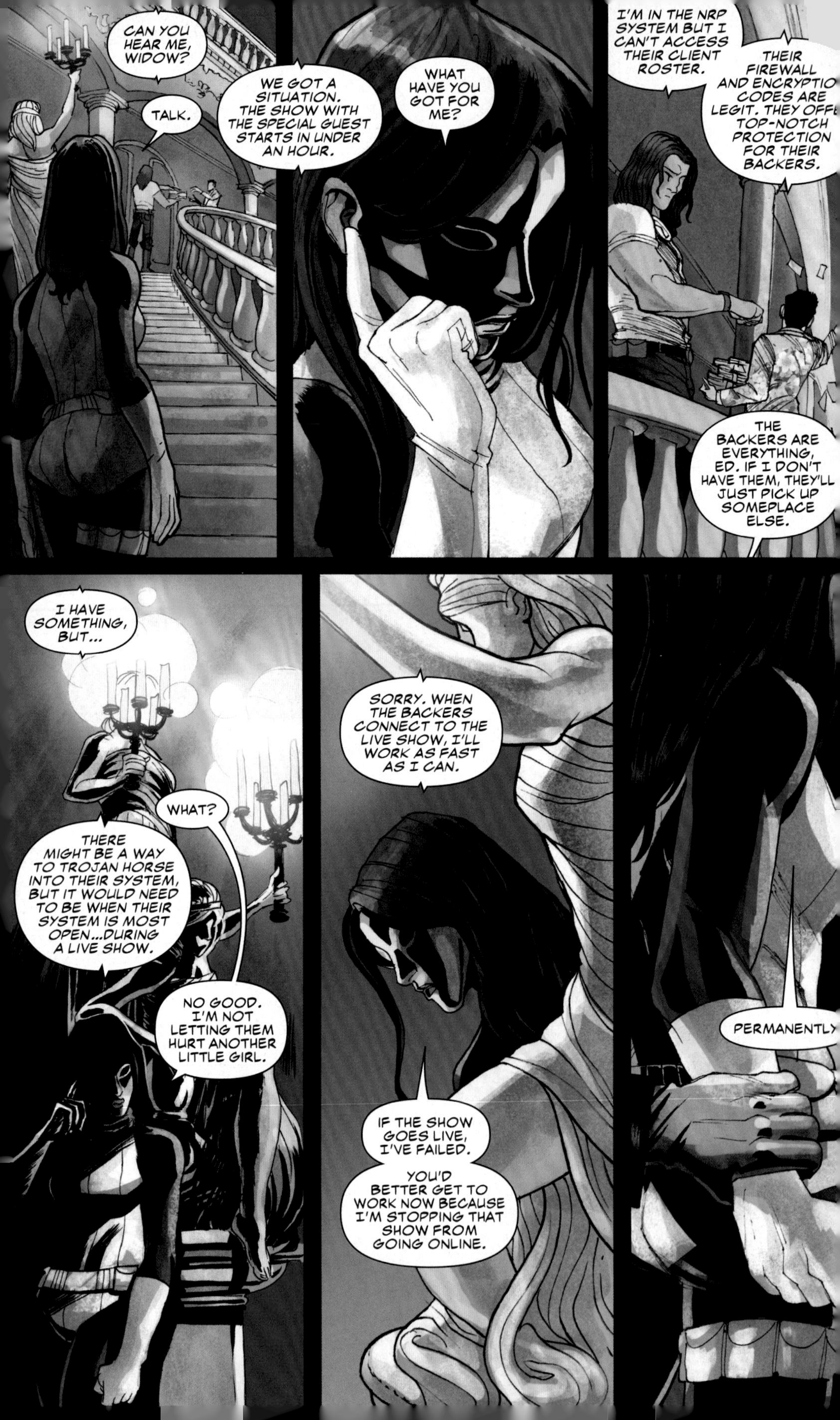
CAN YOU HEAR ME, WIDOW?
TALK.
WE GOT A SITUATION. THE SHOW WITH THE SPECIAL GUEST STARTS IN UNDER AN HOUR.
WHAT HAVE YOU GOT FOR ME?
I'M IN THE NRP SYSTEM BUT I CAN'T ACCESS THEIR CLIENT ROSTER.
THEIR FIREWALL AND ENCRYPTIO CODES ARE LEGIT. THEY OFFE TOP-NOTCH PROTECTION FOR THEIR BACKERS.
THE BACKERS ARE EVERYTHING, ED. IF I DON'T HAVE THEM, THEY'LL JUST PICK UP SOMEPLACE ELSE.
I HAVE SOMETHING, BUT...
WHAT?
THERE MIGHT BE A WAY TO TROJAN HORSE INTO THEIR SYSTEM, BUT IT WOULD NEED TO BE WHEN THEIR SYSTEM IS MOST OPEN...DURING A LIVE SHOW.
NO GOOD. I'M NOT LETTING THEM HURT ANOTHER LITTLE GIRL.
SORRY. WHEN THE BACKERS CONNECT TO THE LIVE SHOW, I'LL WORK AS FAST AS I CAN.
IF THE SHOW GOES LIVE, I'VE FAILED.
YOU'D BETTER GET TO WORK NOW BECAUSE I'M STOPPING THAT SHOW FROM GOING ONLINE.
PERMANENTLY

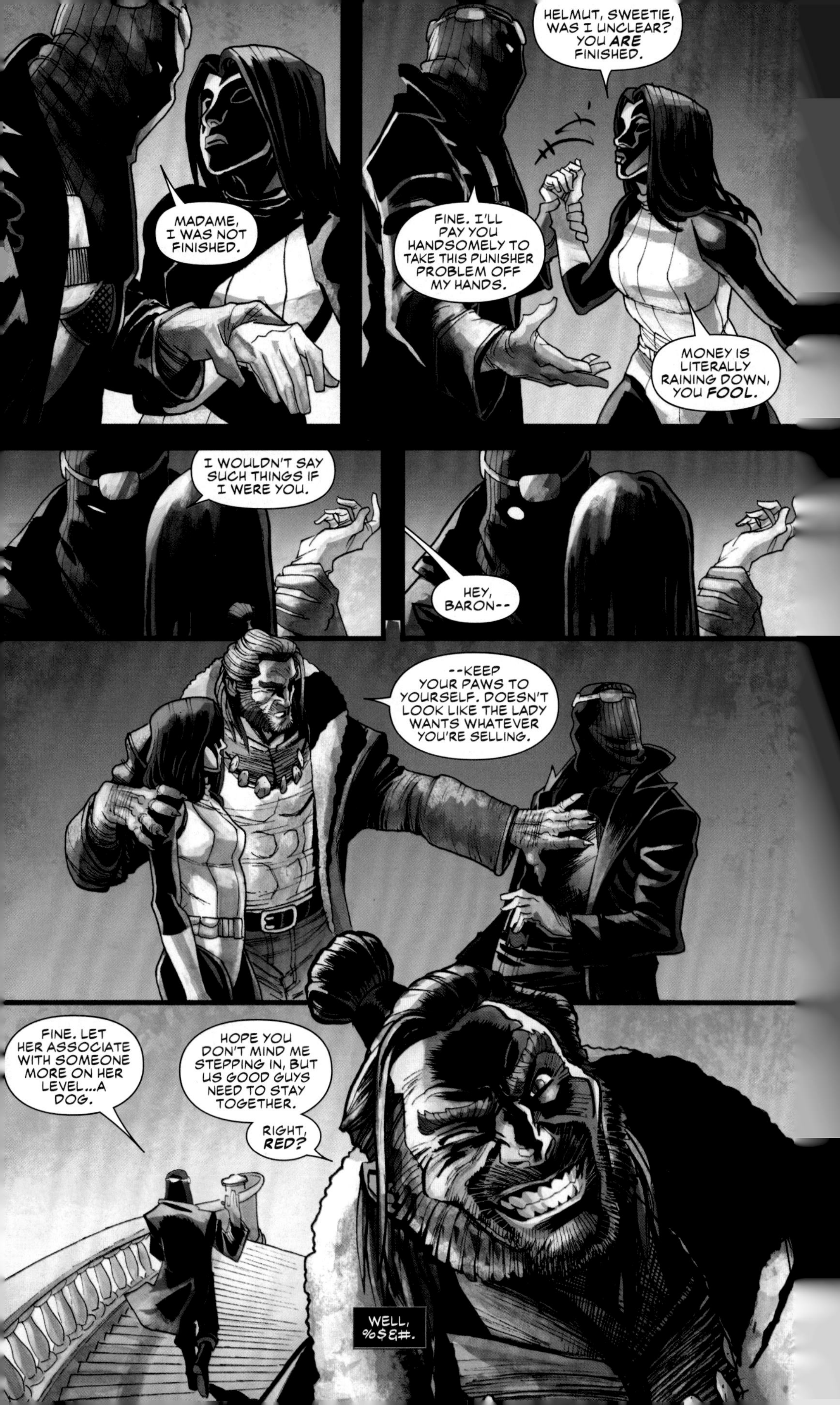
MADAME, I WAS NOT FINISHED.
HELMUT, SWEETIE, WAS I UNCLEAR? YOU ARE FINISHED.
FINE. I'LL PAY YOU HANDSOMELY TO TAKE THIS PUNISHER PROBLEM OFF MY HANDS.
MONEY IS LITERALLY RAINING DOWN, YOU FOOL.
I WOULDN'T SAY SUCH THINGS IF I WERE YOU.
HEY, BARON--
--KEEP YOUR PAWS TO YOURSELF. DOESN'T LOOK LIKE THE LADY WANTS WHATEVER YOU'RE SELLING.
FINE. LET HER ASSOCIATE WITH SOMEONE MORE ON HER LEVEL...A DOG.
HOPE YOU DON'T MIND ME STEPPING IN, BUT US GOOD GUYS NEED TO STAY TOGETHER.
RIGHT, RED?
WELL, %$&#.

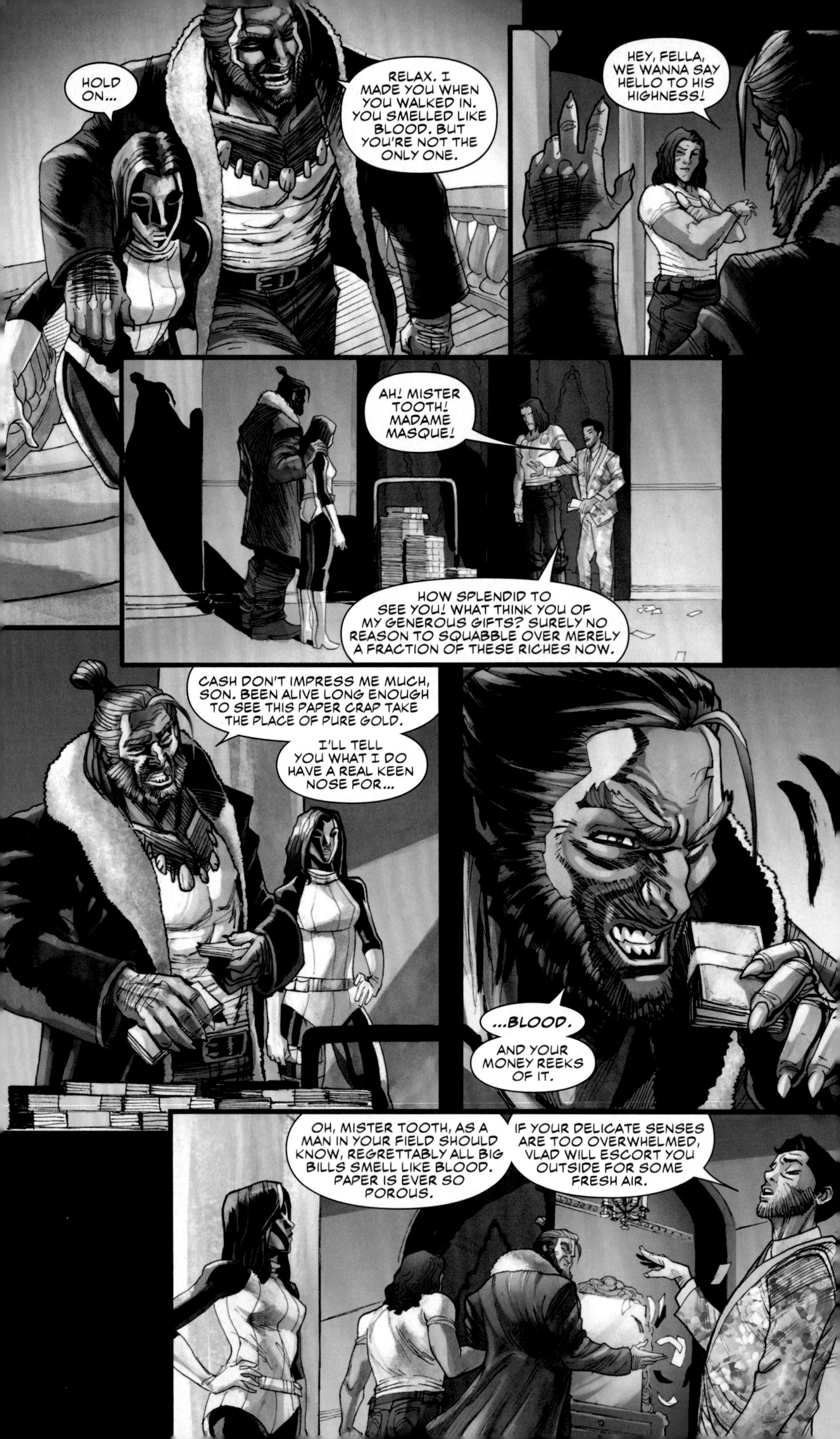
HOLD ON...
RELAX. I MADE YOU WHEN YOU WALKED IN. YOU SMELLED LIKE BLOOD. BUT YOU'RE NOT THE ONLY ONE.
HEY, FELLA, WE WANNA SAY HELLO TO HIS HIGHNESS!
AH! MISTER TOOTH! MADAME MASQUE!
HOW SPLENDID TO SEE YOU! WHAT THINK YOU OF MY GENEROUS GIFTS? SURELY NO REASON TO SQUABBLE OVER MERELY A FRACTION OF THESE RICHES NOW.
CASH DON'T IMPRESS ME MUCH, SON. BEEN ALIVE LONG ENOUGH TO SEE THIS PAPER CRAP TAKE THE PLACE OF PURE GOLD.
I'LL TELL YOU WHAT I DO HAVE A REAL KEEN NOSE FOR...
...BLOOD.
AND YOUR MONEY REEKS OF IT.
OH, MISTER TOOTH, AS A MAN IN YOUR FIELD SHOULD KNOW, REGRETTABLY ALL BIG BILLS SMELL LIKE BLOOD. PAPER IS EVER SO POROUS.
IF YOUR DELICATE SENSES ARE TOO OVERWHELMED, VLAD WILL ESCORT YOU OUTSIDE FOR SOME FRESH AIR.

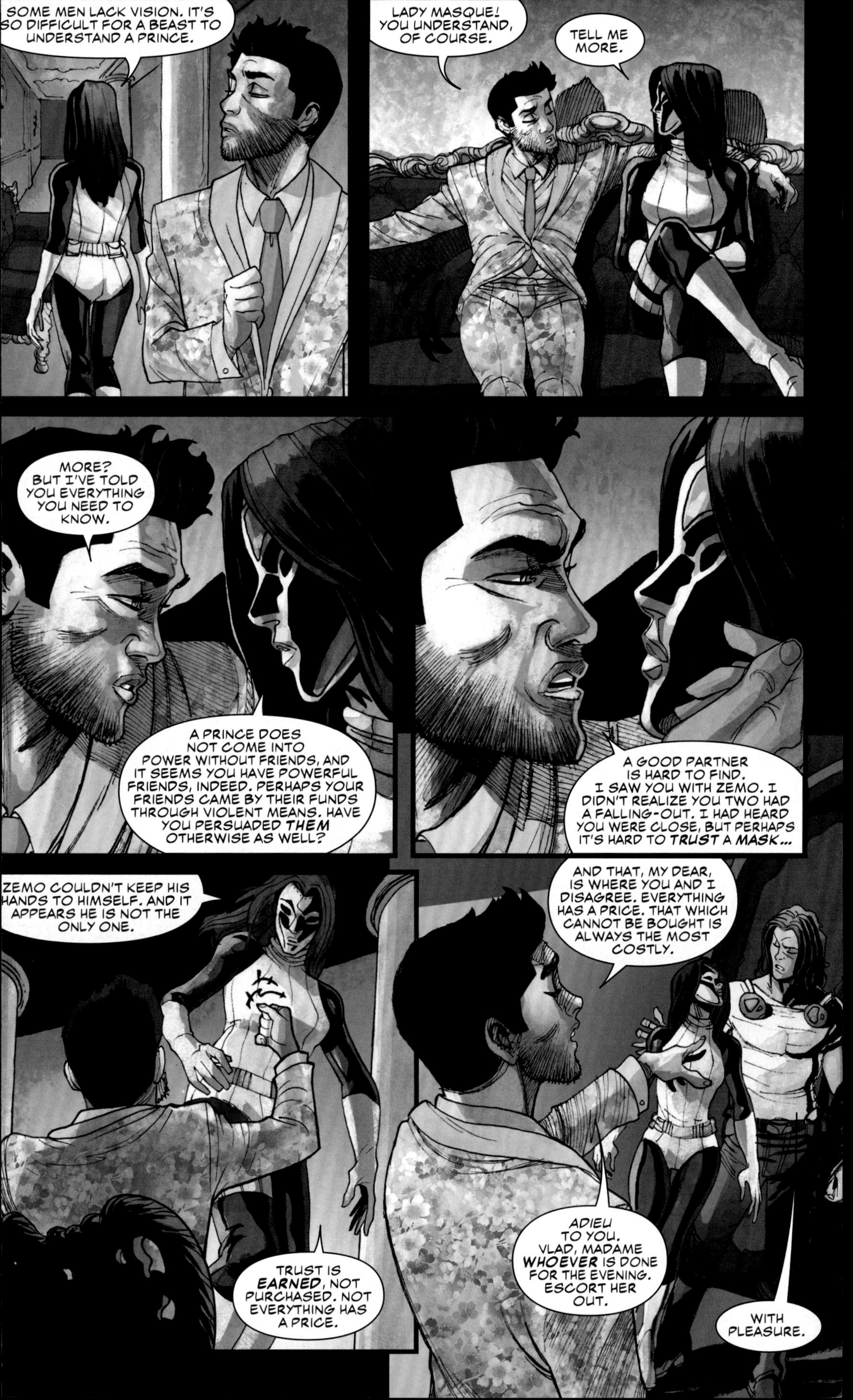
SOME MEN LACK VISION. IT'S SO DIFFICULT FOR A BEAST TO UNDERSTAND A PRINCE.
LADY MASQUE! YOU UNDERSTAND, OF COURSE.
TELL ME MORE.
MORE? BUT I'VE TOLD YOU EVERYTHING YOU NEED TO KNOW.
A PRINCE DOES NOT COME INTO POWER WITHOUT FRIENDS, AND IT SEEMS YOU HAVE POWERFUL FRIENDS, INDEED. PERHAPS YOUR FRIENDS CAME BY THEIR FUNDS THROUGH VIOLENT MEANS. HAVE YOU PERSUADED ***THEM*** OTHERWISE AS WELL?
A GOOD PARTNER IS HARD TO FIND. I SAW YOU WITH ZEMO. I DIDN'T REALIZE YOU TWO HAD A FALLING-OUT. I HAD HEARD YOU WERE CLOSE, BUT PERHAPS IT'S HARD TO ***TRUST*** A ***MASK...***
ZEMO COULDN'T KEEP HIS HANDS TO HIMSELF. AND IT APPEARS HE IS NOT THE ONLY ONE.
TRUST IS ***EARNED***, NOT PURCHASED. NOT EVERYTHING HAS A PRICE.
AND THAT, MY DEAR, IS WHERE YOU AND I DISAGREE. EVERYTHING HAS A PRICE. THAT WHICH CANNOT BE BOUGHT IS ALWAYS THE MOST COSTLY.
ADIEU TO YOU. VLAD, MADAME ***WHOEVER*** IS DONE FOR THE EVENING. ESCORT HER OUT.
WITH PLEASURE.

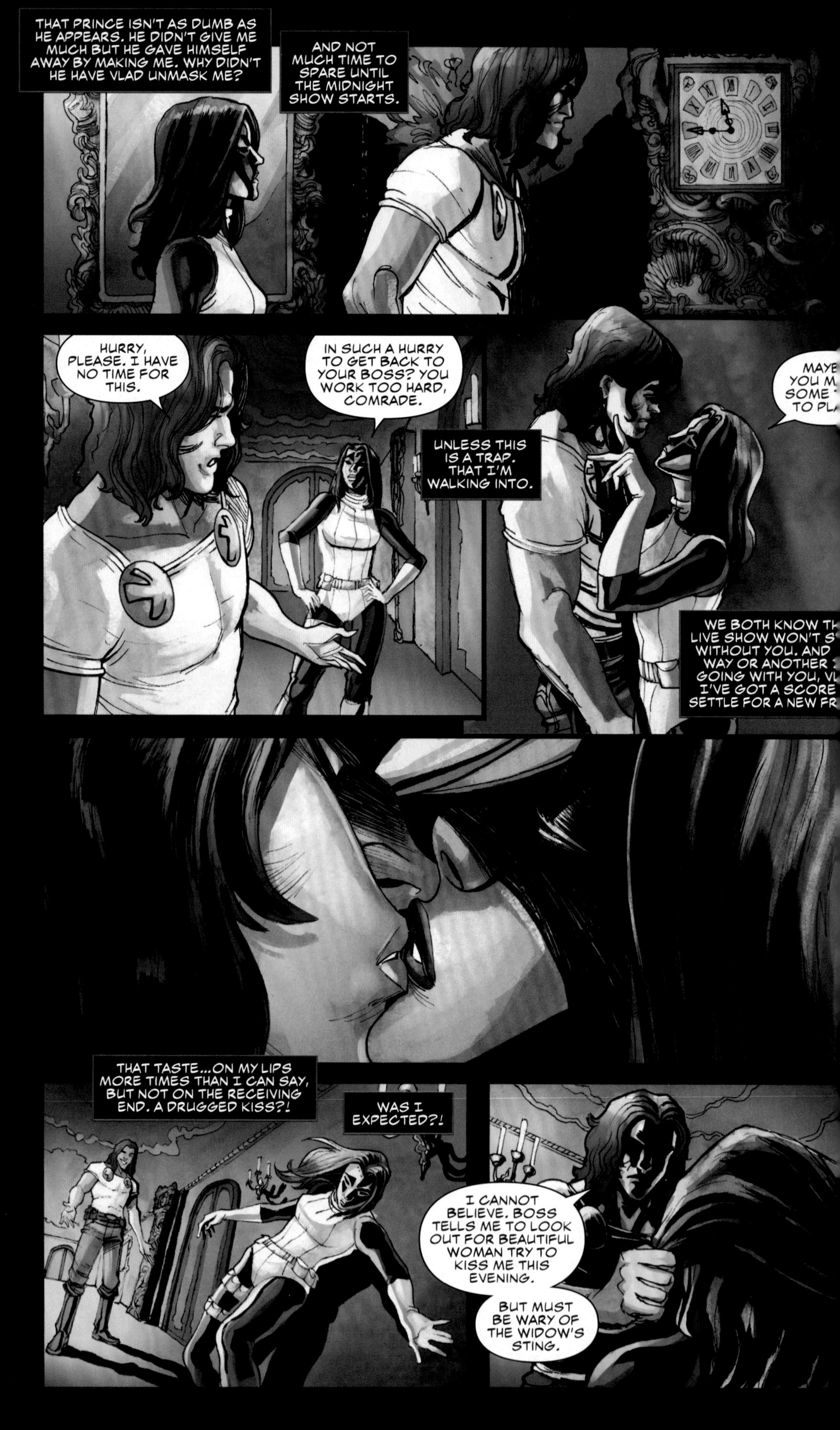
THAT PRINCE ISN'T AS DUMB AS HE APPEARS. HE DIDN'T GIVE ME MUCH BUT HE GAVE HIMSELF AWAY BY MAKING ME. WHY DIDN'T HE HAVE VLAD UNMASK ME?
AND NOT MUCH TIME TO SPARE UNTIL THE MIDNIGHT SHOW STARTS.
HURRY, PLEASE. I HAVE NO TIME FOR THIS.
IN SUCH A HURRY TO GET BACK TO YOUR BOSS? YOU WORK TOO HARD, COMRADE.
UNLESS THIS IS A TRAP. THAT I'M WALKING INTO.
WE BOTH KNOW LIVE SHOW WON'T WITHOUT YOU. AND WAY OR ANOTHER GOING WITH YOU, I'VE GOT A SCORE SETTLE FOR A NEW
THAT TASTE...ON MY LIPS MORE TIMES THAN I CAN SAY, BUT NOT ON THE RECEIVING END. A DRUGGED KISS?!
WAS I EXPECTED?!
I CANNOT BELIEVE. BOSS TELLS ME TO LOOK OUT FOR BEAUTIFUL WOMAN TRY TO KISS ME THIS EVENING.
BUT MUST BE WARY OF THE WIDOW'S STING.

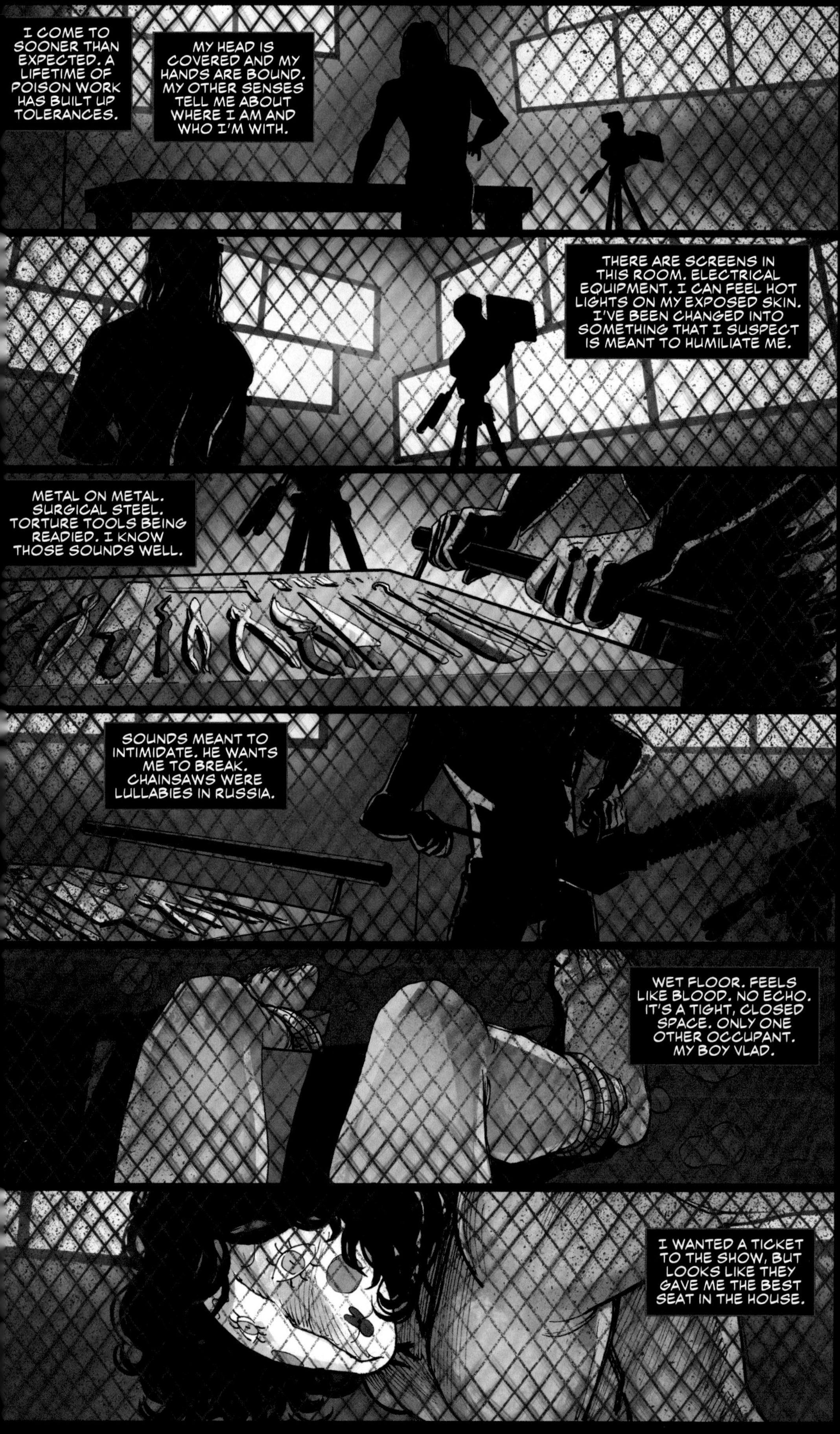
I COME TO SOONER THAN EXPECTED. A LIFETIME OF POISON WORK HAS BUILT UP TOLERANCES.
MY HEAD IS COVERED AND MY HANDS ARE BOUND. MY OTHER SENSES TELL ME ABOUT WHERE I AM AND WHO I'M WITH.
THERE ARE SCREENS IN THIS ROOM. ELECTRICAL EQUIPMENT. I CAN FEEL HOT LIGHTS ON MY EXPOSED SKIN. I'VE BEEN CHANGED INTO SOMETHING THAT I SUSPECT IS MEANT TO HUMILIATE ME.
METAL ON METAL. SURGICAL STEEL. TORTURE TOOLS BEING READIED. I KNOW THOSE SOUNDS WELL.
SOUNDS MEANT TO INTIMIDATE. HE WANTS ME TO BREAK. CHAINSAWS WERE LULLABIES IN RUSSIA.
WET FLOOR. FEELS LIKE BLOOD. NO ECHO. IT'S A TIGHT, CLOSED SPACE. ONLY ONE OTHER OCCUPANT. MY BOY VLAD.
I WANTED A TICKET TO THE SHOW, BUT LOOKS LIKE THEY GAVE ME THE BEST SEAT IN THE HOUSE.

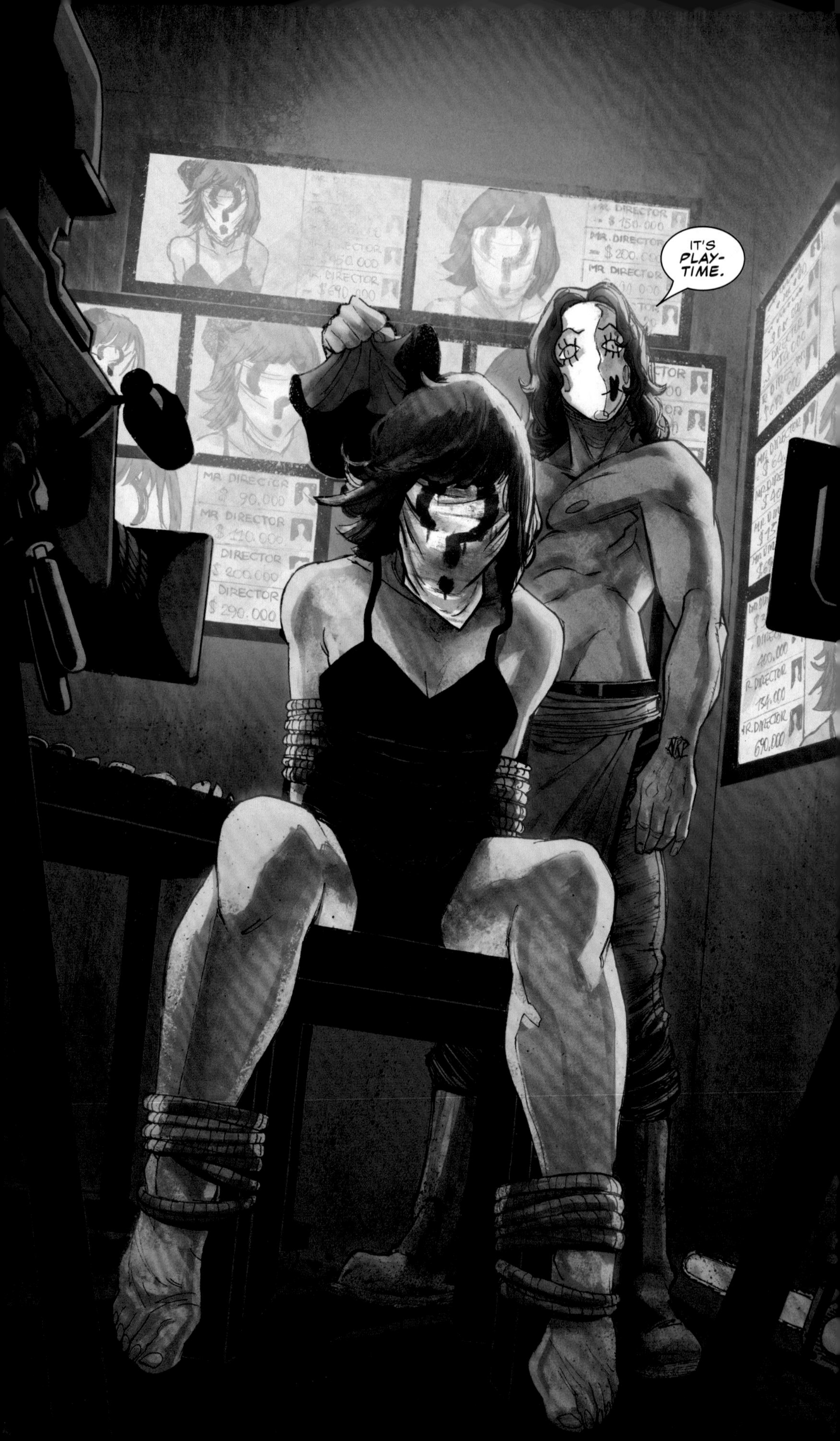
IT'S PLAY-TIME.

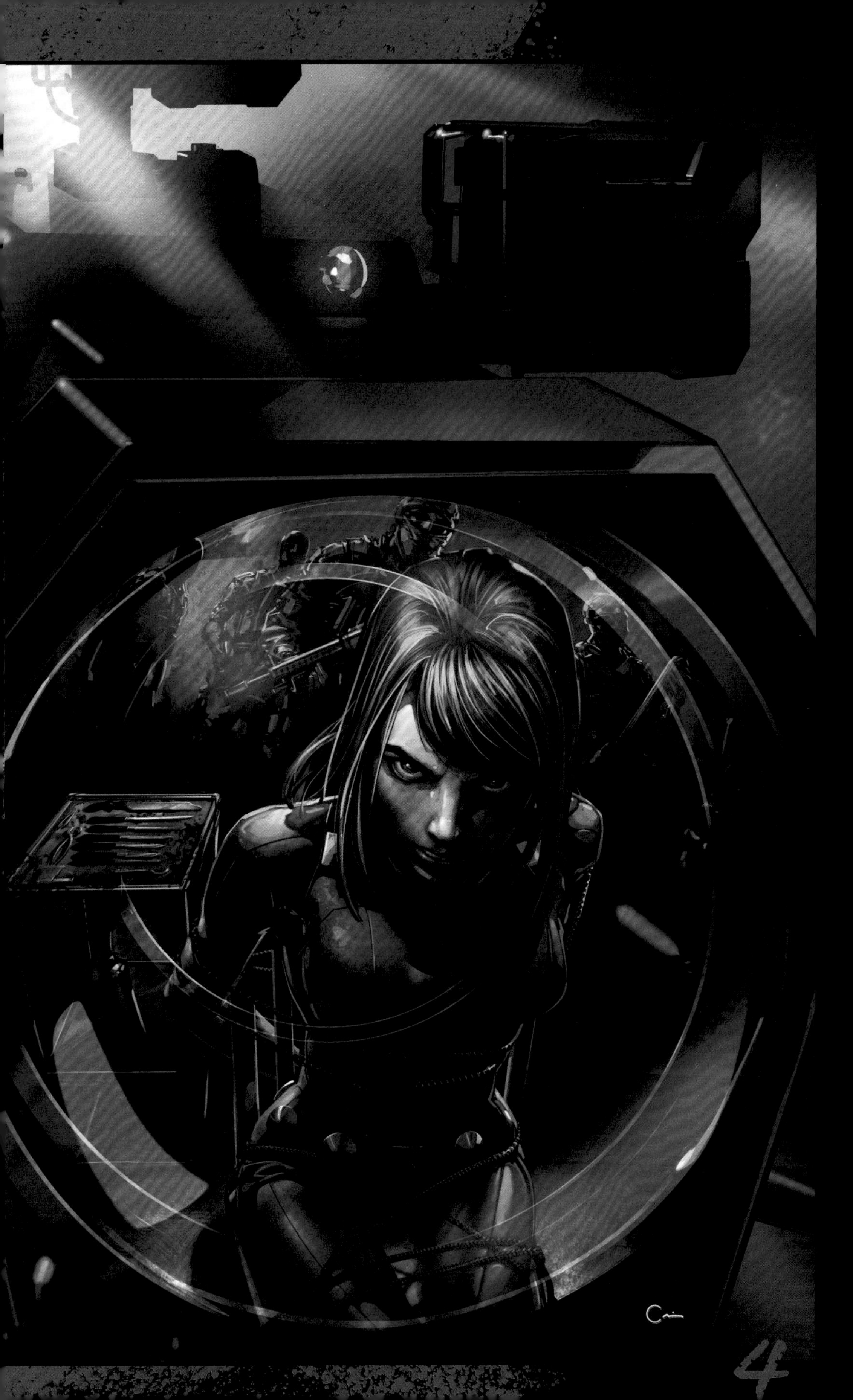
4

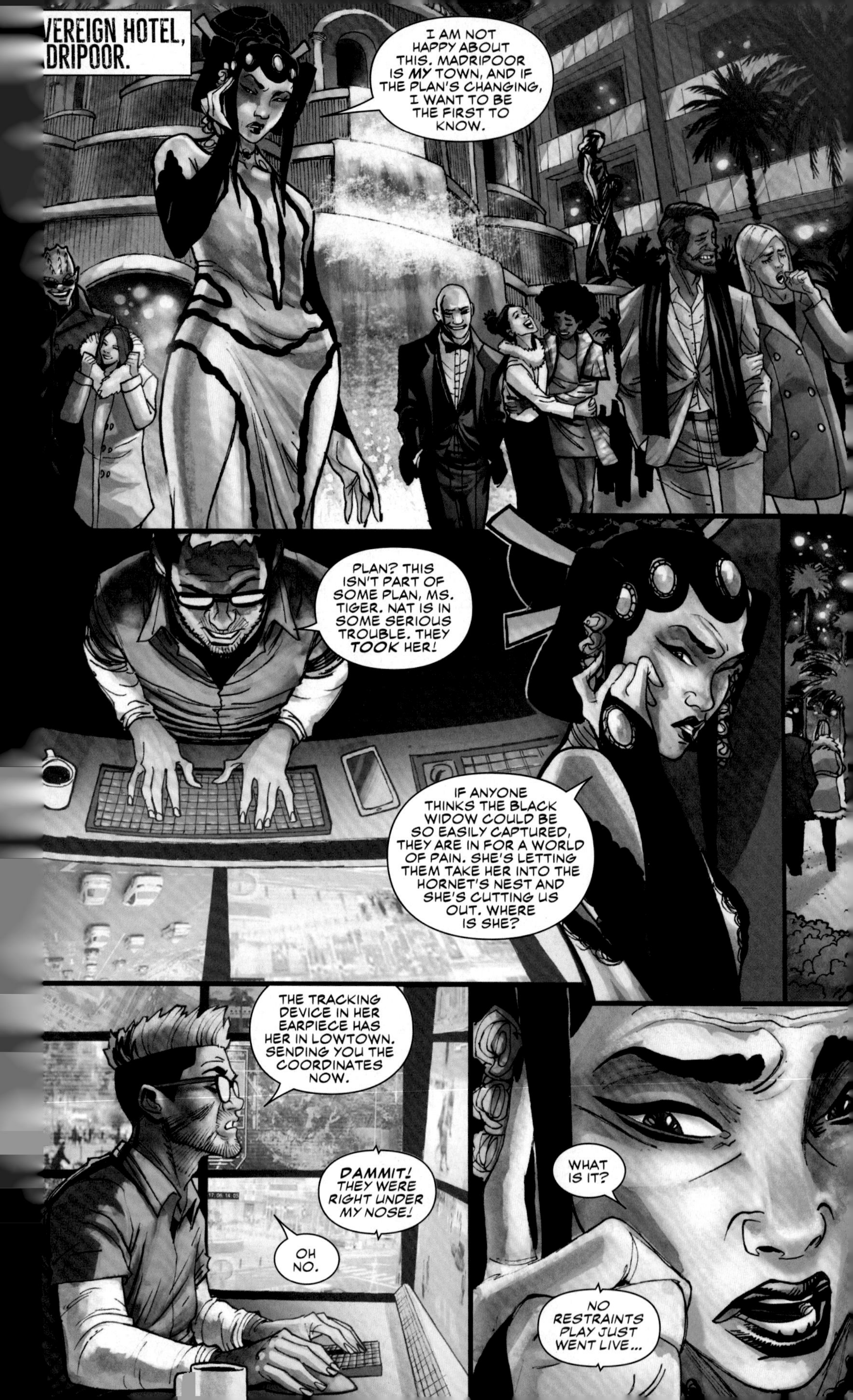
VEREIGN HOTEL, ADRIPOOR.
I AM NOT HAPPY ABOUT THIS. MADRIPOOR IS MY TOWN, AND IF THE PLAN'S CHANGING, I WANT TO BE THE FIRST TO KNOW.
PLAN? THIS ISN'T PART OF SOME PLAN, MS. TIGER. NAT IS IN SOME SERIOUS TROUBLE. THEY TOOK HER!
IF ANYONE THINKS THE BLACK WIDOW COULD BE SO EASILY CAPTURED, THEY ARE IN FOR A WORLD OF PAIN. SHE'S LETTING THEM TAKE HER INTO THE HORNET'S NEST AND SHE'S CUTTING US OUT. WHERE IS SHE?
THE TRACKING DEVICE IN HER EARPIECE HAS HER IN LOWTOWN. SENDING YOU THE COORDINATES NOW.
DAMMIT! THEY WERE RIGHT UNDER MY NOSE!
OH NO.
WHAT IS IT?
NO RESTRAINTS PLAY JUST WENT LIVE...

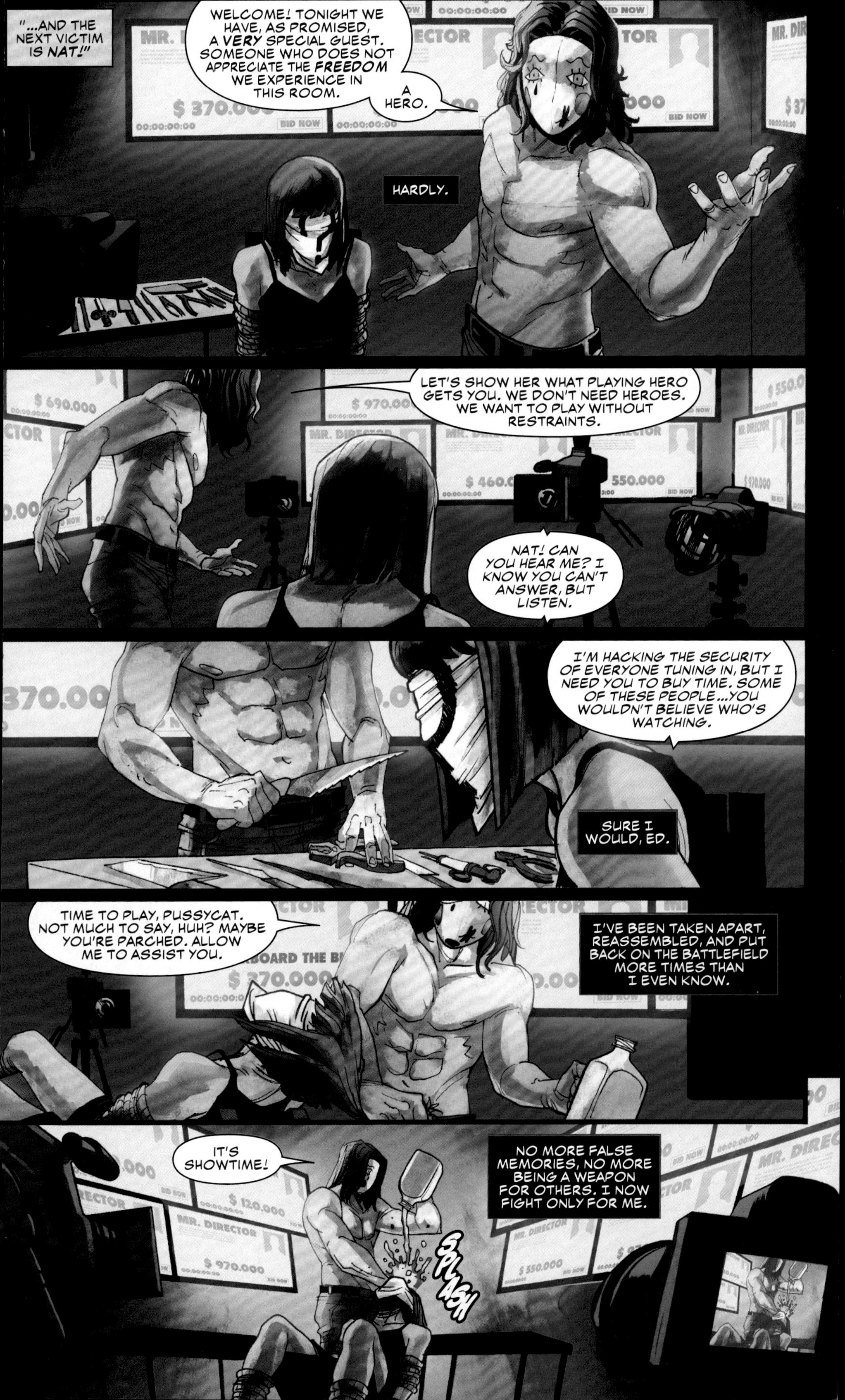
"...AND THE NEXT VICTIM IS NAT!"
WELCOME! TONIGHT WE HAVE, AS PROMISED, A VERY SPECIAL GUEST. SOMEONE WHO DOES NOT APPRECIATE THE FREEDOM WE EXPERIENCE IN THIS ROOM.
A HERO.
HARDLY.
LET'S SHOW HER WHAT PLAYING HERO GETS YOU. WE DON'T NEED HEROES. WE WANT TO PLAY WITHOUT RESTRAINTS.
NAT! CAN YOU HEAR ME? I KNOW YOU CAN'T ANSWER, BUT LISTEN.
I'M HACKING THE SECURITY OF EVERYONE TUNING IN, BUT I NEED YOU TO BUY TIME. SOME OF THESE PEOPLE...YOU WOULDN'T BELIEVE WHO'S WATCHING.
SURE I WOULD, ED.
TIME TO PLAY, PUSSYCAT. NOT MUCH TO SAY, HUH? MAYBE YOU'RE PARCHED. ALLOW ME TO ASSIST YOU.
I'VE BEEN TAKEN APART, REASSEMBLED, AND PUT BACK ON THE BATTLEFIELD MORE TIMES THAN I EVEN KNOW.
IT'S SHOWTIME!
NO MORE FALSE MEMORIES, NO MORE BEING A WEAPON FOR OTHERS. I NOW FIGHT ONLY FOR ME.
SPLASH

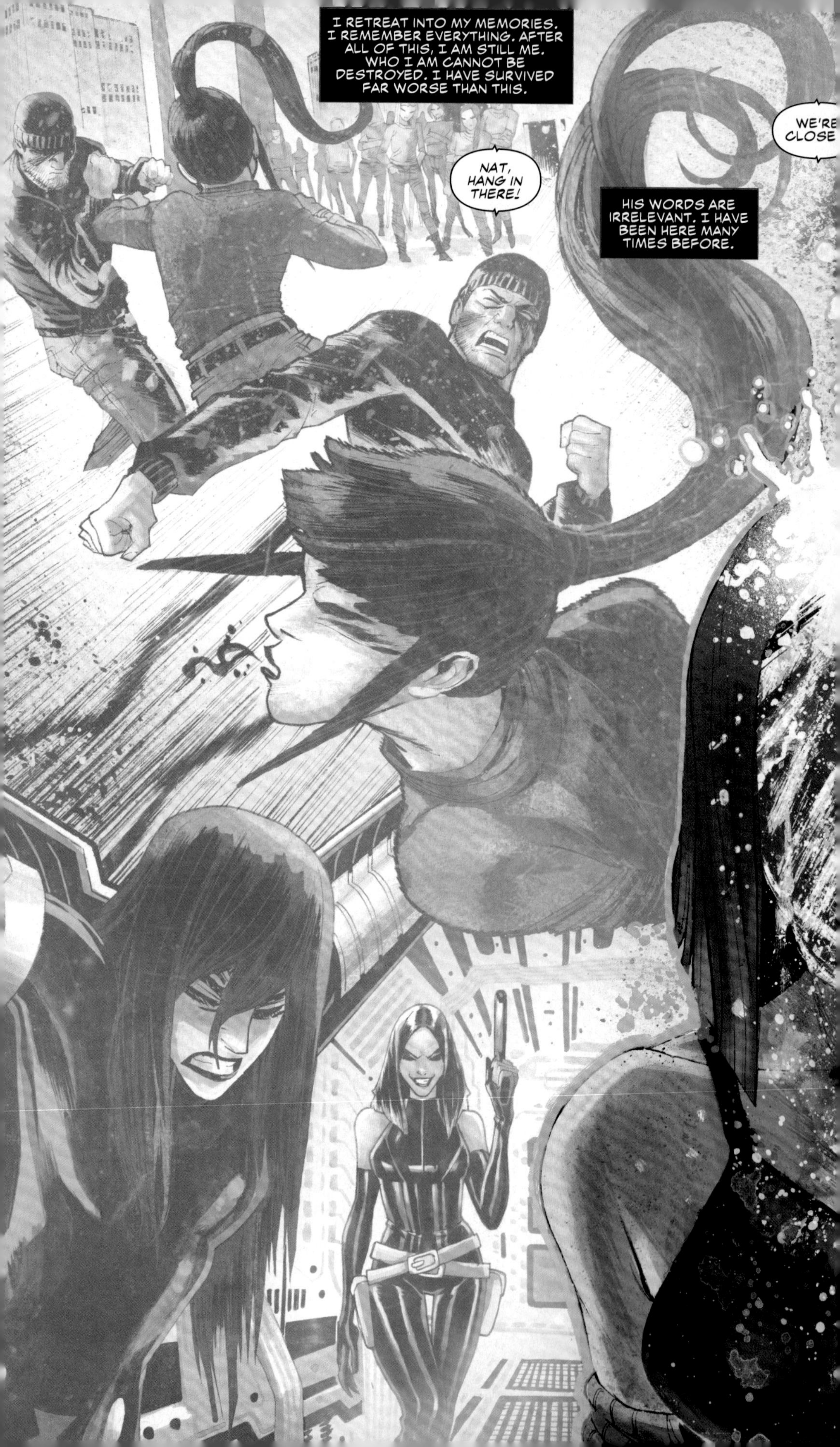
I RETREAT INTO MY MEMORIES. I REMEMBER EVERYTHING. AFTER ALL OF THIS, I AM STILL ME. WHO I AM CANNOT BE DESTROYED. I HAVE SURVIVED FAR WORSE THAN THIS.
NAT, HANG IN THERE!
WE'RE CLOSE
HIS WORDS ARE IRRELEVANT. I HAVE BEEN HERE MANY TIMES BEFORE.

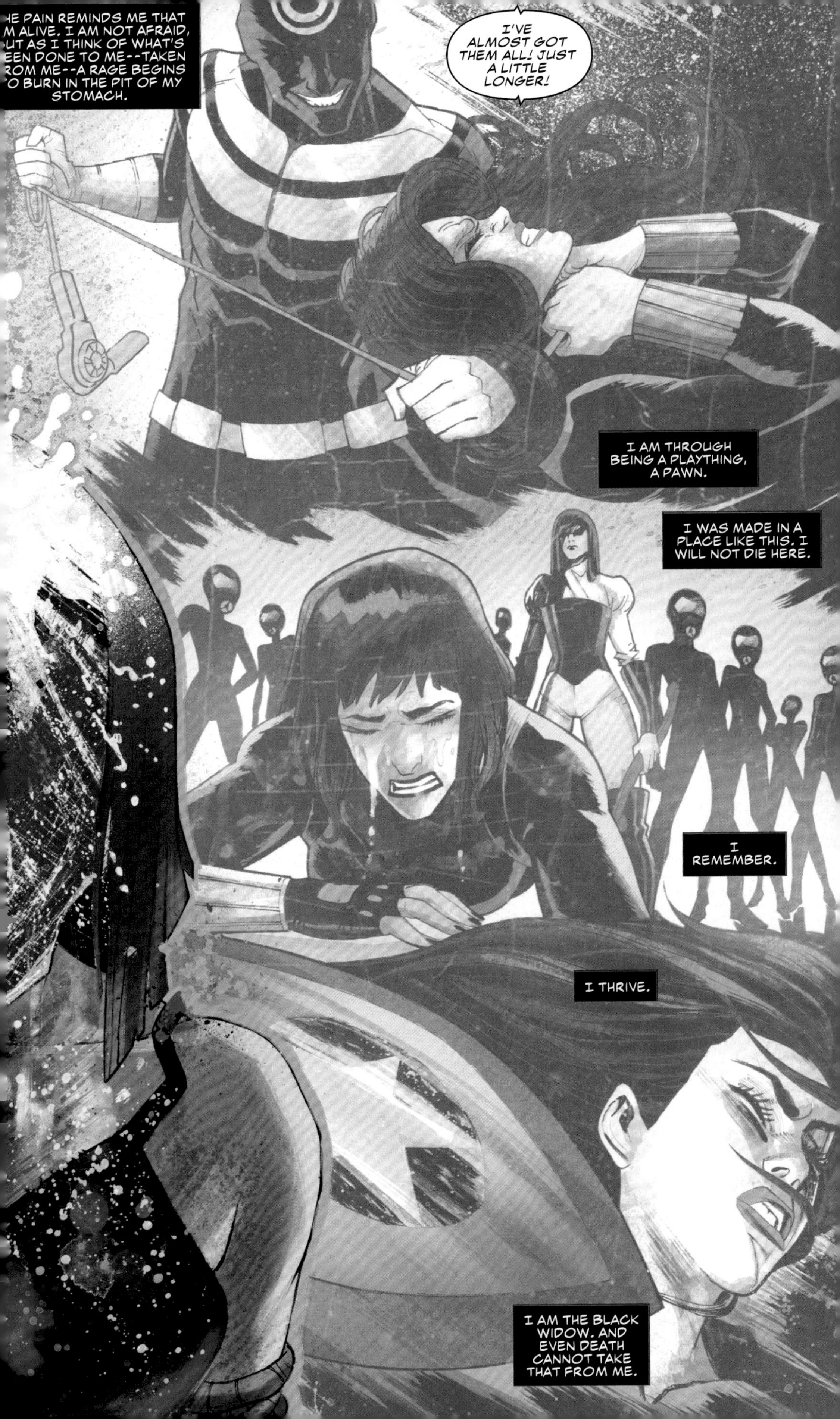

HE PAIN REMINDS ME THAT M ALIVE. I AM NOT AFRAID, UT AS I THINK OF WHAT'S EEN DONE TO ME--TAKEN ROM ME--A RAGE BEGINS O BURN IN THE PIT OF MY STOMACH.
I'VE ALMOST GOT THEM ALL! JUST A LITTLE LONGER!
I AM THROUGH BEING A PLAYTHING, A PAWN.
I WAS MADE IN A PLACE LIKE THIS. I WILL NOT DIE HERE.
I REMEMBER.
I THRIVE.
I AM THE BLACK WIDOW. AND EVEN DEATH CANNOT TAKE THAT FROM ME.

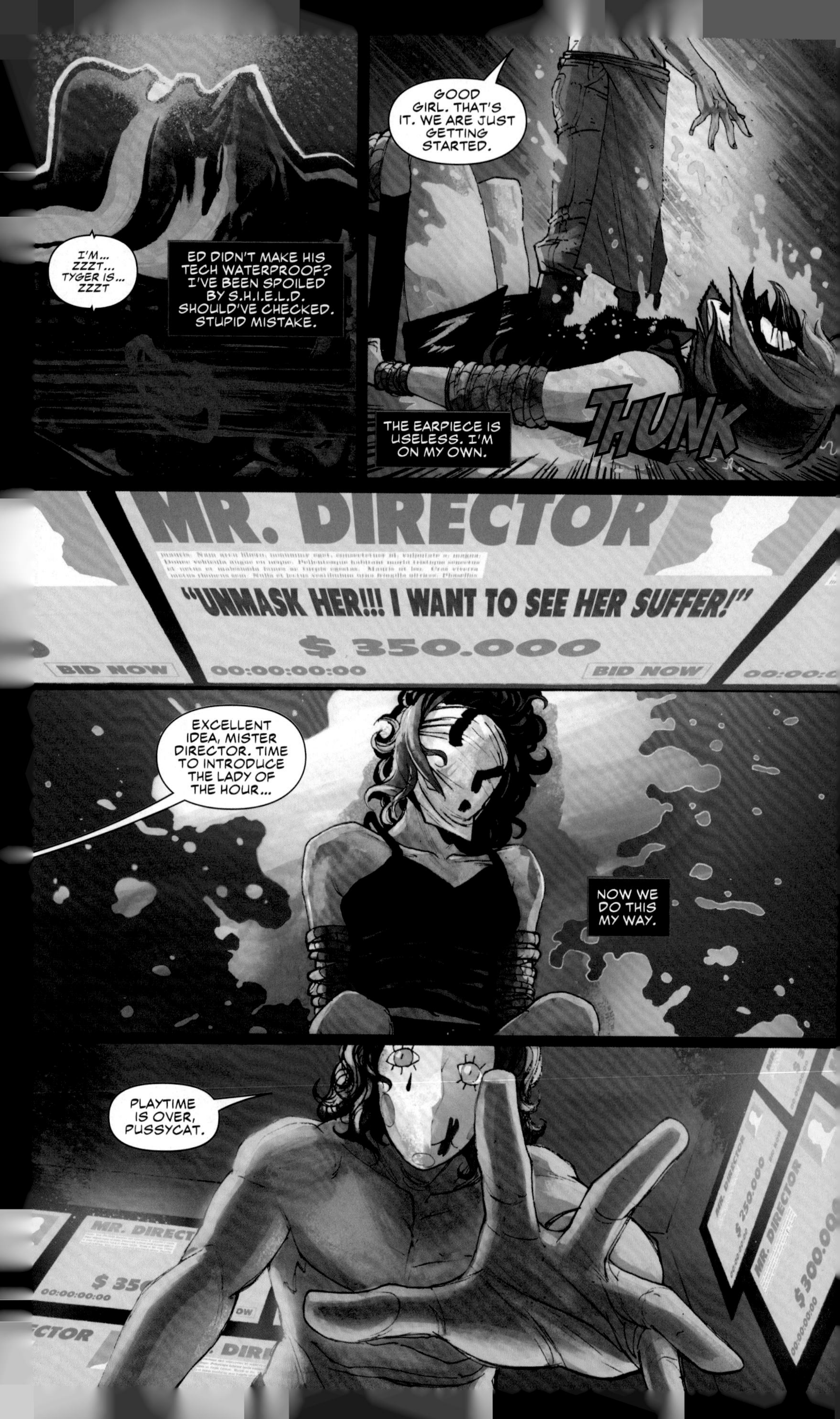

I'M... ZZZT... TYGER IS... ZZZT
ED DIDN'T MAKE HIS TECH WATERPROOF? I'VE BEEN SPOILED BY S.H.I.E.L.D. SHOULD'VE CHECKED. STUPID MISTAKE.
GOOD GIRL. THAT'S IT. WE ARE JUST GETTING STARTED.
THE EARPIECE IS USELESS. I'M ON MY OWN.
THUNK
MR. DIRECTOR
"UNMASK HER!!! I WANT TO SEE HER SUFFER!"
$ 350.000
BID NOW
00:00:00:00
BID NOW
EXCELLENT IDEA, MISTER DIRECTOR. TIME TO INTRODUCE THE LADY OF THE HOUR...
NOW WE DO THIS MY WAY.
PLAYTIME IS OVER, PUSSYCAT.
MR. DIRECTOR
$ 250.000
MR. DIRECTOR
$ 300.000

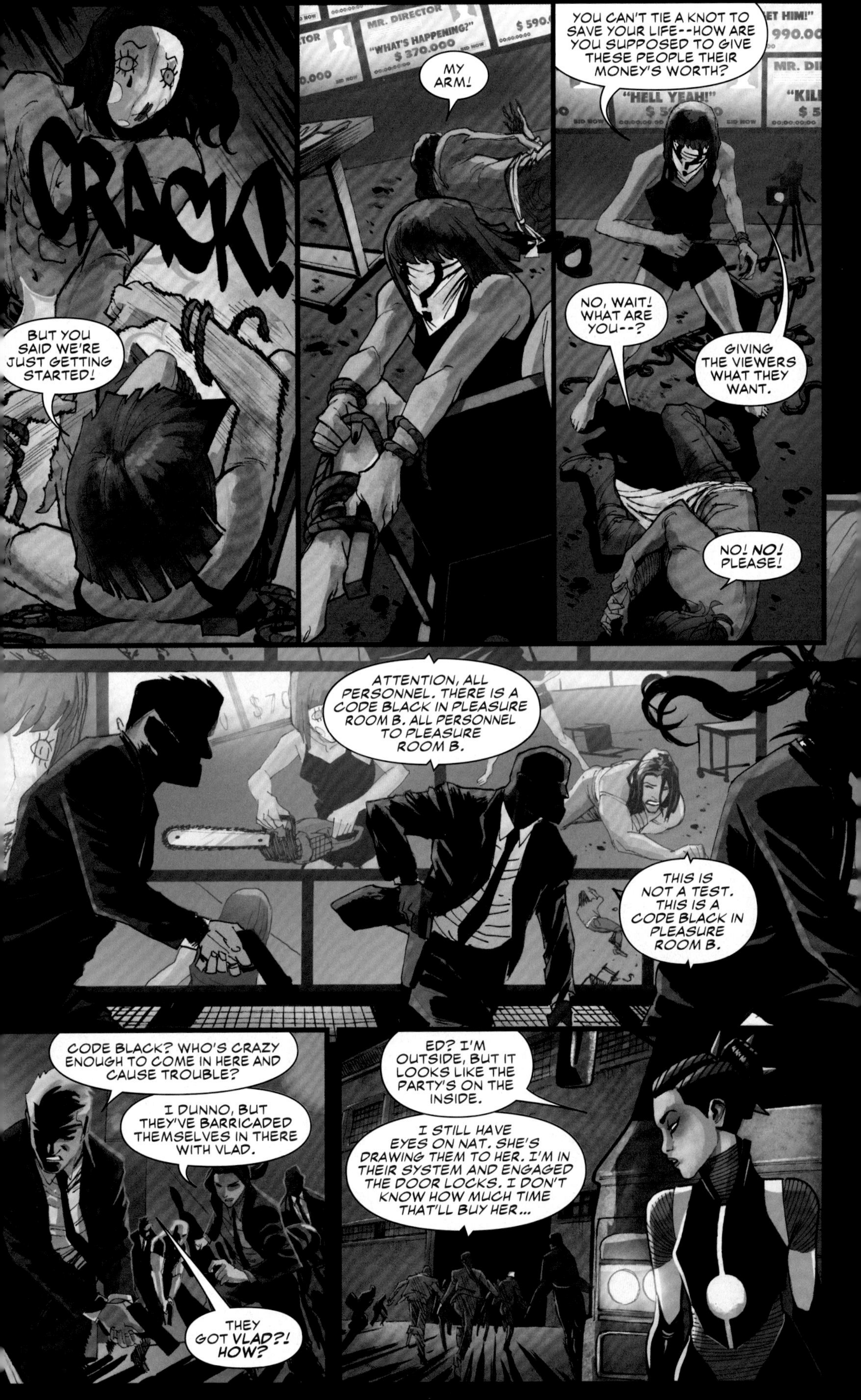
CRACK!
BUT YOU SAID WE'RE JUST GETTING STARTED!
MY ARM!
YOU CAN'T TIE A KNOT TO SAVE YOUR LIFE--HOW ARE YOU SUPPOSED TO GIVE THESE PEOPLE THEIR MONEY'S WORTH?
NO, WAIT! WHAT ARE YOU--?
GIVING THE VIEWERS WHAT THEY WANT.
NO! NO! PLEASE!
ATTENTION, ALL PERSONNEL. THERE IS A CODE BLACK IN PLEASURE ROOM B. ALL PERSONNEL TO PLEASURE ROOM B.
THIS IS NOT A TEST. THIS IS A CODE BLACK IN PLEASURE ROOM B.
CODE BLACK? WHO'S CRAZY ENOUGH TO COME IN HERE AND CAUSE TROUBLE?
I DUNNO, BUT THEY'VE BARRICADED THEMSELVES IN THERE WITH VLAD.
THEY GOT VLAD?! HOW?
ED? I'M OUTSIDE, BUT IT LOOKS LIKE THE PARTY'S ON THE INSIDE.
I STILL HAVE EYES ON NAT. SHE'S DRAWING THEM TO HER. I'M IN THEIR SYSTEM AND ENGAGED THE DOOR LOCKS. I DON'T KNOW HOW MUCH TIME THAT'LL BUY HER...

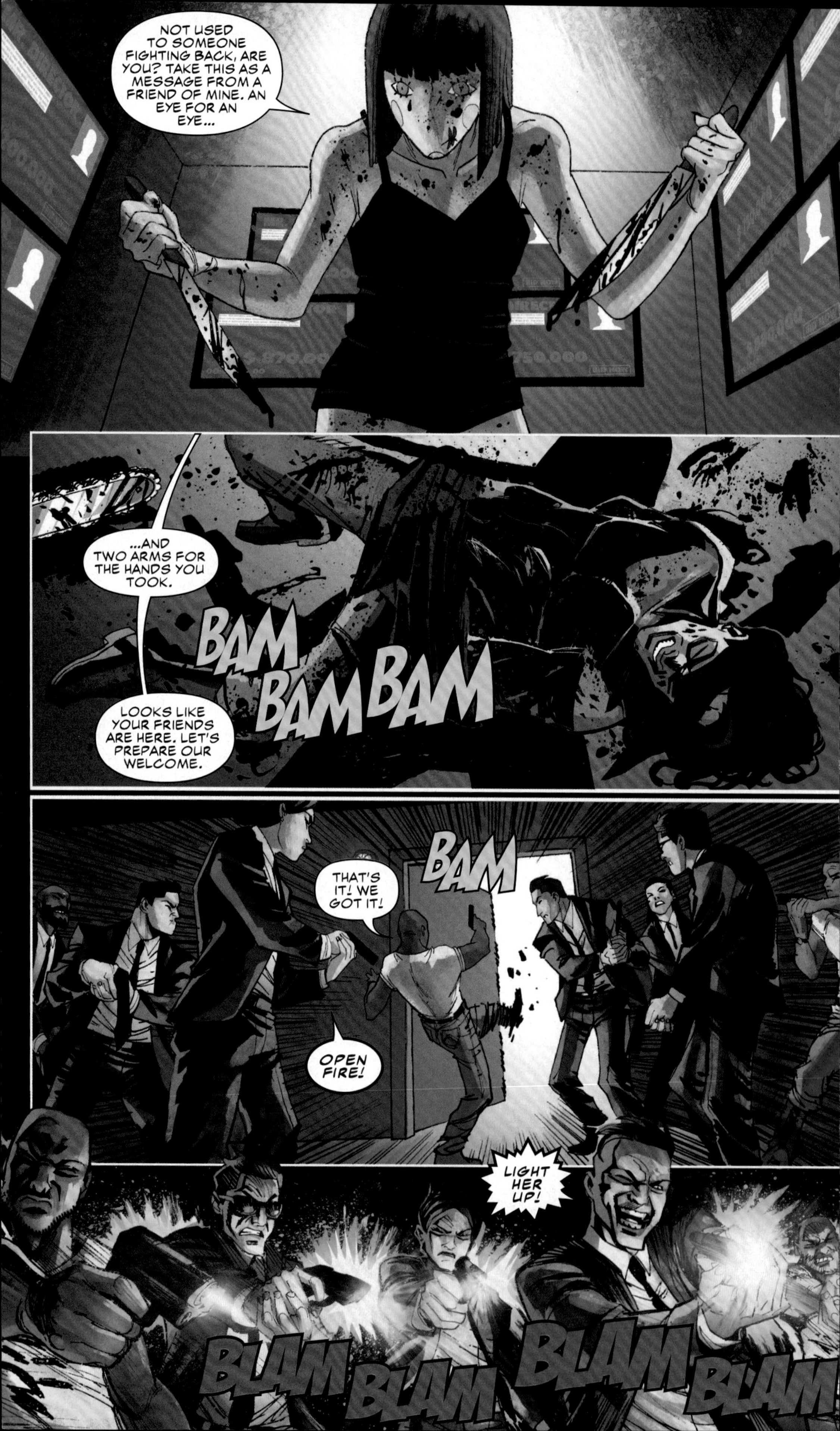
NOT USED TO SOMEONE FIGHTING BACK, ARE YOU? TAKE THIS AS A MESSAGE FROM A FRIEND OF MINE. AN EYE FOR AN EYE...
...AND TWO ARMS FOR THE HANDS YOU TOOK.
BAM BAM BAM
LOOKS LIKE YOUR FRIENDS ARE HERE. LET'S PREPARE OUR WELCOME.
BAM
THAT'S IT! WE GOT IT!
OPEN FIRE!
LIGHT HER UP!
BLAM BLAM BLAM BLAM

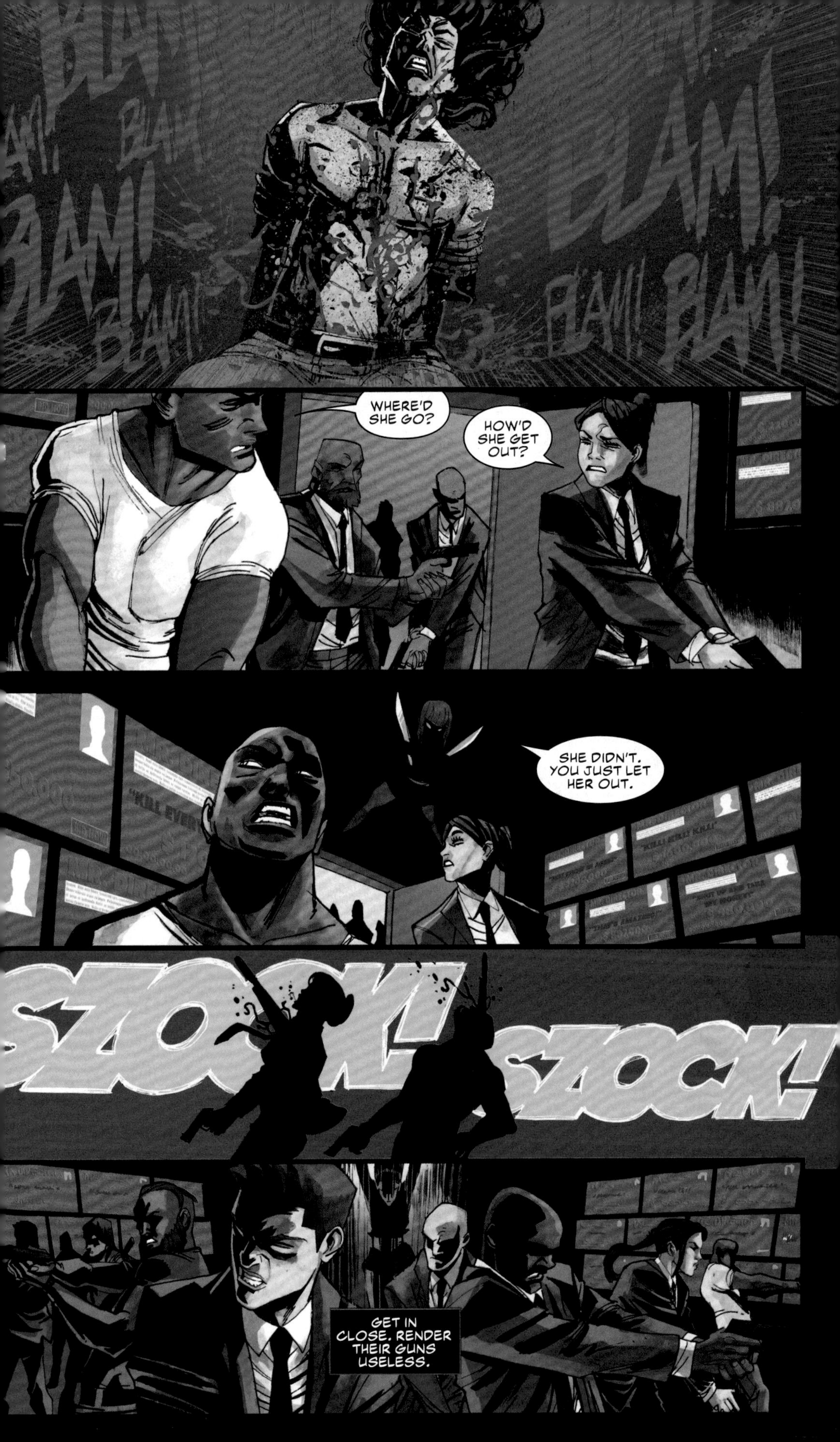

BLAM! BLAM! BLAM! BLAM! BLAM! BLAM! BLAM! BLAM!
WHERE'D SHE GO?
HOW'D SHE GET OUT?
SHE DIDN'T. YOU JUST LET HER OUT.
SZOCK! SZOCK!
GET IN CLOSE. RENDER THEIR GUNS USELESS.

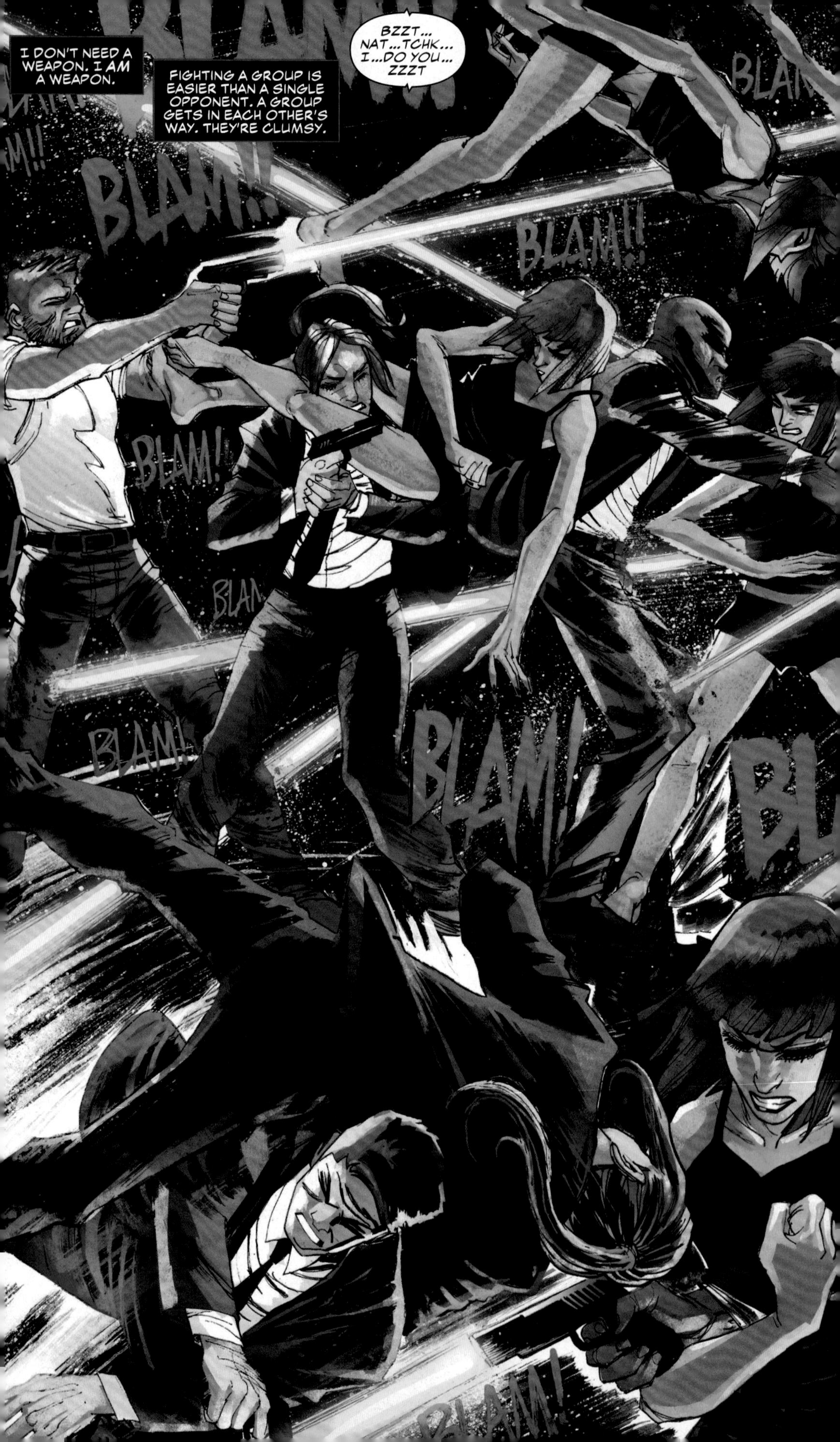
I DON'T NEED A WEAPON. I AM A WEAPON.
FIGHTING A GROUP IS EASIER THAN A SINGLE OPPONENT. A GROUP GETS IN EACH OTHER'S WAY. THEY'RE CLUMSY.
BZZT... NAT...TCHK... I...DO YOU... ZZZT
BLAM!!
BLAM!!
BLAM!!
BLAM!
BLAM!
BLAM!

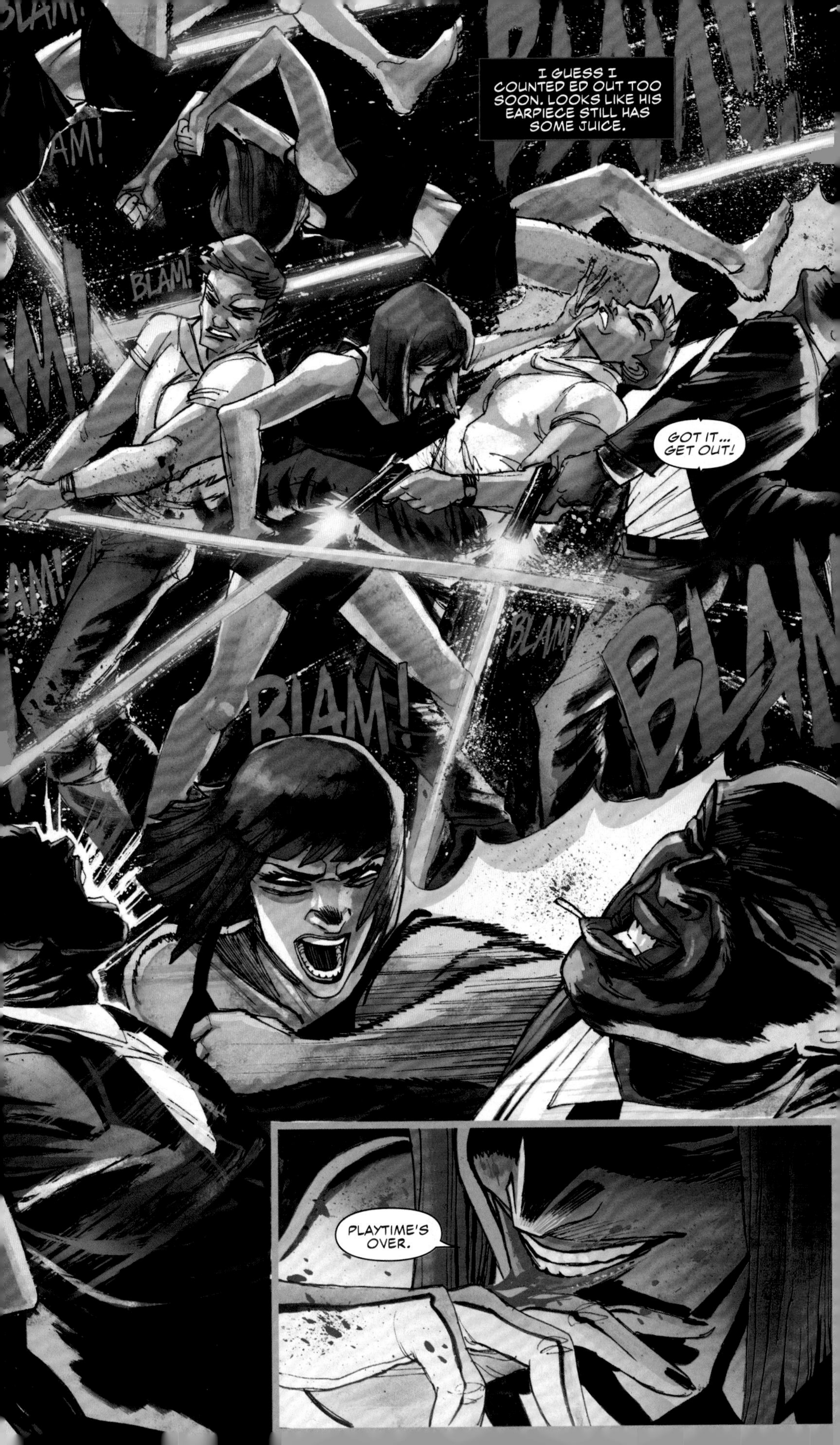
BLAM!
I GUESS I COUNTED ED OUT TOO SOON. LOOKS LIKE HIS EARPIECE STILL HAS SOME JUICE.
BLAM!
BLAM!
GOT IT... GET OUT!
BLAM!
BLAM!
BLAM!
PLAYTIME'S OVER.

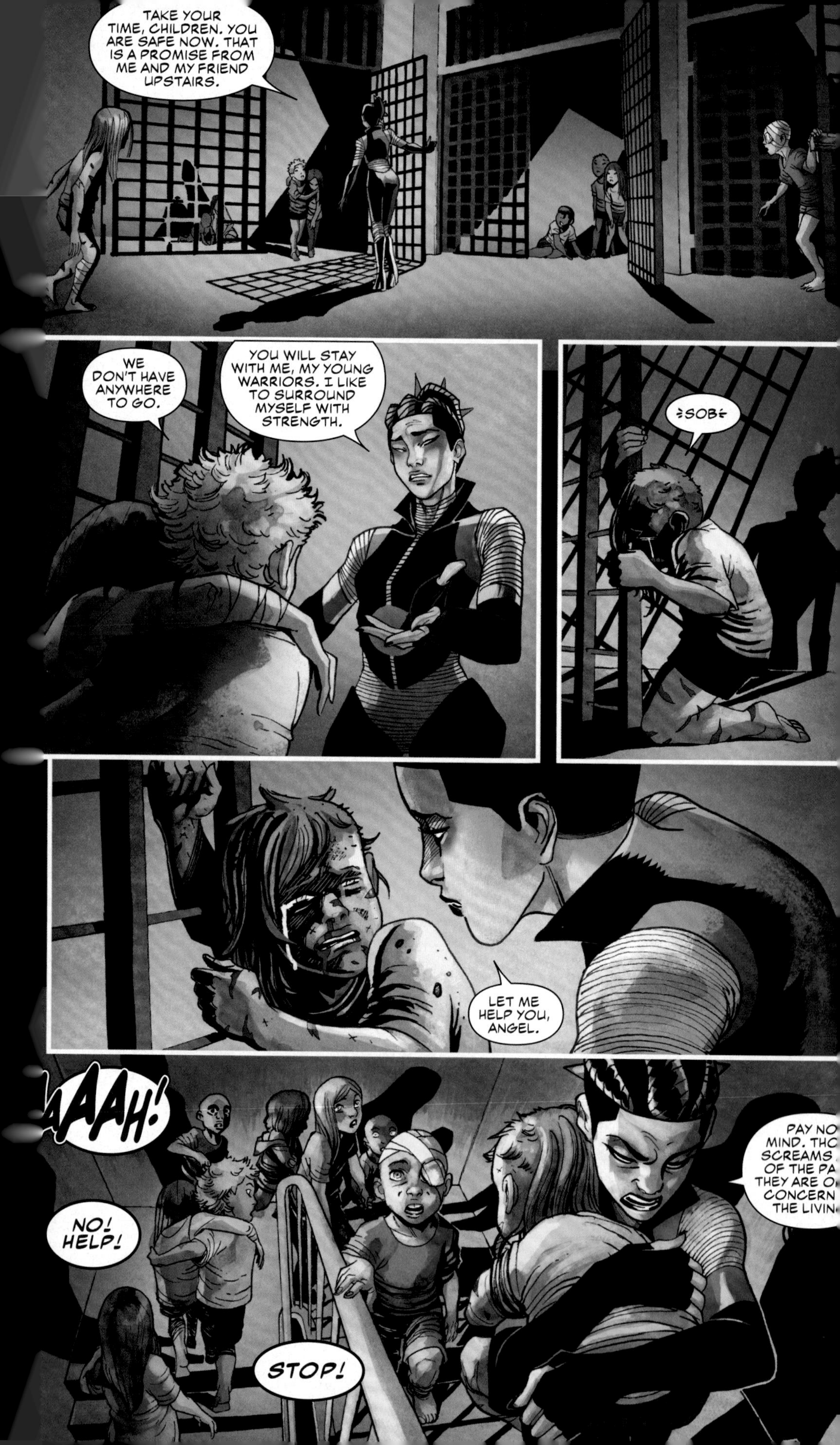
TAKE YOUR TIME, CHILDREN. YOU ARE SAFE NOW. THAT IS A PROMISE FROM ME AND MY FRIEND UPSTAIRS.
WE DON'T HAVE ANYWHERE TO GO.
YOU WILL STAY WITH ME, MY YOUNG WARRIORS. I LIKE TO SURROUND MYSELF WITH STRENGTH.
SOB
LET ME HELP YOU, ANGEL.
AAAH!
PAY NO MIND. THO SCREAMS OF THE PA THEY ARE O CONCERN THE LIVIN
NO! HELP!
STOP!

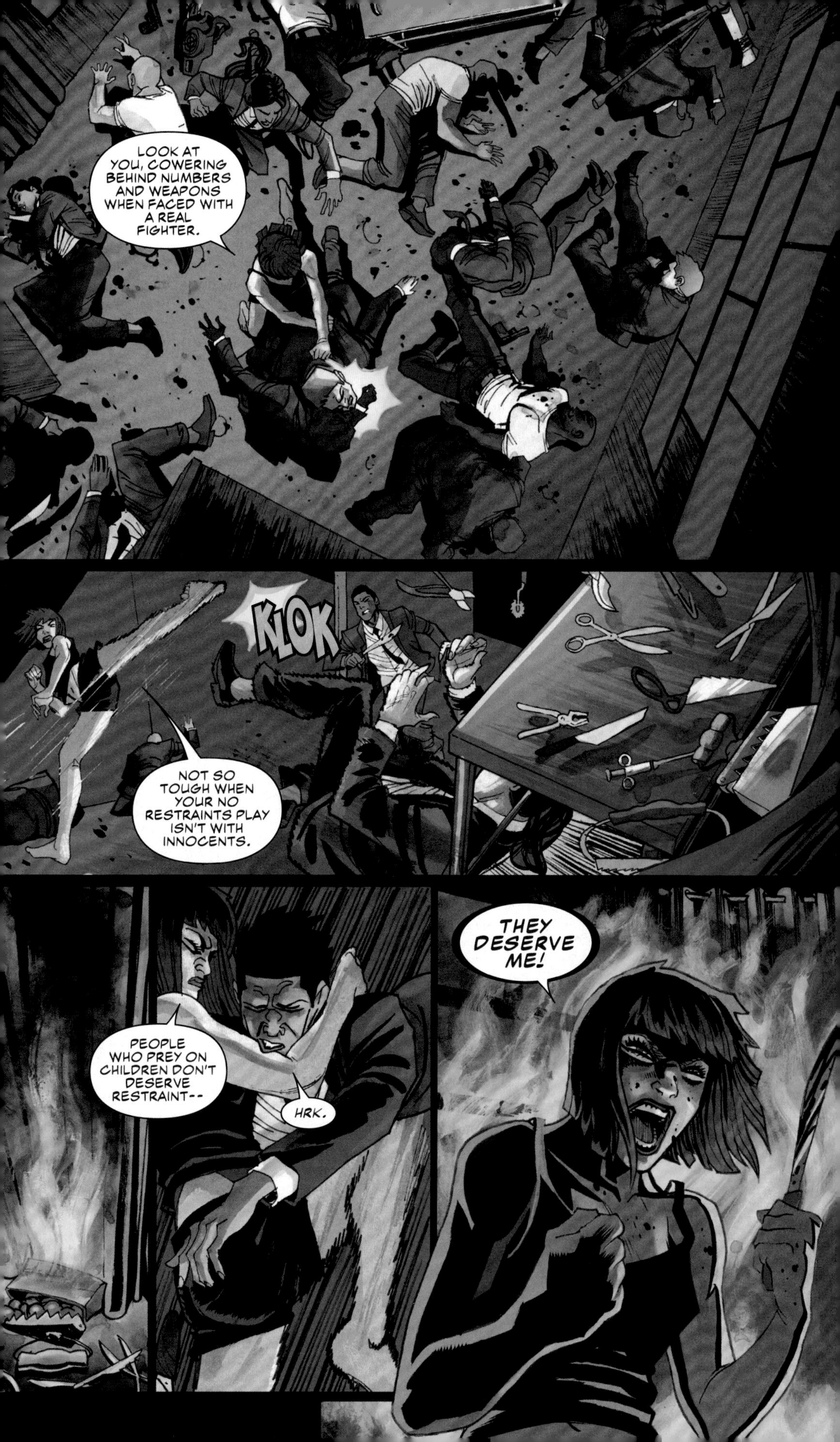
LOOK AT YOU, COWERING BEHIND NUMBERS AND WEAPONS WHEN FACED WITH A REAL FIGHTER.
KLOK
NOT SO TOUGH WHEN YOUR NO RESTRAINTS PLAY ISN'T WITH INNOCENTS.
PEOPLE WHO PREY ON CHILDREN DON'T DESERVE RESTRAINT--
HRK.
THEY DESERVE ME!

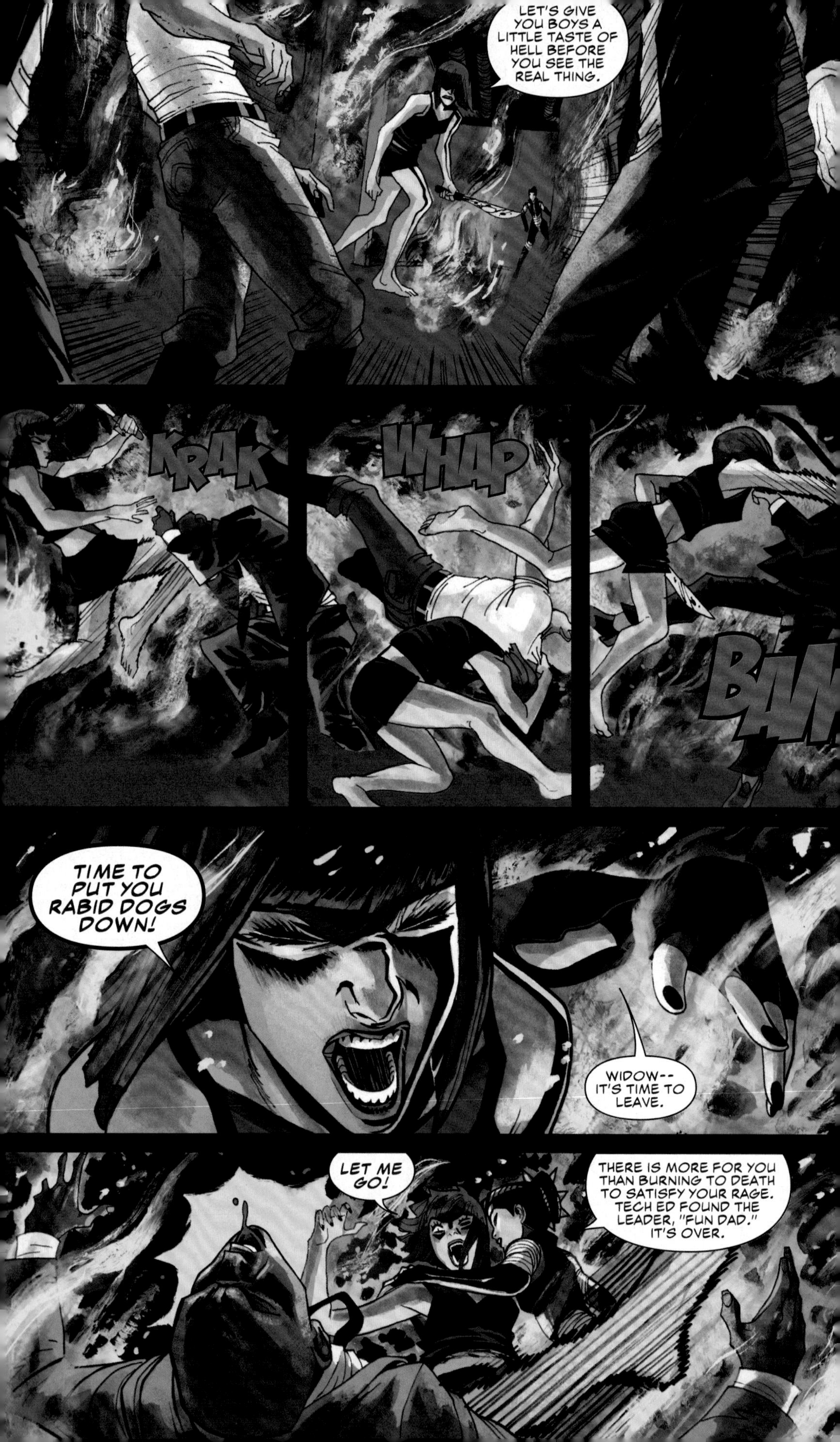
LET'S GIVE YOU BOYS A LITTLE TASTE OF HELL BEFORE YOU SEE THE REAL THING.
KRAK
WHAP
BAM
TIME TO PUT YOU RABID DOGS DOWN!
WIDOW-- IT'S TIME TO LEAVE.
LET ME GO!
THERE IS MORE FOR YOU THAN BURNING TO DEATH TO SATISFY YOUR RAGE. TECH ED FOUND THE LEADER, "FUN DAD." IT'S OVER.

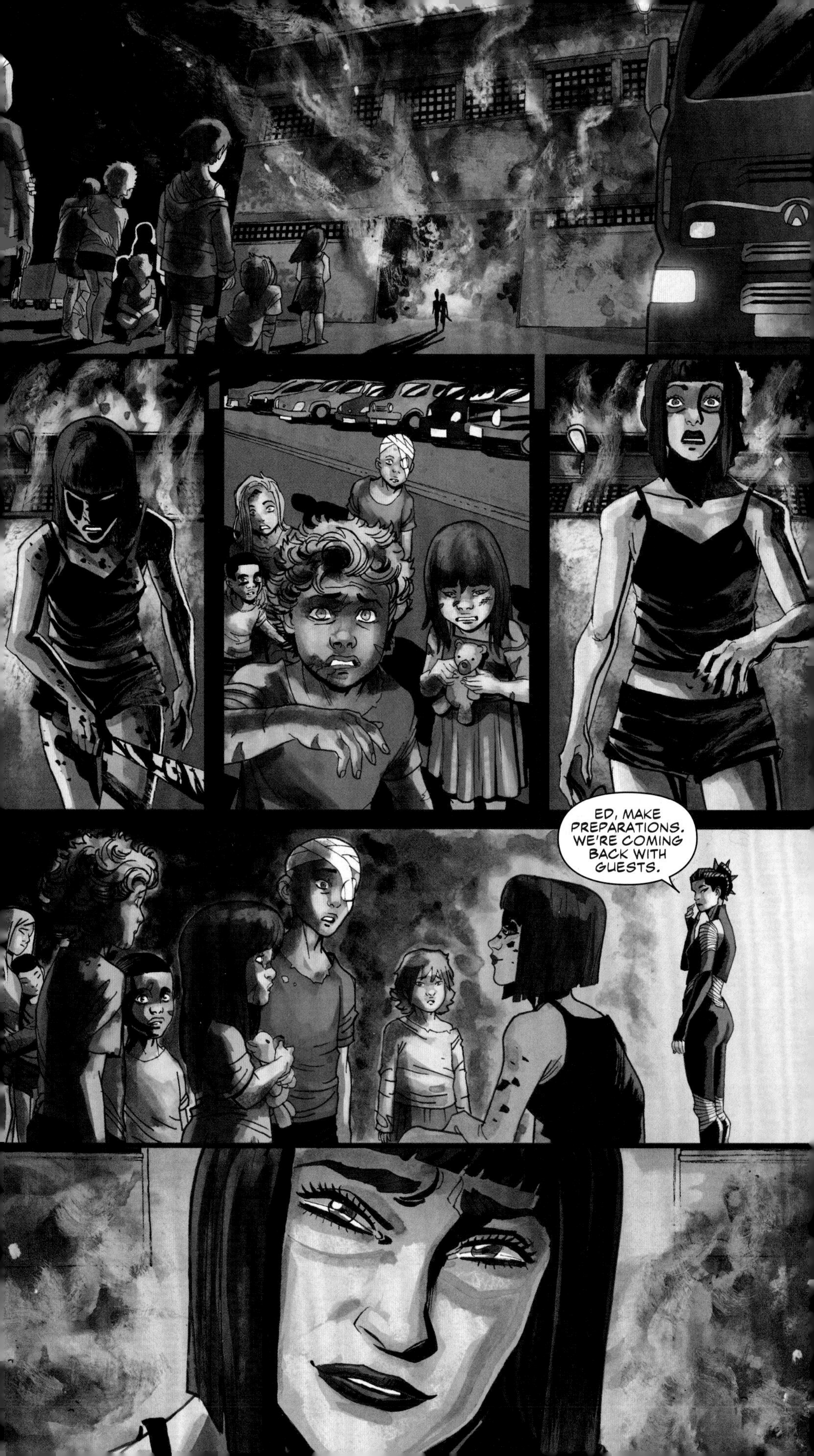
ED, MAKE PREPARATIONS. WE'RE COMING BACK WITH GUESTS.

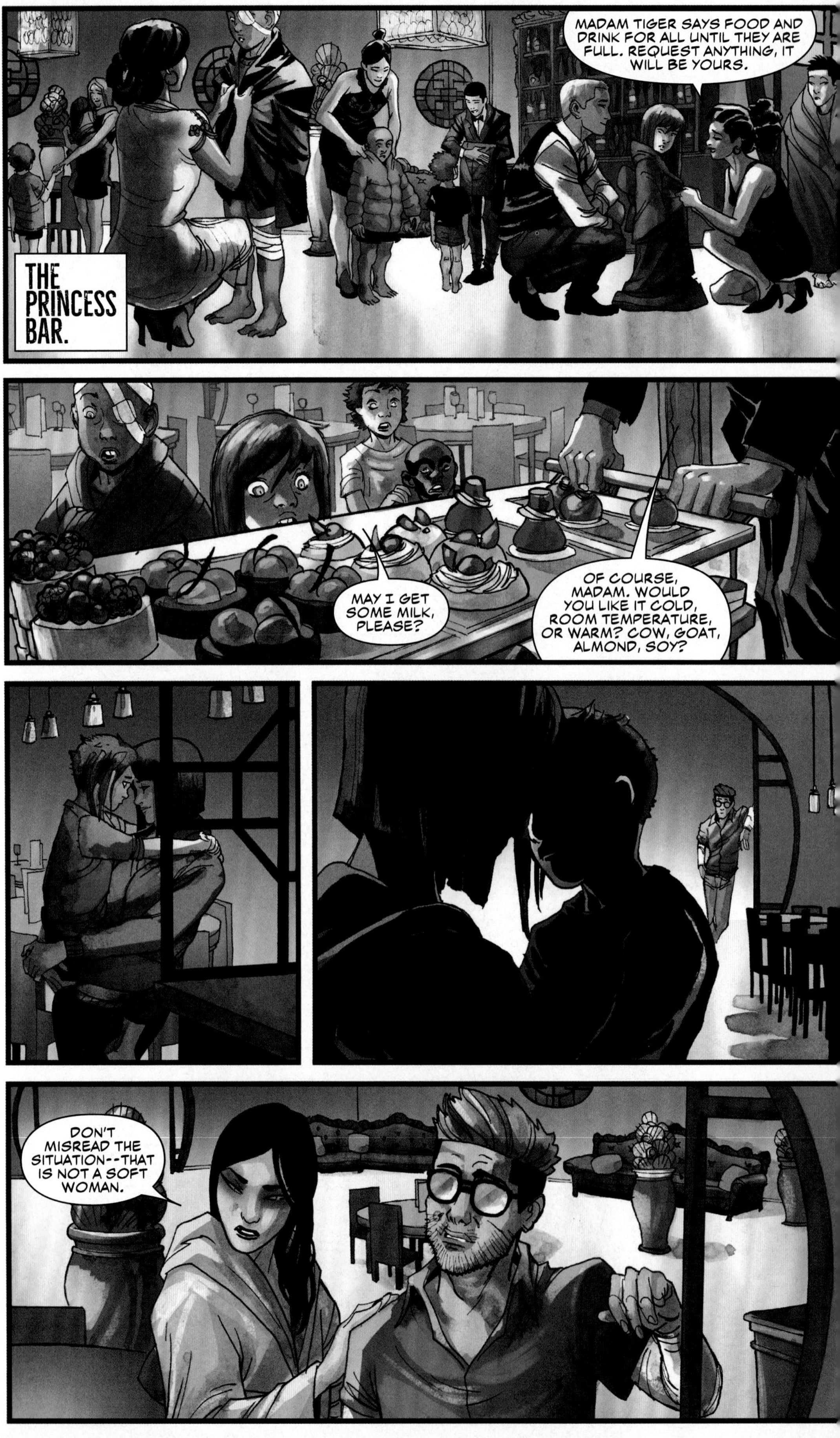
THE PRINCESS BAR.
MADAM TIGER SAYS FOOD AND DRINK FOR ALL UNTIL THEY ARE FULL. REQUEST ANYTHING, IT WILL BE YOURS.
MAY I GET SOME MILK, PLEASE?
OF COURSE, MADAM. WOULD YOU LIKE IT COLD, ROOM TEMPERATURE, OR WARM? COW, GOAT, ALMOND, SOY?
DON'T MISREAD THE SITUATION--THAT IS NOT A SOFT WOMAN.

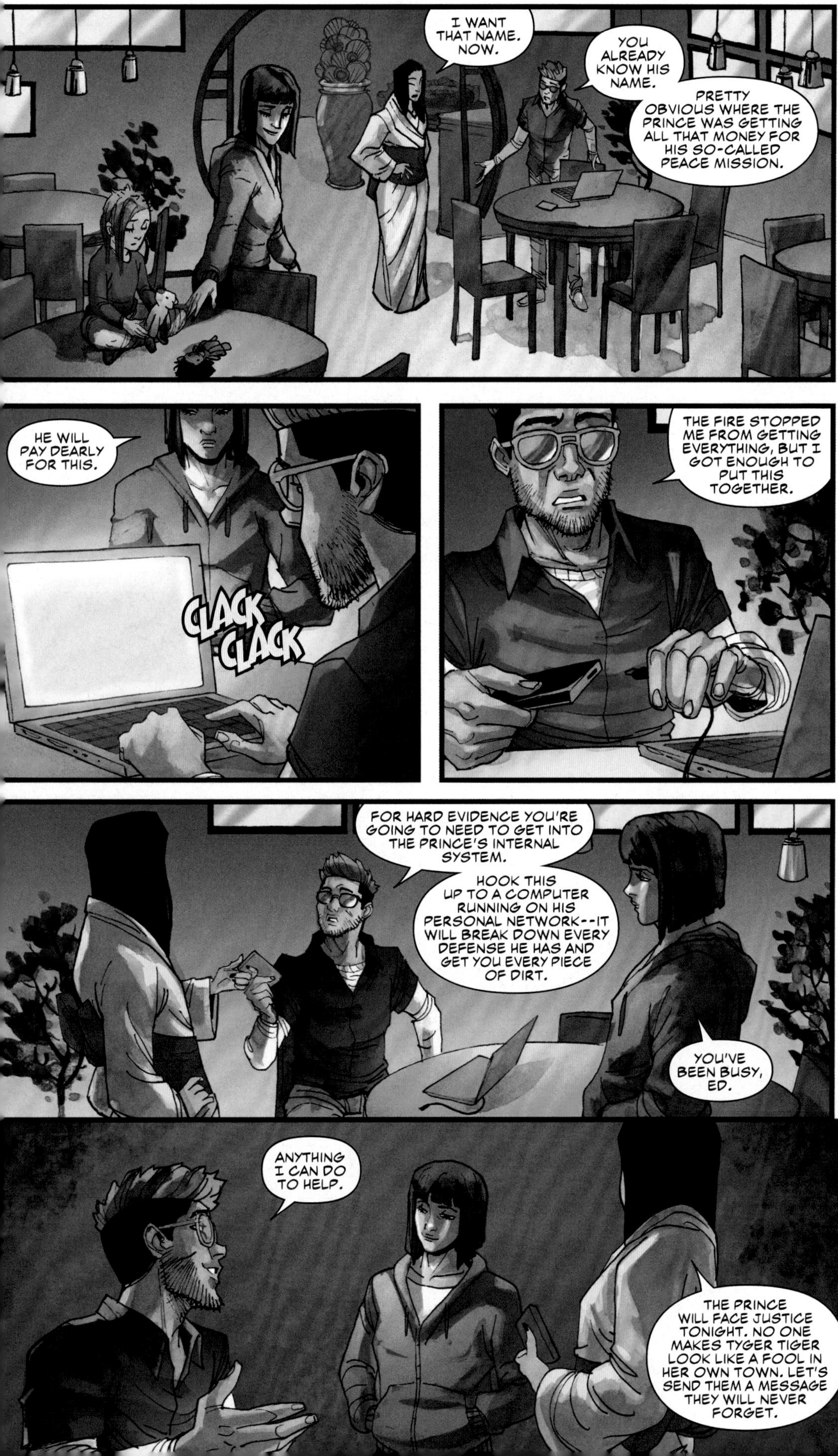
I WANT THAT NAME. NOW.
YOU ALREADY KNOW HIS NAME.
PRETTY OBVIOUS WHERE THE PRINCE WAS GETTING ALL THAT MONEY FOR HIS SO-CALLED PEACE MISSION.
HE WILL PAY DEARLY FOR THIS.
CLACK CLACK
THE FIRE STOPPED ME FROM GETTING EVERYTHING, BUT I GOT ENOUGH TO PUT THIS TOGETHER.
FOR HARD EVIDENCE YOU'RE GOING TO NEED TO GET INTO THE PRINCE'S INTERNAL SYSTEM.
HOOK THIS UP TO A COMPUTER RUNNING ON HIS PERSONAL NETWORK--IT WILL BREAK DOWN EVERY DEFENSE HE HAS AND GET YOU EVERY PIECE OF DIRT.
YOU'VE BEEN BUSY, ED.
ANYTHING I CAN DO TO HELP.
THE PRINCE WILL FACE JUSTICE TONIGHT. NO ONE MAKES TYGER TIGER LOOK LIKE A FOOL IN HER OWN TOWN. LET'S SEND THEM A MESSAGE THEY WILL NEVER FORGET.

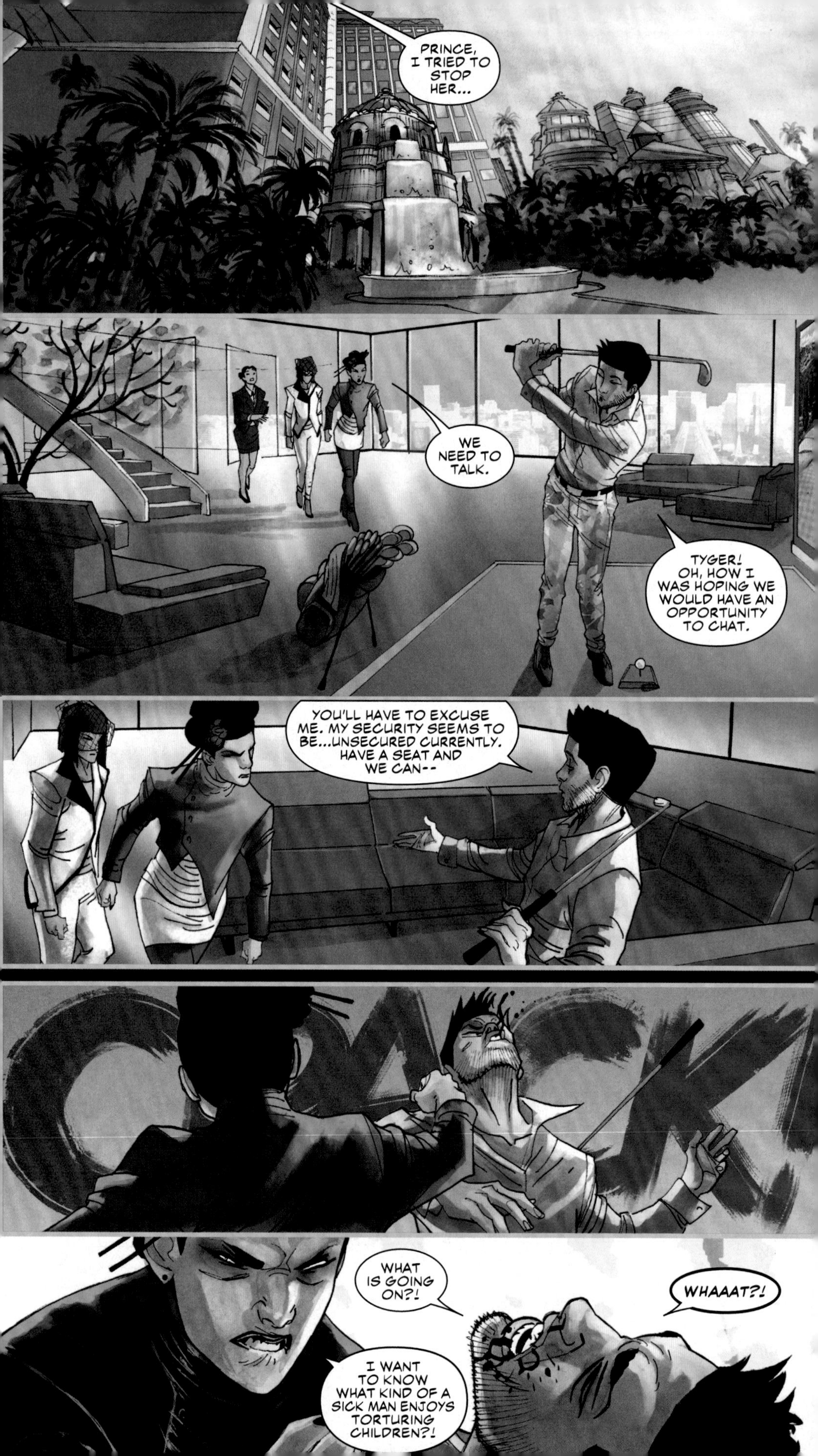
PRINCE, I TRIED TO STOP HER...
WE NEED TO TALK.
TYGER! OH, HOW I WAS HOPING WE WOULD HAVE AN OPPORTUNITY TO CHAT.
YOU'LL HAVE TO EXCUSE ME. MY SECURITY SEEMS TO BE...UNSECURED CURRENTLY. HAVE A SEAT AND WE CAN--
WHAT IS GOING ON?!
WHAAAT?!
I WANT TO KNOW WHAT KIND OF A SICK MAN ENJOYS TORTURING CHILDREN?!

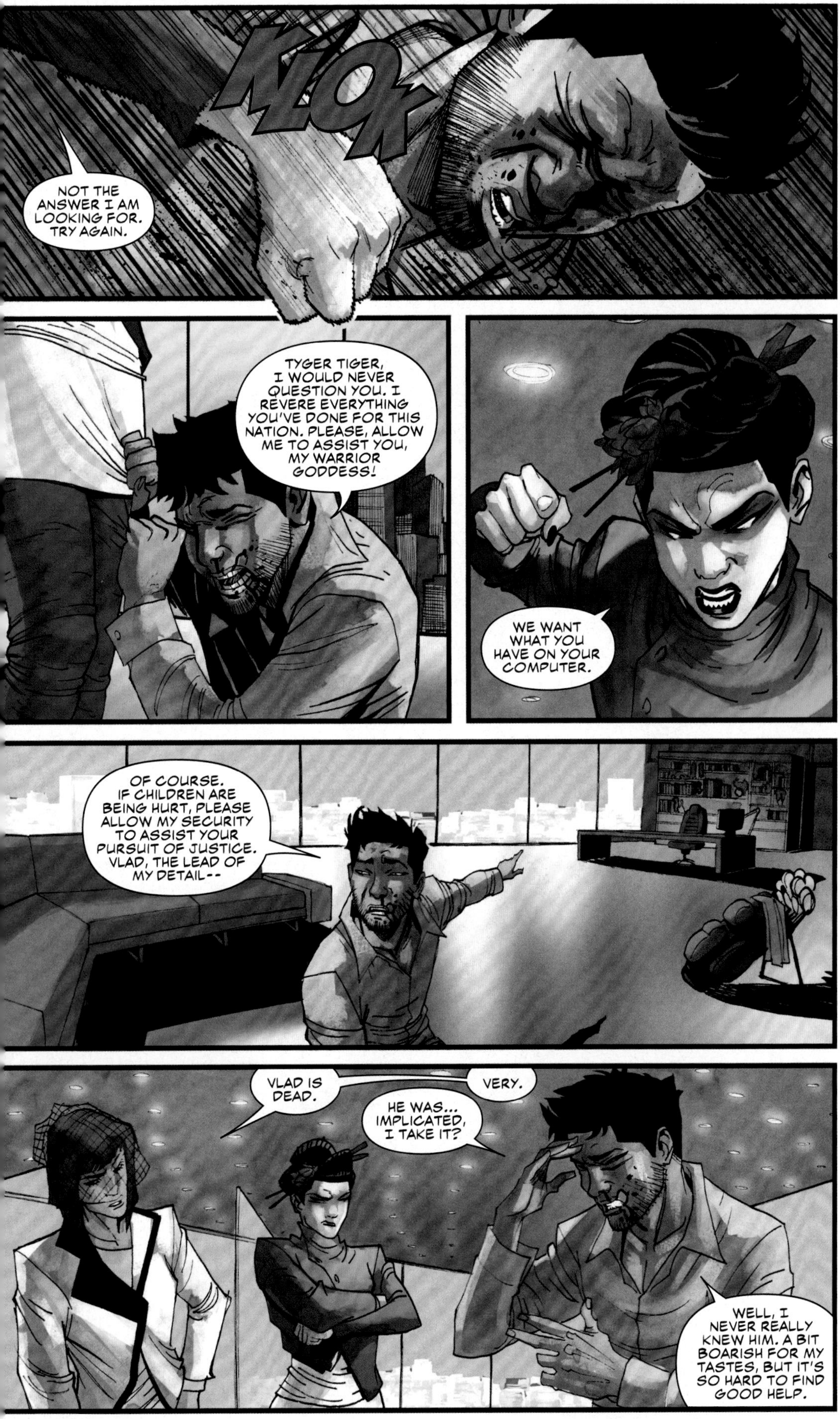
KLOK
NOT THE ANSWER I AM LOOKING FOR. TRY AGAIN.
TYGER TIGER, I WOULD NEVER QUESTION YOU. I REVERE EVERYTHING YOU'VE DONE FOR THIS NATION. PLEASE, ALLOW ME TO ASSIST YOU, MY WARRIOR GODDESS!
WE WANT WHAT YOU HAVE ON YOUR COMPUTER.
OF COURSE. IF CHILDREN ARE BEING HURT, PLEASE ALLOW MY SECURITY TO ASSIST YOUR PURSUIT OF JUSTICE. VLAD, THE LEAD OF MY DETAIL--
VLAD IS DEAD.
VERY.
HE WAS... IMPLICATED, I TAKE IT?
WELL, I NEVER REALLY KNEW HIM. A BIT BOARISH FOR MY TASTES, BUT IT'S SO HARD TO FIND GOOD HELP.

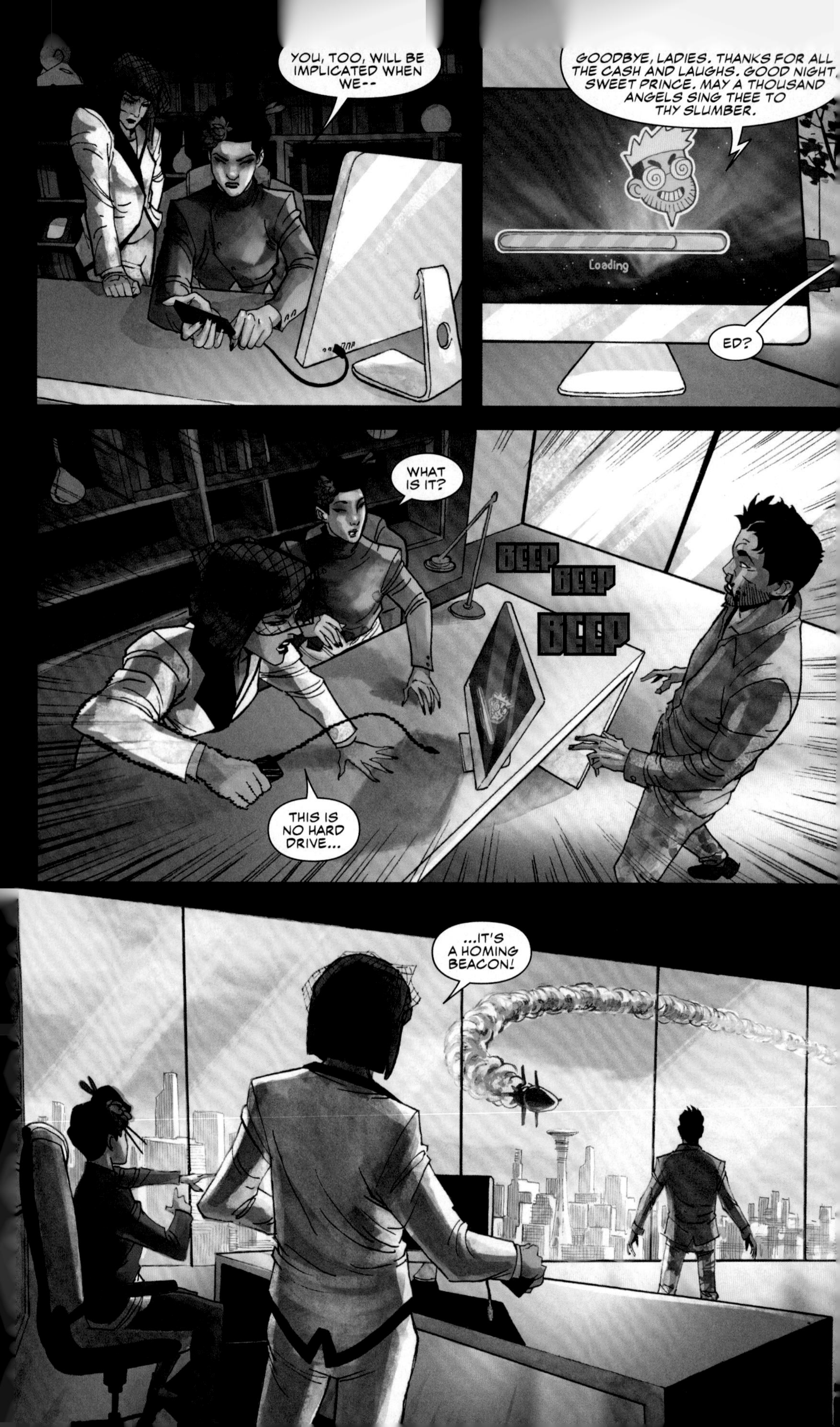
YOU, TOO, WILL BE IMPLICATED WHEN WE--
GOODBYE, LADIES. THANKS FOR ALL THE CASH AND LAUGHS. GOOD NIGHT, SWEET PRINCE. MAY A THOUSAND ANGELS SING THEE TO THY SLUMBER.
Loading
ED?
WHAT IS IT?
BEEP
BEEP
BEEP
THIS IS NO HARD DRIVE...
...IT'S A HOMING BEACON!

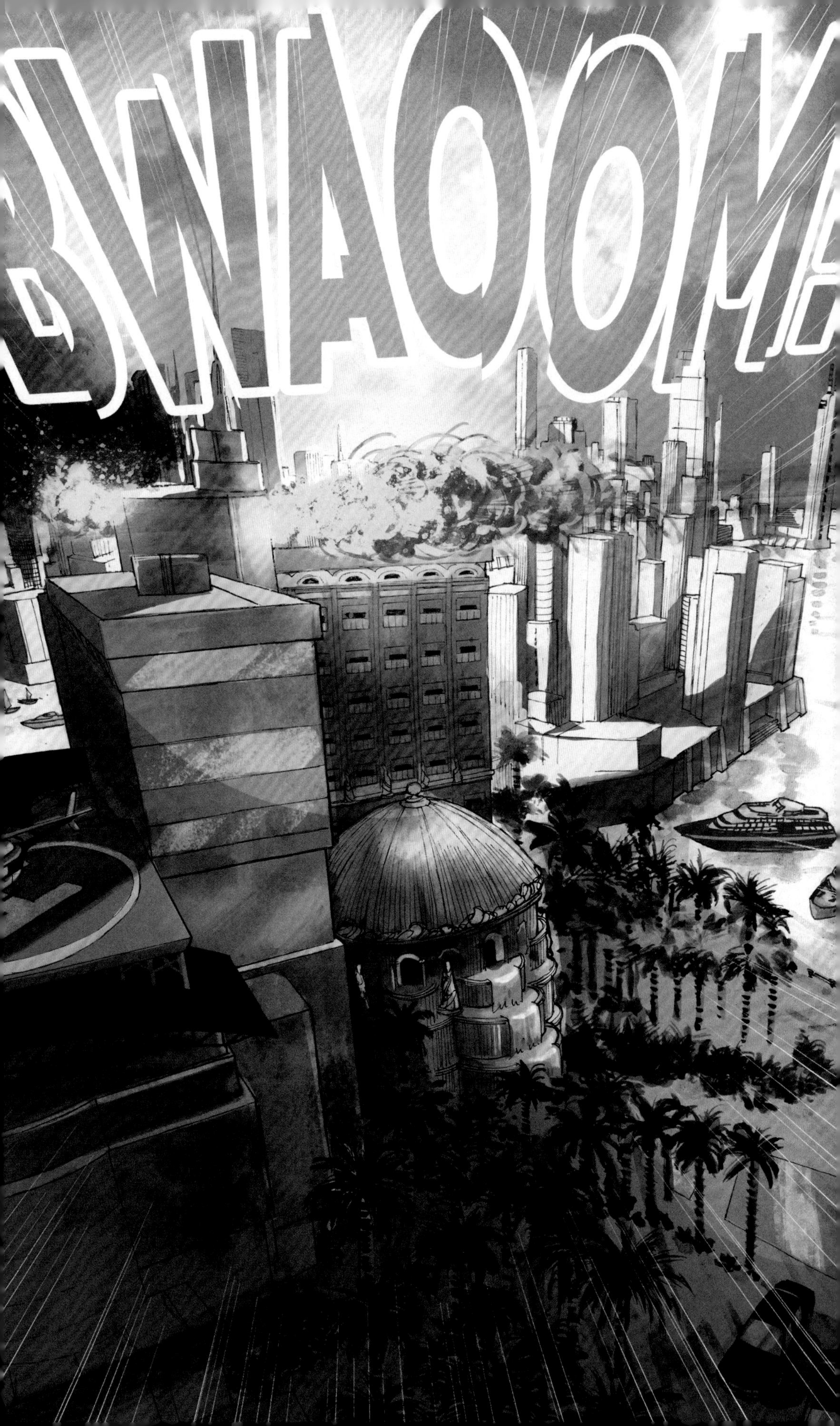
WAOOM

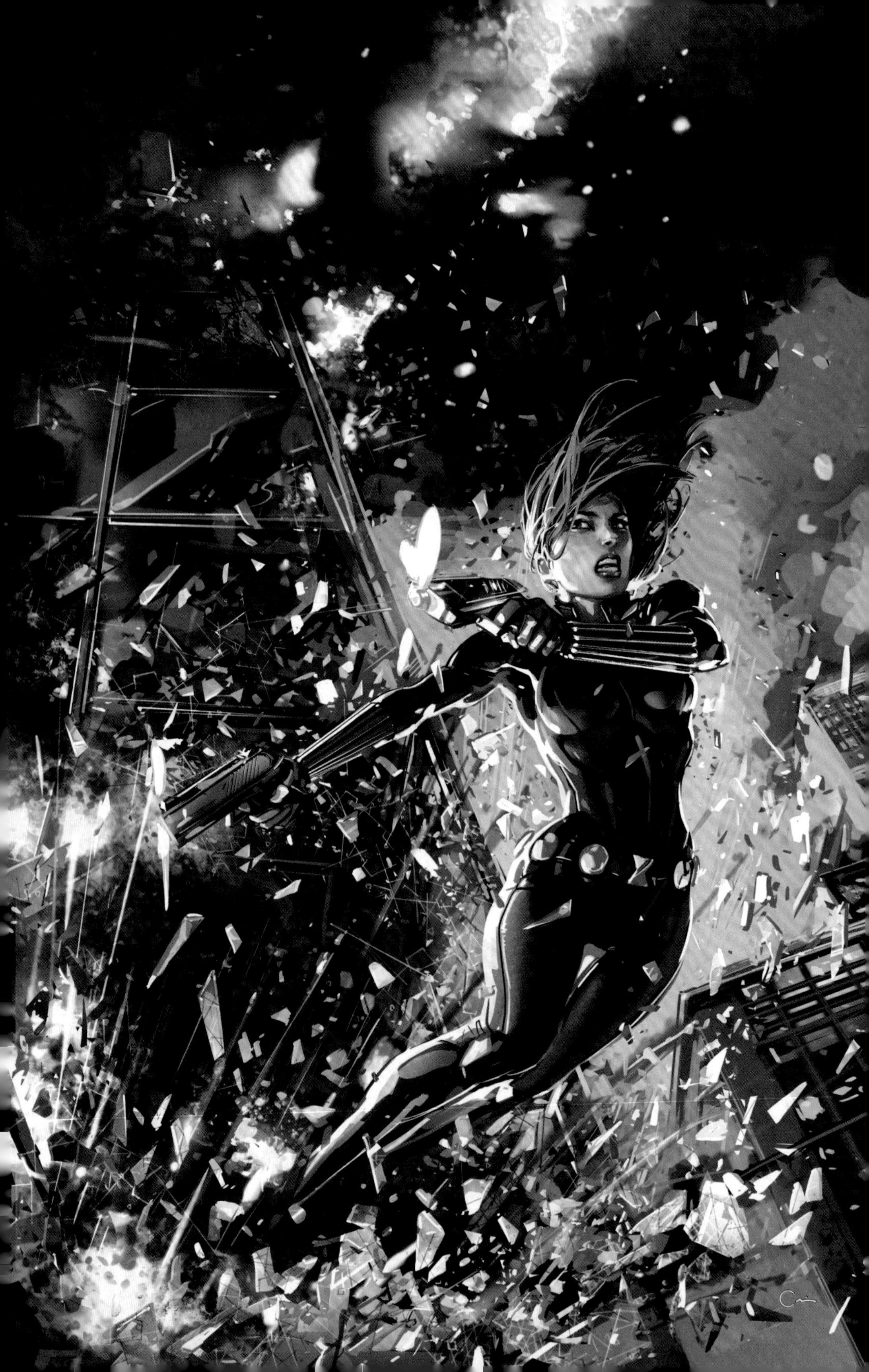

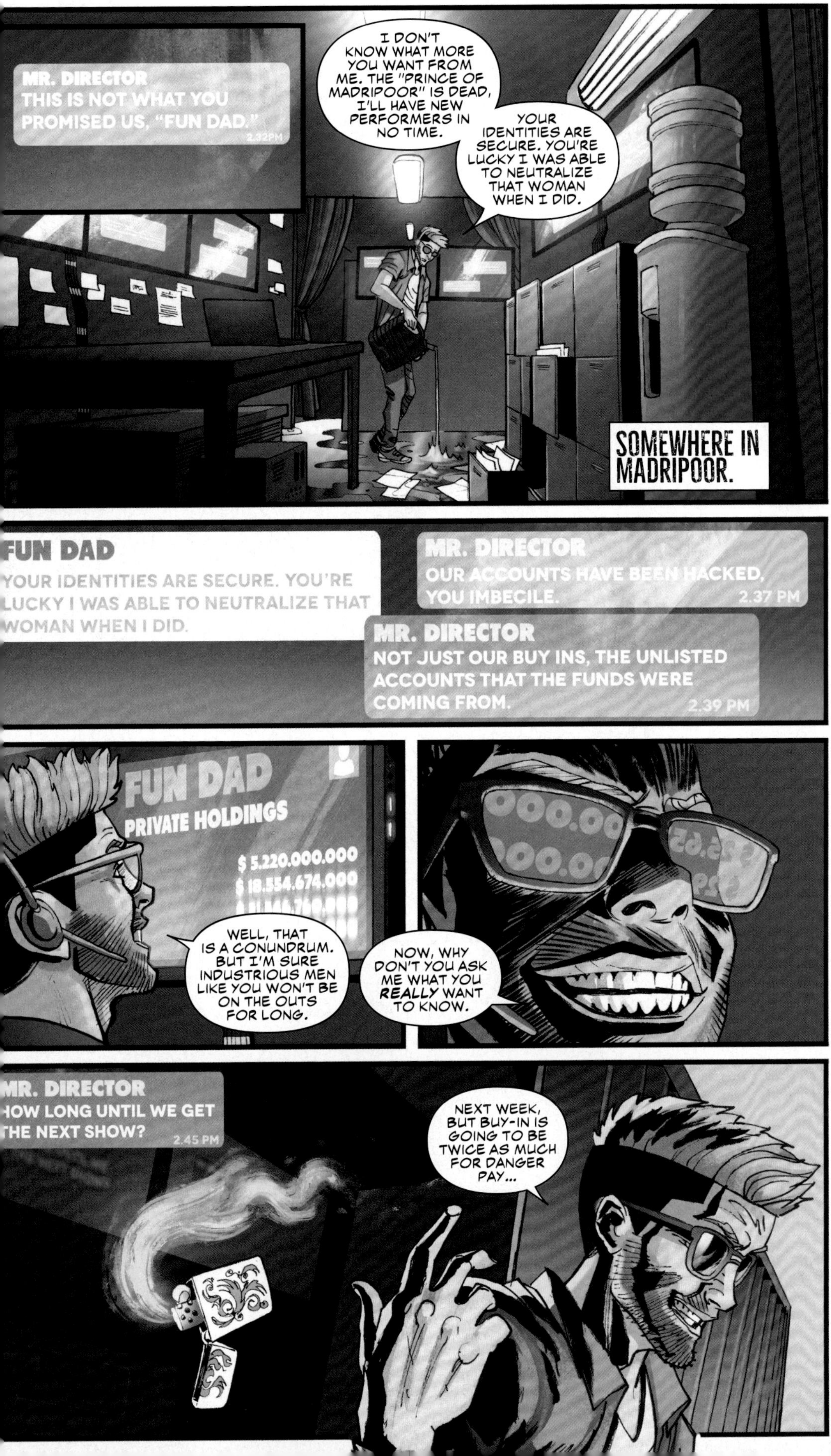
MR. DIRECTOR
THIS IS NOT WHAT YOU PROMISED US, "FUN DAD."
2.32PM
I DON'T KNOW WHAT MORE YOU WANT FROM ME. THE "PRINCE OF MADRIPOOR" IS DEAD, I'LL HAVE NEW PERFORMERS IN NO TIME.
YOUR IDENTITIES ARE SECURE. YOU'RE LUCKY I WAS ABLE TO NEUTRALIZE THAT WOMAN WHEN I DID.
SOMEWHERE IN MADRIPOOR.
FUN DAD
YOUR IDENTITIES ARE SECURE. YOU'RE LUCKY I WAS ABLE TO NEUTRALIZE THAT WOMAN WHEN I DID.
MR. DIRECTOR
OUR ACCOUNTS HAVE BEEN HACKED, YOU IMBECILE.
2.37 PM
MR. DIRECTOR
NOT JUST OUR BUY INS, THE UNLISTED ACCOUNTS THAT THE FUNDS WERE COMING FROM.
2.39 PM
FUN DAD
PRIVATE HOLDINGS
$ 5.220.000.000
$ 18.554.674.000
WELL, THAT IS A CONUNDRUM. BUT I'M SURE INDUSTRIOUS MEN LIKE YOU WON'T BE ON THE OUTS FOR LONG.
NOW, WHY DON'T YOU ASK ME WHAT YOU REALLY WANT TO KNOW.
MR. DIRECTOR
HOW LONG UNTIL WE GET THE NEXT SHOW?
2.45 PM
NEXT WEEK, BUT BUY-IN IS GOING TO BE TWICE AS MUCH FOR DANGER PAY...

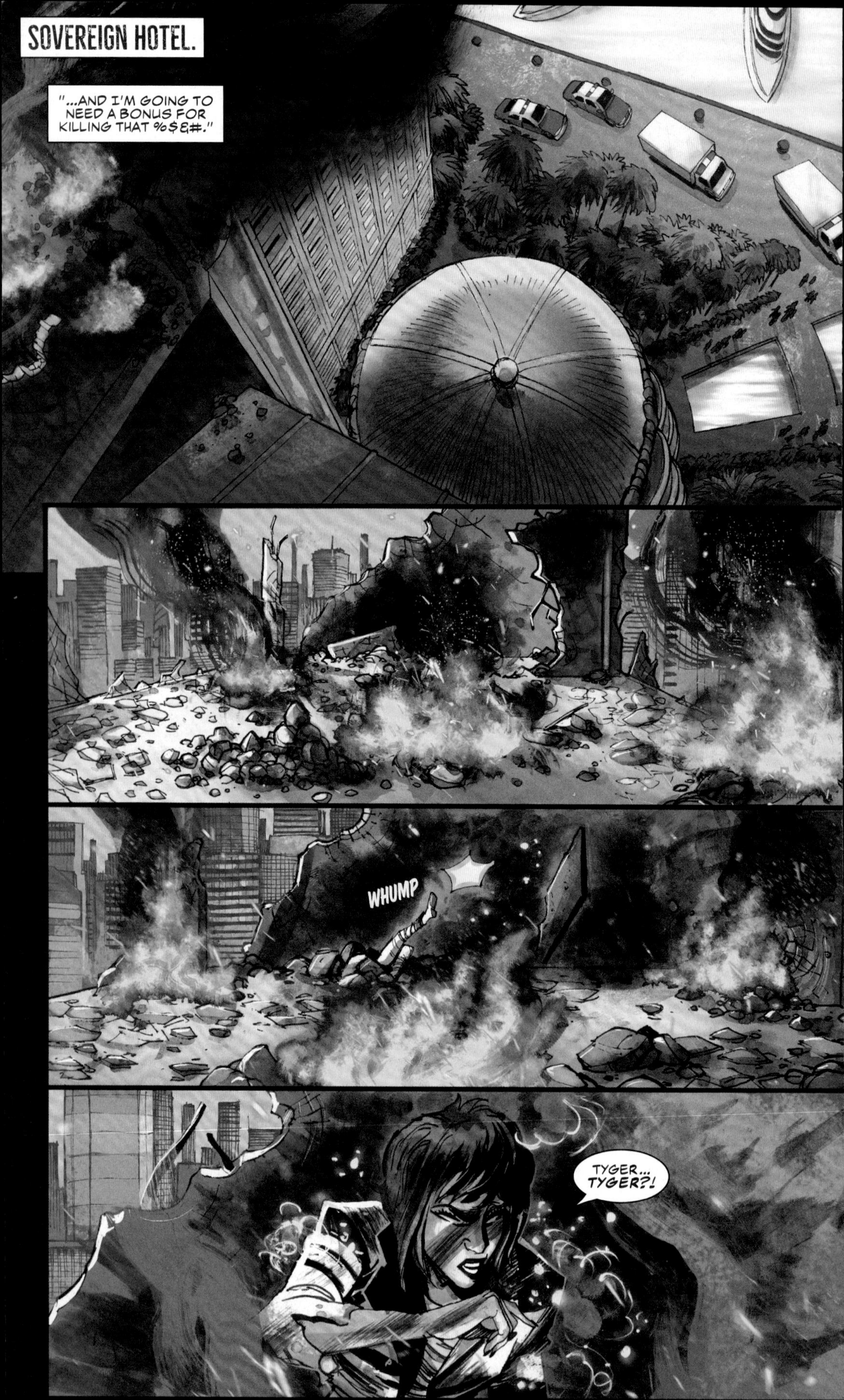
SOVEREIGN HOTEL.
"...AND I'M GOING TO NEED A BONUS FOR KILLING THAT %$&#."
WHUMP
TYGER... TYGER?!

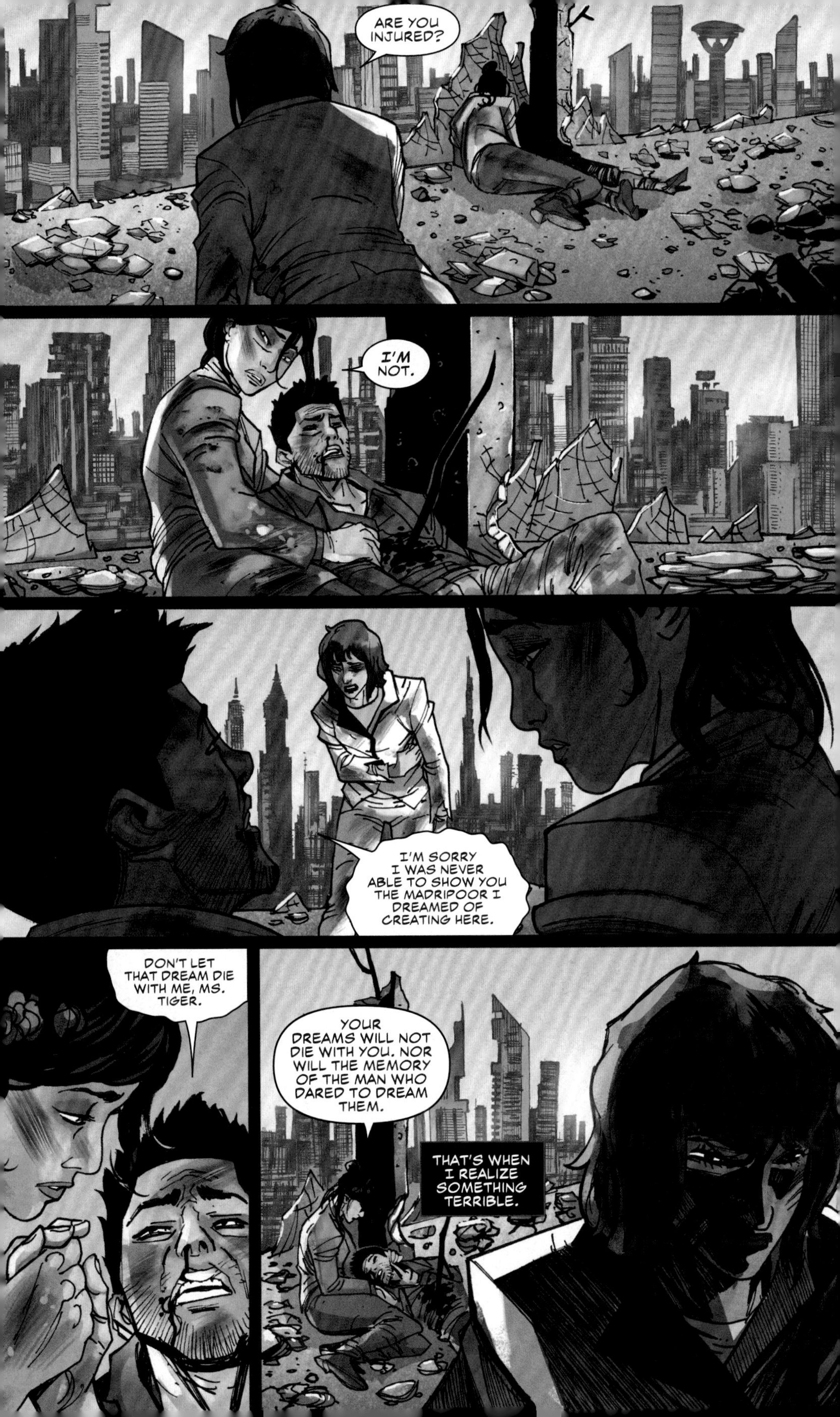
ARE YOU INJURED?
I'M NOT.
I'M SORRY I WAS NEVER ABLE TO SHOW YOU THE MADRIPOOR I DREAMED OF CREATING HERE.
DON'T LET THAT DREAM DIE WITH ME, MS. TIGER.
YOUR DREAMS WILL NOT DIE WITH YOU. NOR WILL THE MEMORY OF THE MAN WHO DARED TO DREAM THEM.
THAT'S WHEN I REALIZE SOMETHING TERRIBLE.

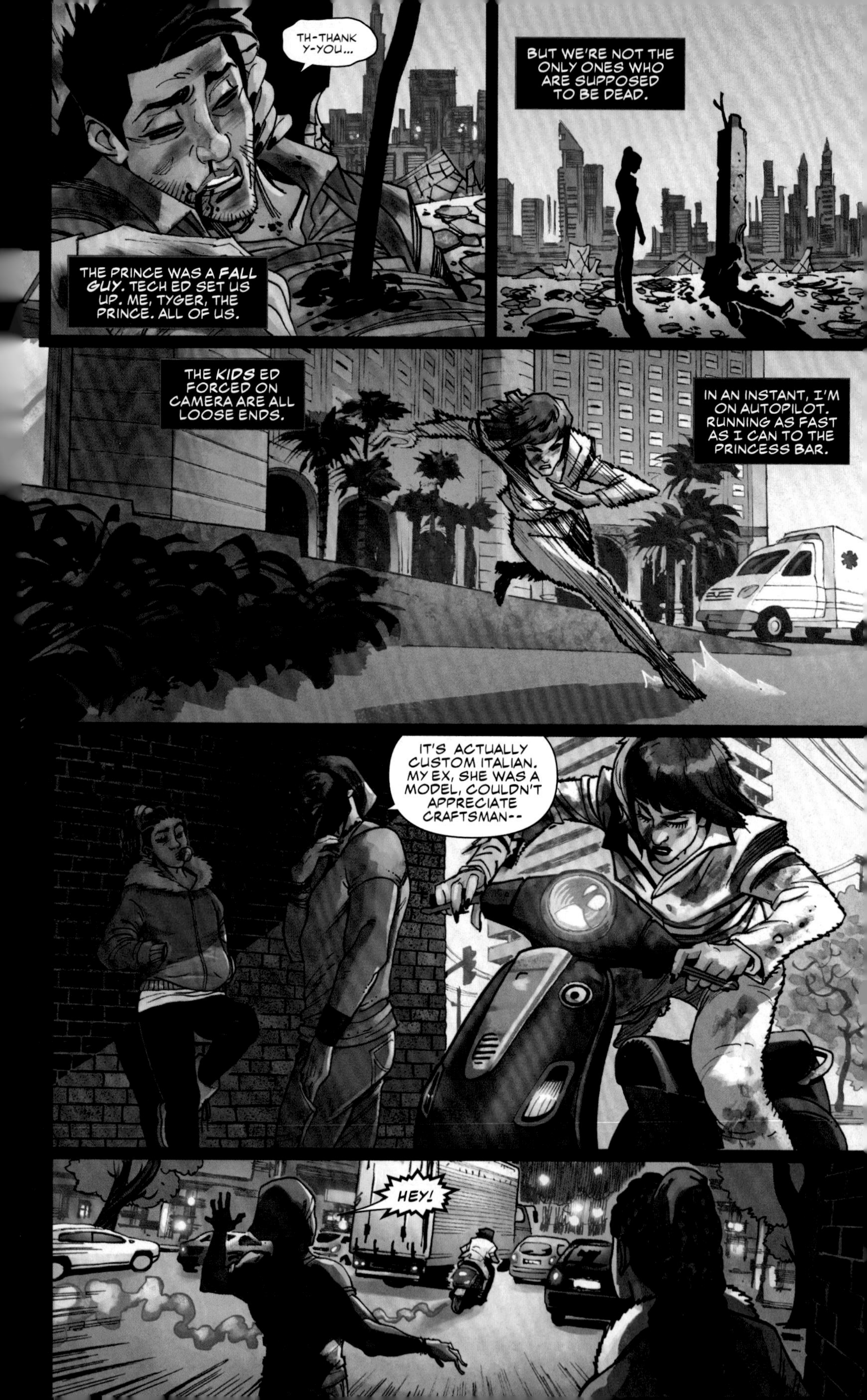
TH-THANK Y-YOU...
THE PRINCE WAS A FALL GUY. TECH ED SET US UP. ME, TYGER, THE PRINCE. ALL OF US.
BUT WE'RE NOT THE ONLY ONES WHO ARE SUPPOSED TO BE DEAD.
THE KIDS ED FORCED ON CAMERA ARE ALL LOOSE ENDS.
IN AN INSTANT, I'M ON AUTOPILOT. RUNNING AS FAST AS I CAN TO THE PRINCESS BAR.
IT'S ACTUALLY CUSTOM ITALIAN. MY EX, SHE WAS A MODEL, COULDN'T APPRECIATE CRAFTSMAN--
HEY!

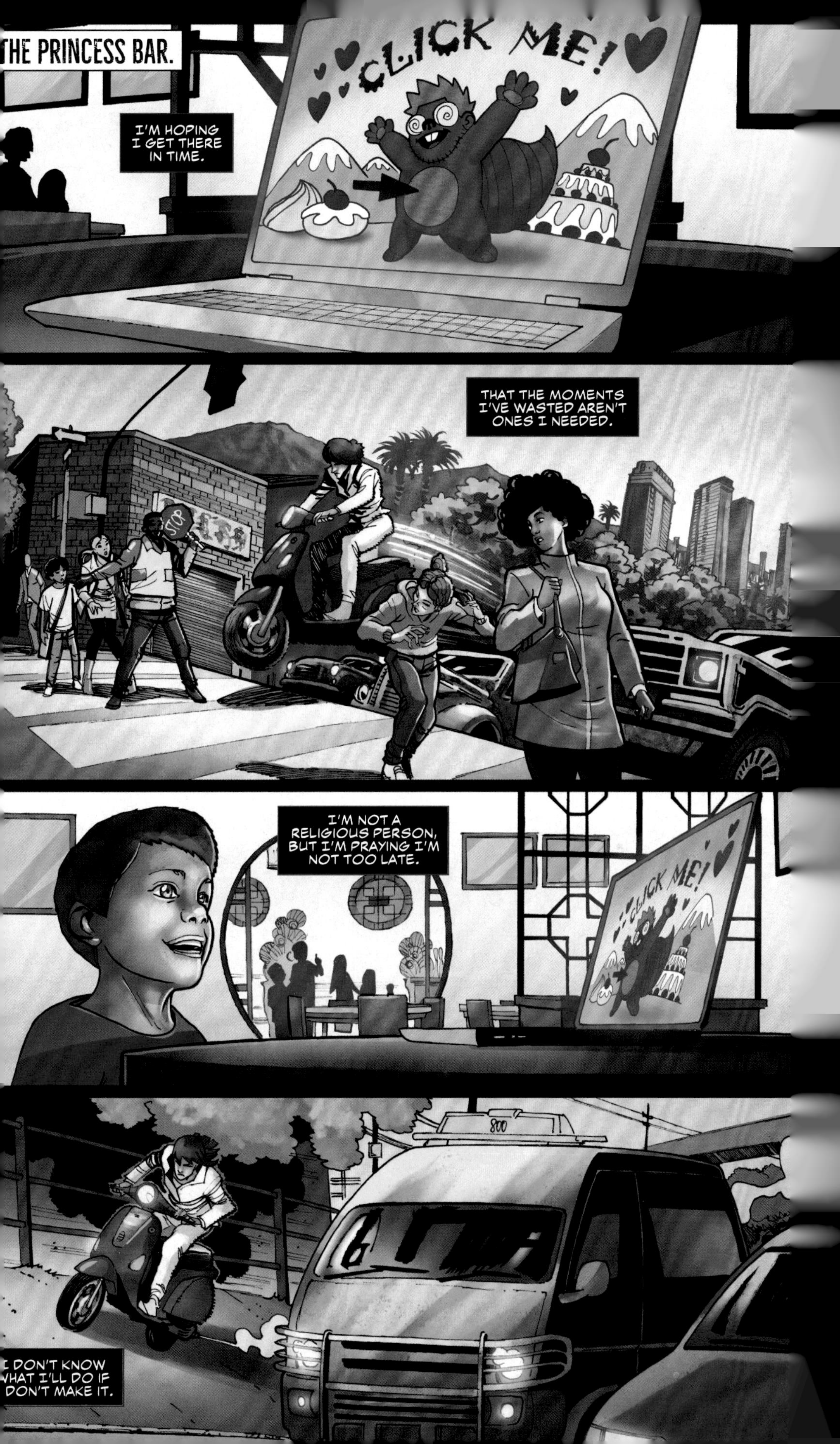
THE PRINCESS BAR.
CLICK ME!
I'M HOPING I GET THERE IN TIME.
THAT THE MOMENTS I'VE WASTED AREN'T ONES I NEEDED.
STOP
I'M NOT A RELIGIOUS PERSON, BUT I'M PRAYING I'M NOT TOO LATE.
CLICK ME!
800
I DON'T KNOW WHAT I'LL DO IF I DON'T MAKE IT.

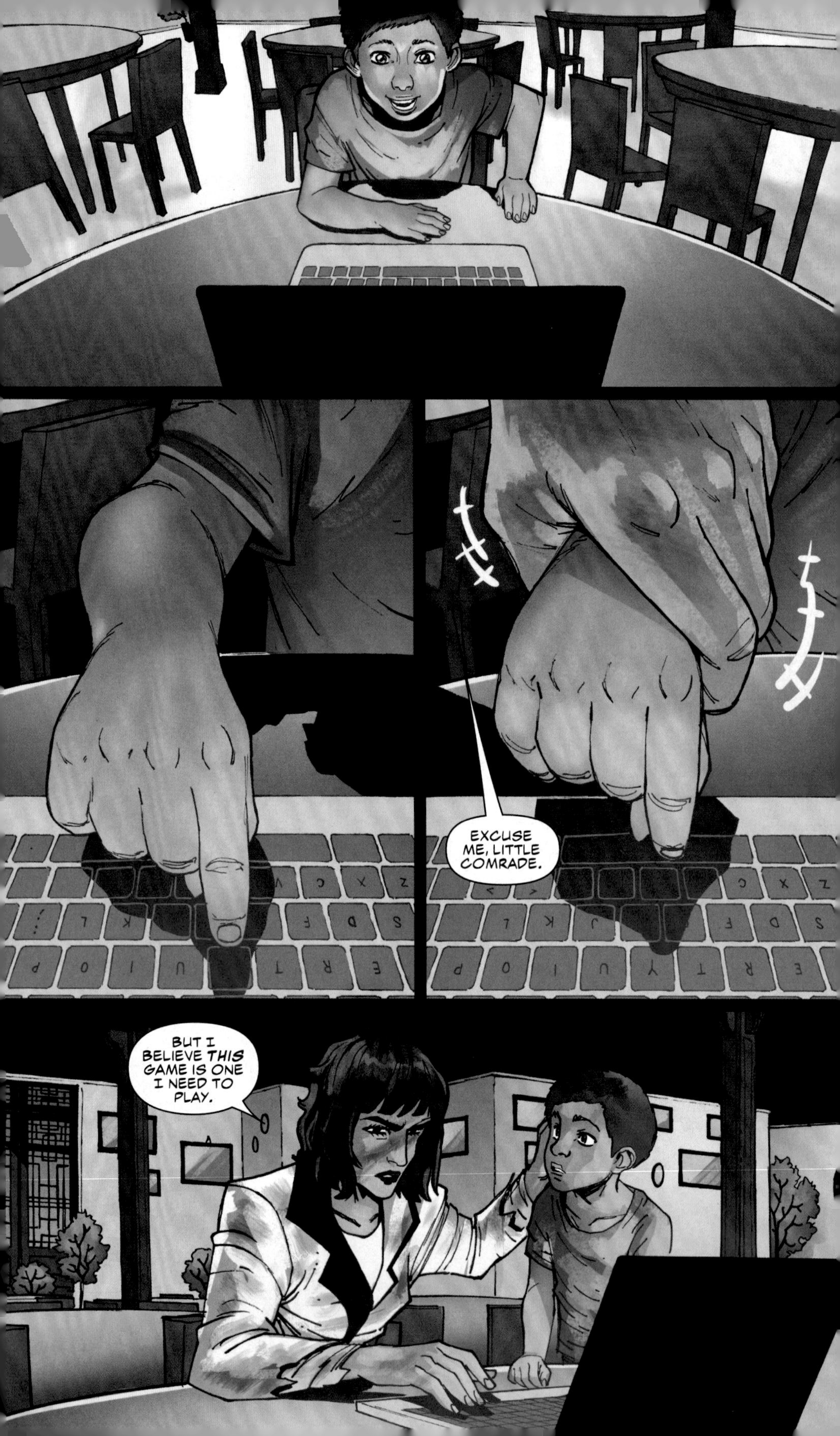
EXCUSE ME, LITTLE COMRADE.
BUT I BELIEVE THIS GAME IS ONE I NEED TO PLAY.

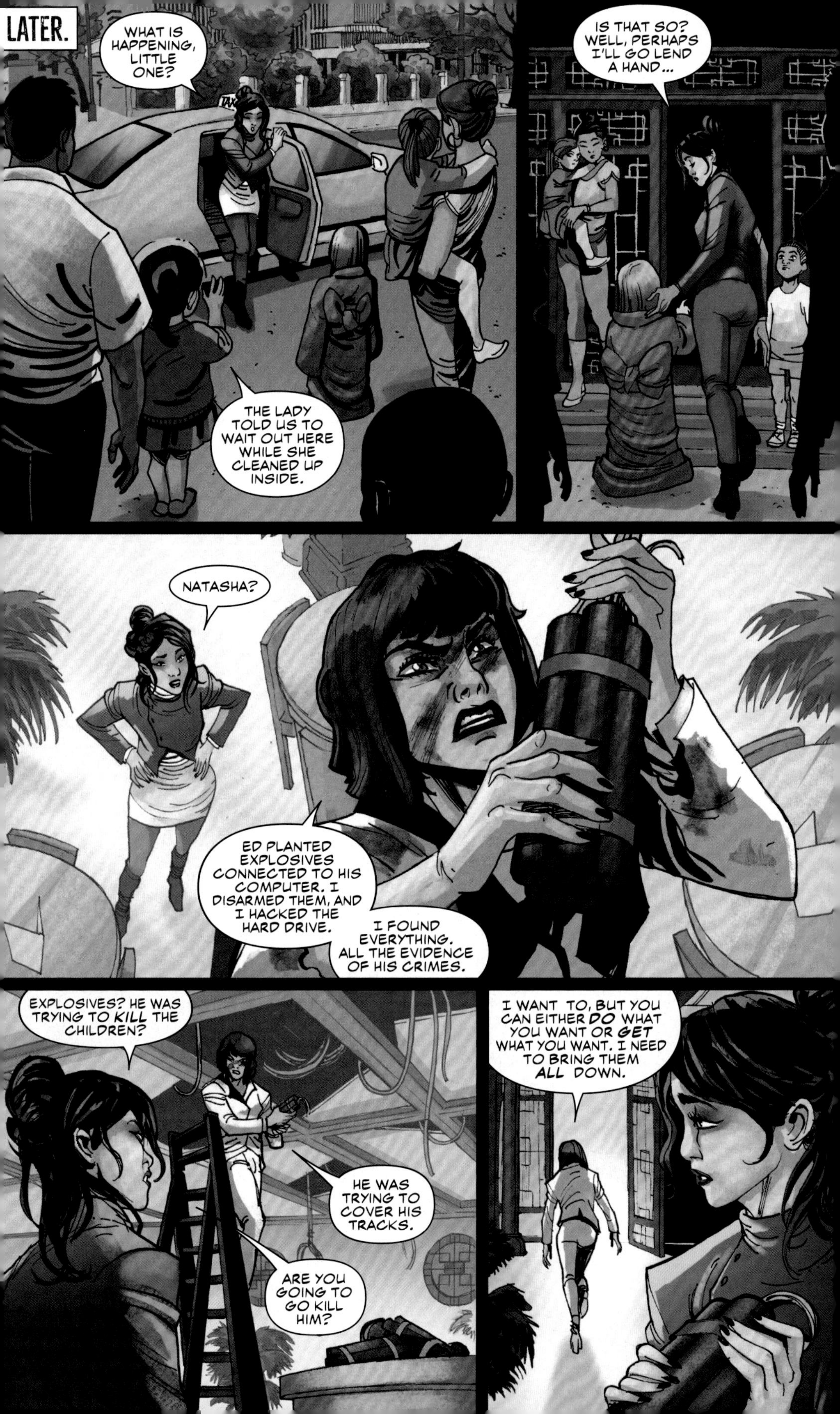
LATER.
WHAT IS HAPPENING, LITTLE ONE?
THE LADY TOLD US TO WAIT OUT HERE WHILE SHE CLEANED UP INSIDE.
IS THAT SO? WELL, PERHAPS I'LL GO LEND A HAND...
NATASHA?
ED PLANTED EXPLOSIVES CONNECTED TO HIS COMPUTER. I DISARMED THEM, AND I HACKED THE HARD DRIVE.
I FOUND EVERYTHING. ALL THE EVIDENCE OF HIS CRIMES.
EXPLOSIVES? HE WAS TRYING TO KILL THE CHILDREN?
HE WAS TRYING TO COVER HIS TRACKS.
ARE YOU GOING TO GO KILL HIM?
I WANT TO, BUT YOU CAN EITHER DO WHAT YOU WANT OR GET WHAT YOU WANT. I NEED TO BRING THEM ALL DOWN.

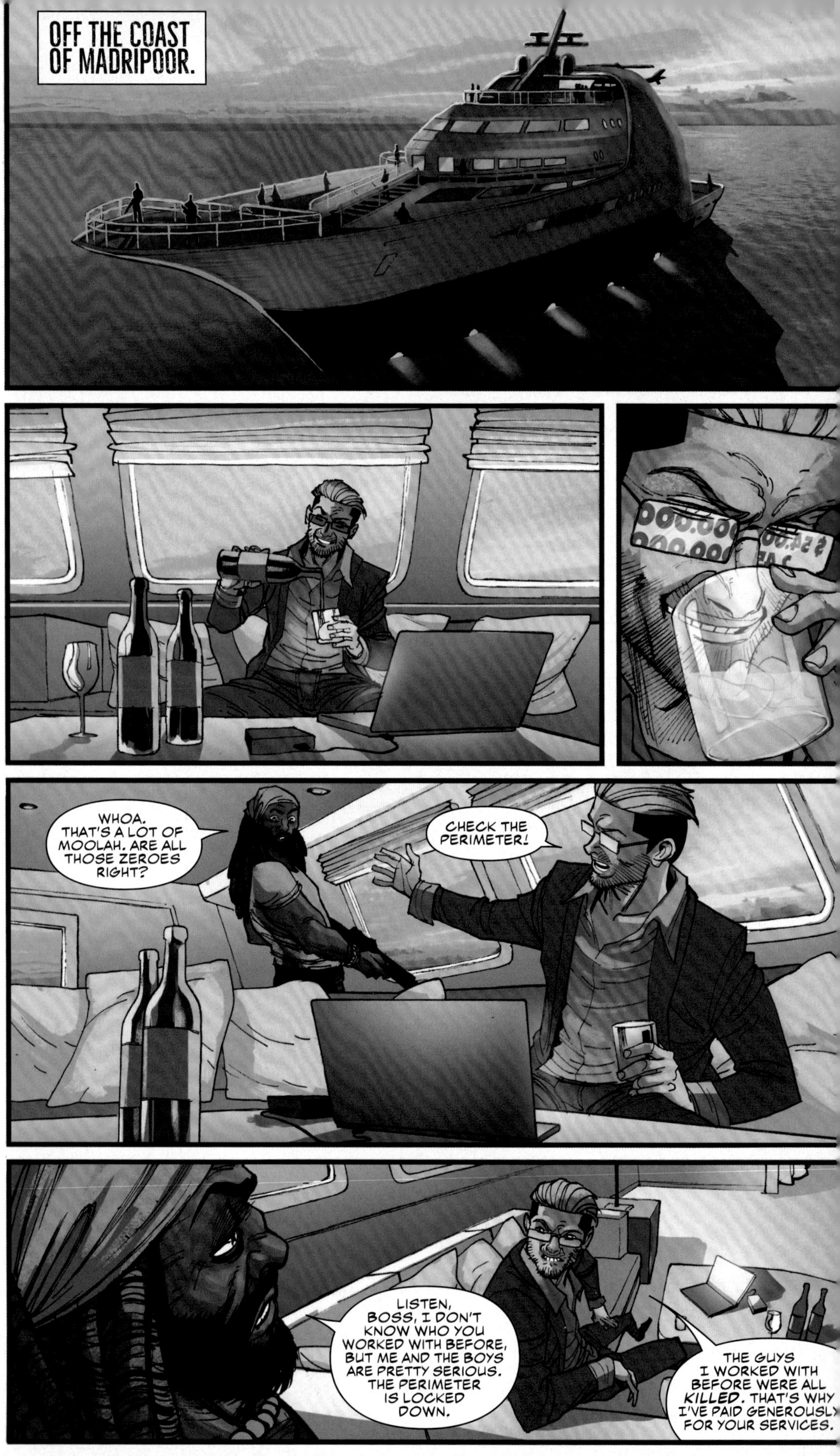
OFF THE COAST OF MADRIPOOR.
WHOA. THAT'S A LOT OF MOOLAH. ARE ALL THOSE ZEROES RIGHT?
CHECK THE PERIMETER!
LISTEN, BOSS, I DON'T KNOW WHO YOU WORKED WITH BEFORE, BUT ME AND THE BOYS ARE PRETTY SERIOUS. THE PERIMETER IS LOCKED DOWN.
THE GUYS I WORKED WITH BEFORE WERE ALL *KILLED*. THAT'S WHY I'VE PAID GENEROUSLY FOR YOUR SERVICES.

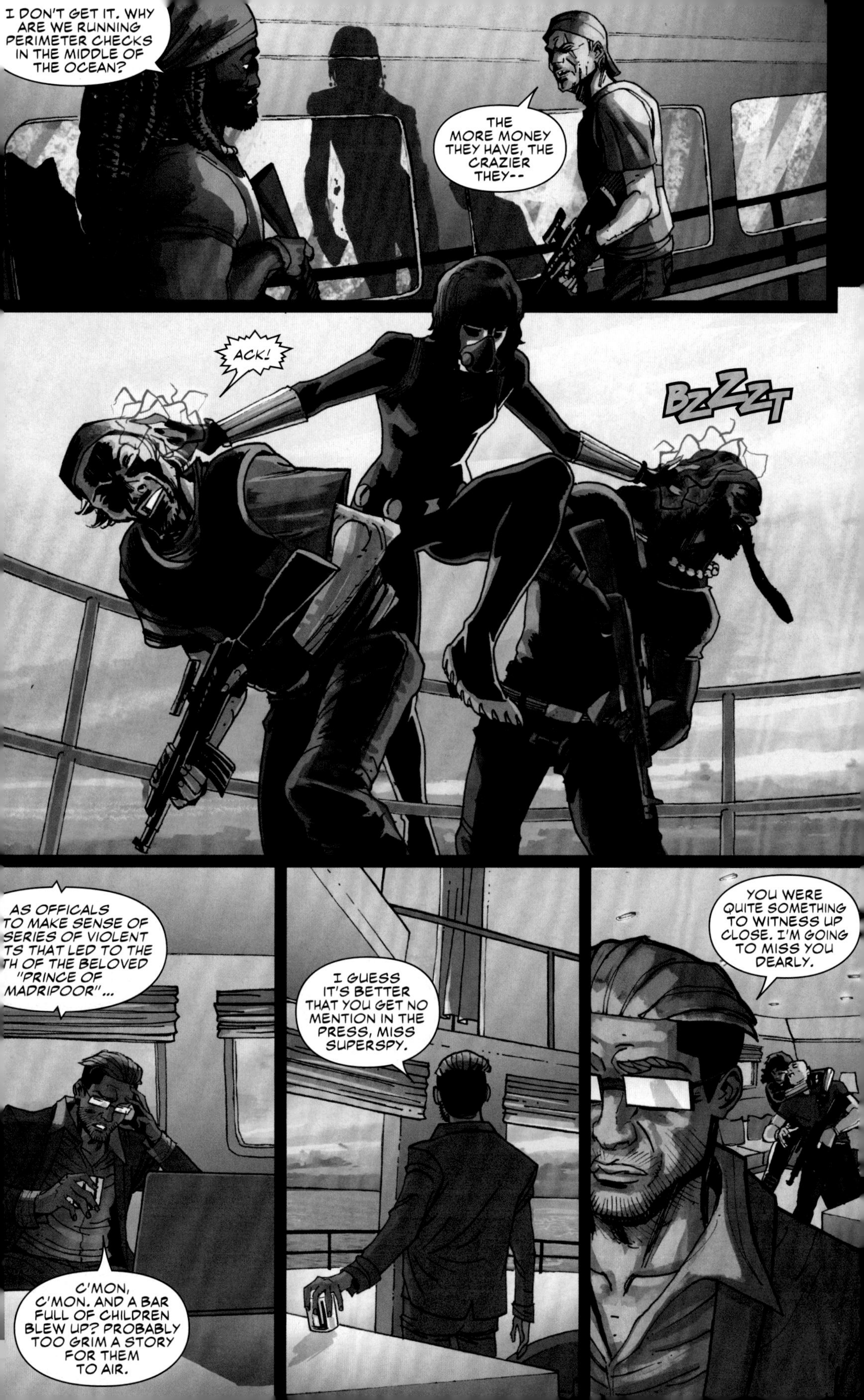

I DON'T GET IT. WHY ARE WE RUNNING PERIMETER CHECKS IN THE MIDDLE OF THE OCEAN?
THE MORE MONEY THEY HAVE, THE CRAZIER THEY--
ACK!
BZZZT
AS OFFICALS TO MAKE SENSE OF SERIES OF VIOLENT TS THAT LED TO THE TH OF THE BELOVED "PRINCE OF MADRIPOOR"...
C'MON, C'MON. AND A BAR FULL OF CHILDREN BLEW UP? PROBABLY TOO GRIM A STORY FOR THEM TO AIR.
I GUESS IT'S BETTER THAT YOU GET NO MENTION IN THE PRESS, MISS SUPERSPY.
YOU WERE QUITE SOMETHING TO WITNESS UP CLOSE. I'M GOING TO MISS YOU DEARLY.

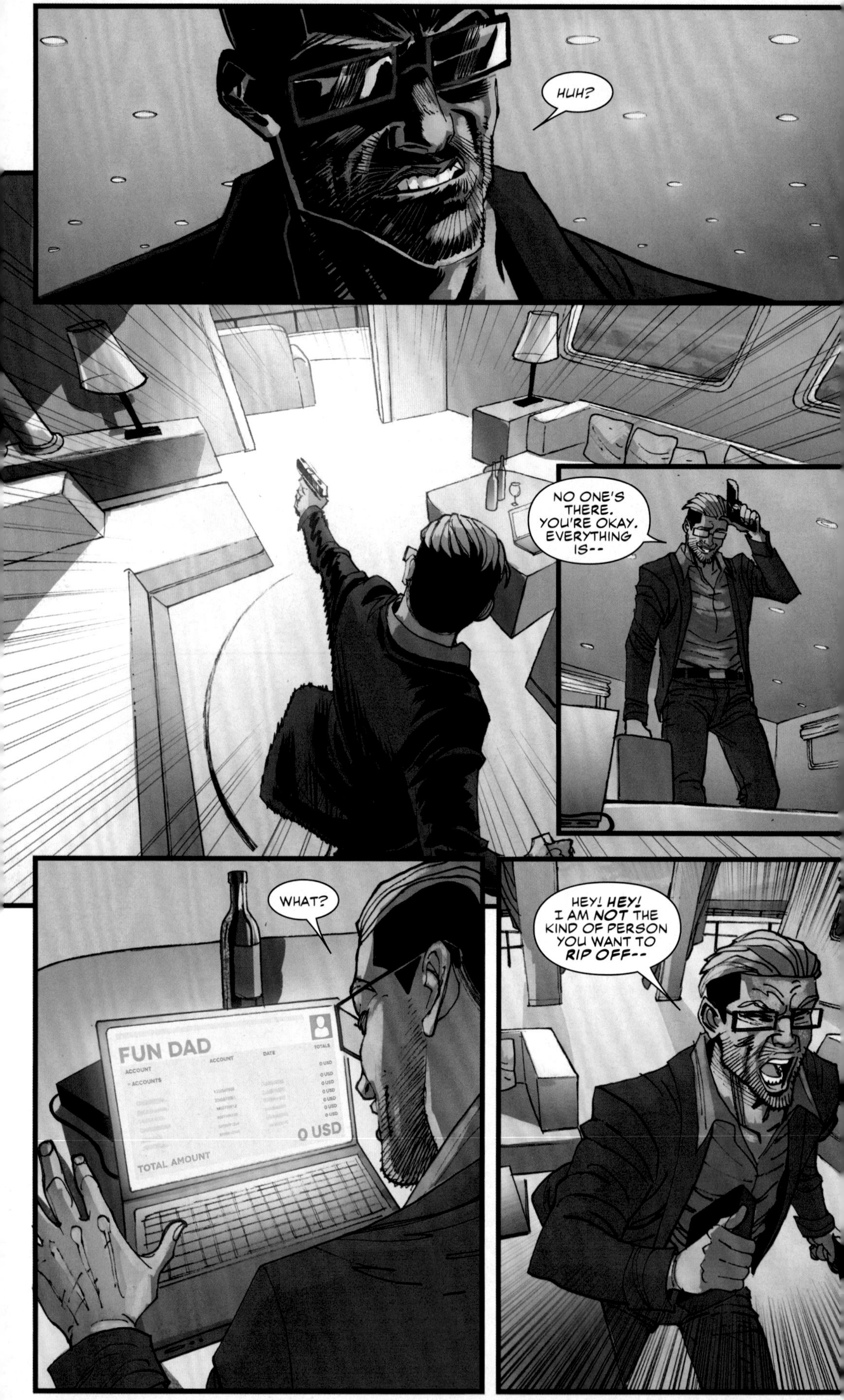
HUH?
NO ONE'S THERE. YOU'RE OKAY. EVERYTHING IS--
WHAT?
FUN DAD
0 USD
TOTAL AMOUNT
HEY! HEY! I AM NOT THE KIND OF PERSON YOU WANT TO RIP OFF--

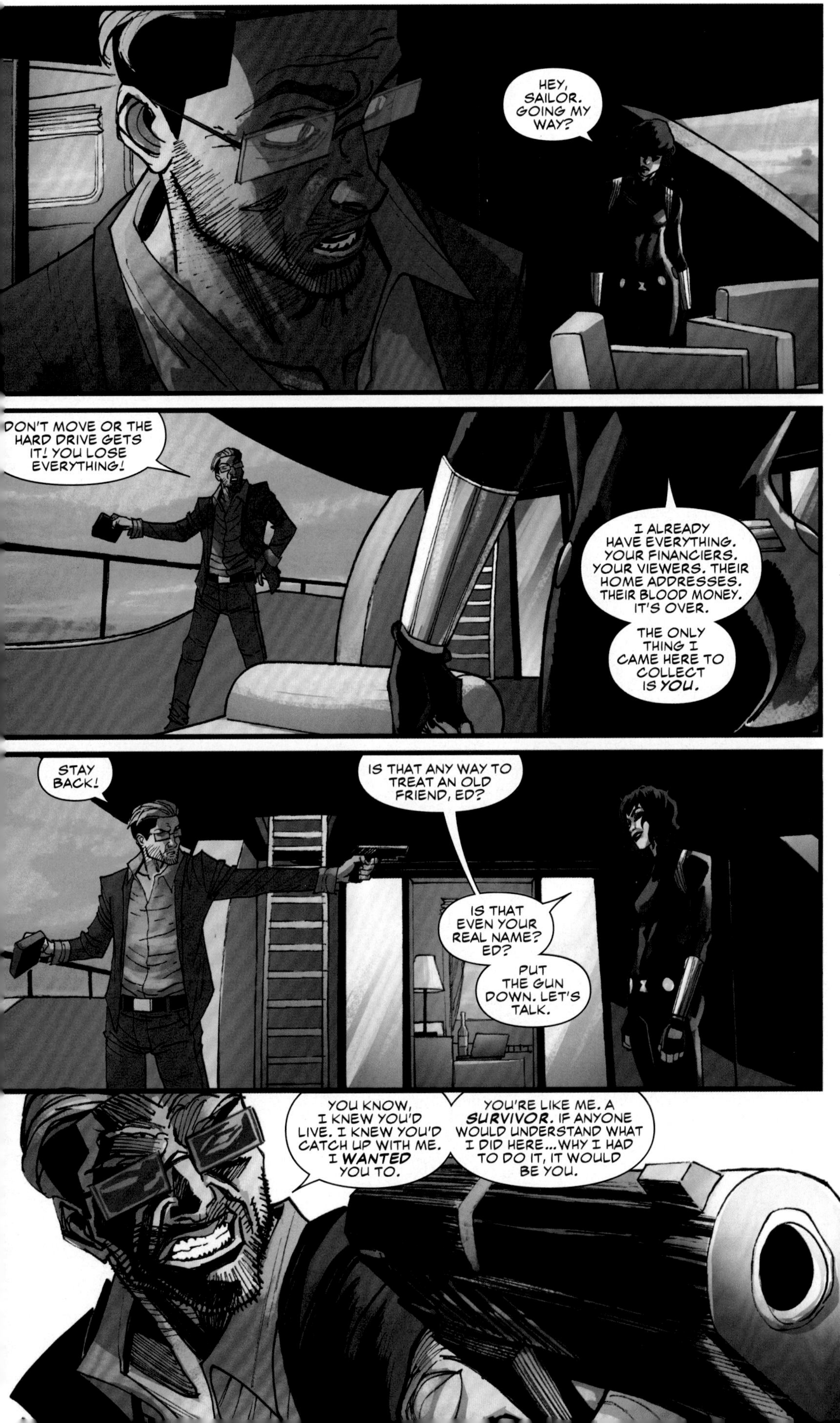
HEY, SAILOR. GOING MY WAY?
DON'T MOVE OR THE HARD DRIVE GETS IT! YOU LOSE EVERYTHING!
I ALREADY HAVE EVERYTHING. YOUR FINANCIERS. YOUR VIEWERS. THEIR HOME ADDRESSES. THEIR BLOOD MONEY. IT'S OVER.
THE ONLY THING I CAME HERE TO COLLECT IS *YOU*.
STAY BACK!
IS THAT ANY WAY TO TREAT AN OLD FRIEND, ED?
IS THAT EVEN YOUR REAL NAME? ED?
PUT THE GUN DOWN. LET'S TALK.
YOU KNOW, I KNEW YOU'D LIVE. I KNEW YOU'D CATCH UP WITH ME. I *WANTED* YOU TO.
YOU'RE LIKE ME. A *SURVIVOR*. IF ANYONE WOULD UNDERSTAND WHAT I DID HERE...WHY I HAD TO DO IT, IT WOULD BE YOU.

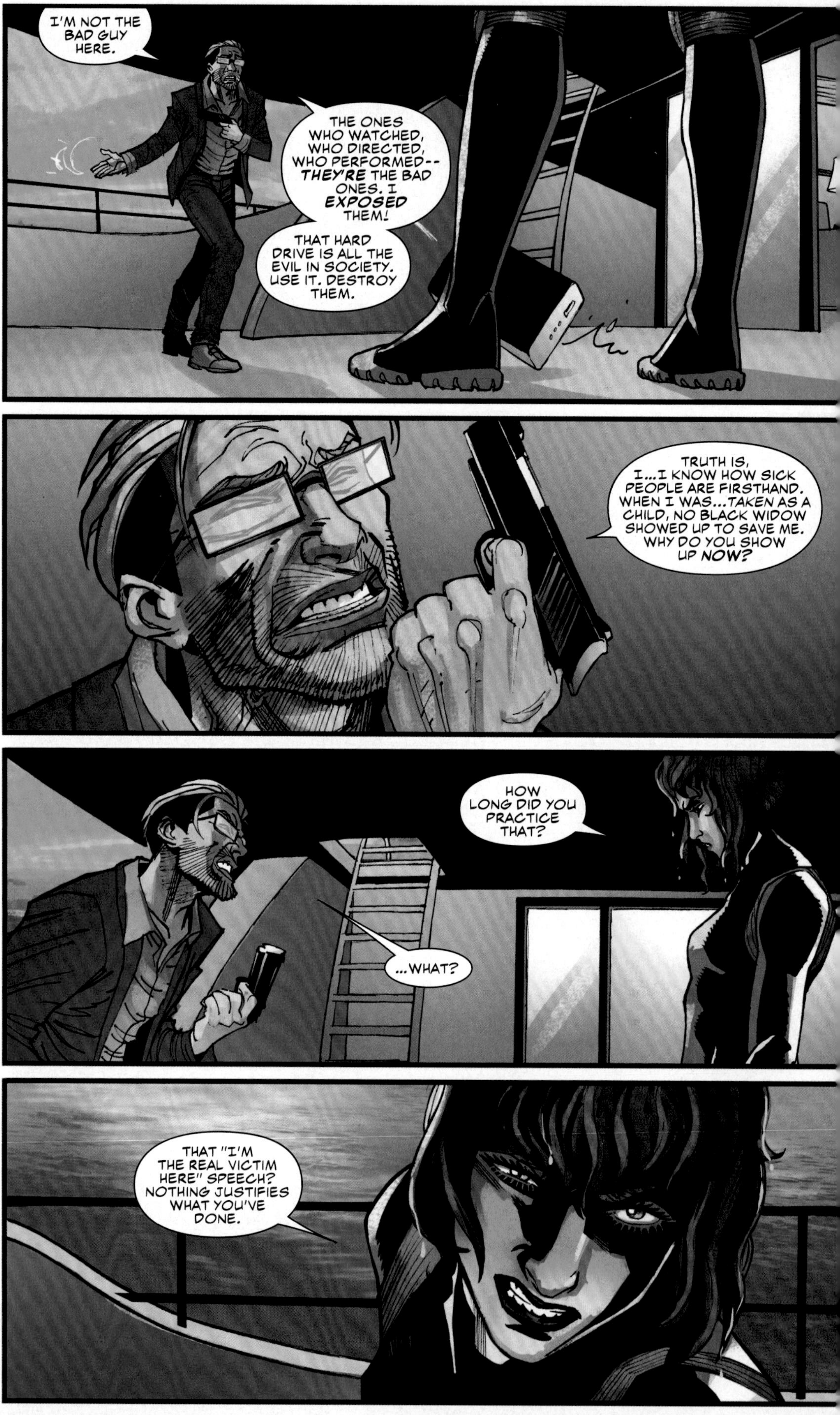
I'M NOT THE BAD GUY HERE.
THE ONES WHO WATCHED, WHO DIRECTED, WHO PERFORMED-- THEY'RE THE BAD ONES. I EXPOSED THEM!
THAT HARD DRIVE IS ALL THE EVIL IN SOCIETY. USE IT. DESTROY THEM.
TRUTH IS, I...I KNOW HOW SICK PEOPLE ARE FIRSTHAND. WHEN I WAS...TAKEN AS A CHILD, NO BLACK WIDOW SHOWED UP TO SAVE ME. WHY DO YOU SHOW UP NOW?
HOW LONG DID YOU PRACTICE THAT?
...WHAT?
THAT "I'M THE REAL VICTIM HERE" SPEECH? NOTHING JUSTIFIES WHAT YOU'VE DONE.

THOSE KIDS WOULD BE BETTER OFF DEAD AND YOU KNOW IT! AFTER WHAT THEY'VE BEEN THROUGH? YOU THINK THERE'S COMING BACK FROM THAT?!

I CAME BACK.

HOW DO YOU THINK THE FELLAS IN PRISON ARE GONNA FEEL ABOUT WHAT YOU DID? DO YOU THINK THEY'LL SEE YOU AS THE VICTIM HERE? NOT A CHILD KILLER?

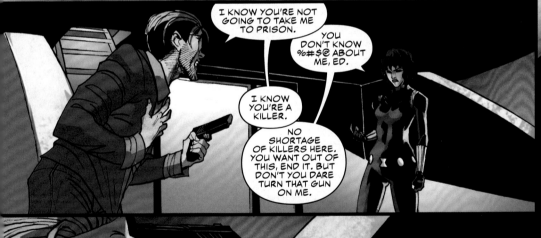

I KNOW YOU'RE NOT GOING TO TAKE ME TO PRISON.

YOU DON'T KNOW %#$@ ABOUT ME, ED.

I KNOW YOU'RE A KILLER.

NO SHORTAGE OF KILLERS HERE. YOU WANT OUT OF THIS, END IT. BUT DON'T YOU DARE TURN THAT GUN ON ME.

YOU WON'T BELIEVE ME, NAT, BUT IS IS HOW I **WANTED** IT O END. I'D DREAMED OF KRUPTING THOSE $%#@ R SO LONG, I DIDN'T PLAN AT CAME NEXT. I COULD NEVER SEE PAST THIS MOMENT.

I JUST WANTED IT TO BE OVER.

WHY WON'T YOU JUST END IT? WHY WON'T YOU SAVE ME?

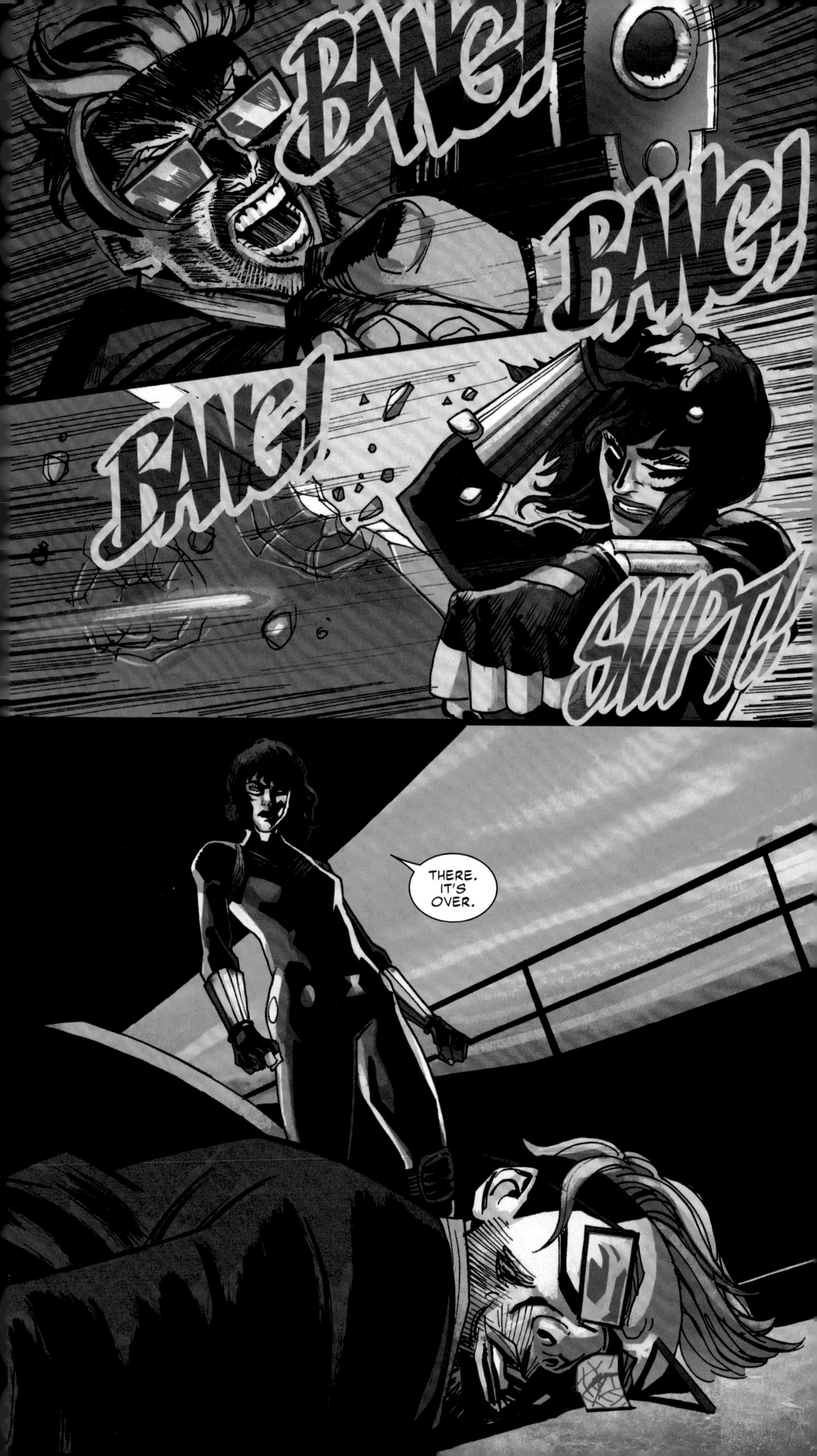
BANG!
BANG!
BANG!
SNIPT!
THERE. IT'S OVER.

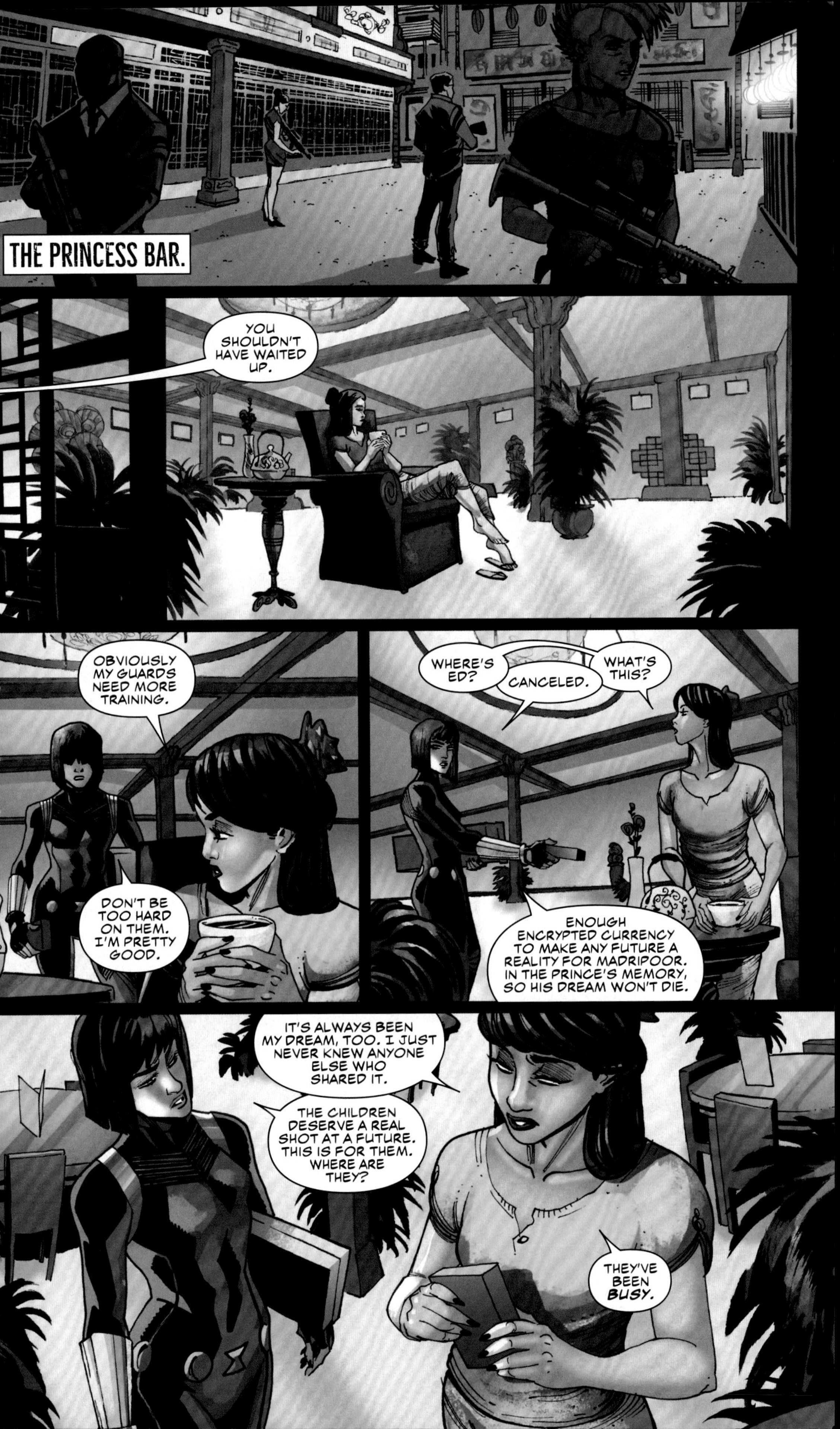
THE PRINCESS BAR.
YOU SHOULDN'T HAVE WAITED UP.
OBVIOUSLY MY GUARDS NEED MORE TRAINING.
DON'T BE TOO HARD ON THEM. I'M PRETTY GOOD.
WHERE'S ED?
CANCELED.
WHAT'S THIS?
ENOUGH ENCRYPTED CURRENCY TO MAKE ANY FUTURE A REALITY FOR MADRIPOOR. IN THE PRINCE'S MEMORY, SO HIS DREAM WON'T DIE.
IT'S ALWAYS BEEN MY DREAM, TOO. I JUST NEVER KNEW ANYONE ELSE WHO SHARED IT.
THE CHILDREN DESERVE A REAL SHOT AT A FUTURE. THIS IS FOR THEM. WHERE ARE THEY?
THEY'VE BEEN *BUSY*.

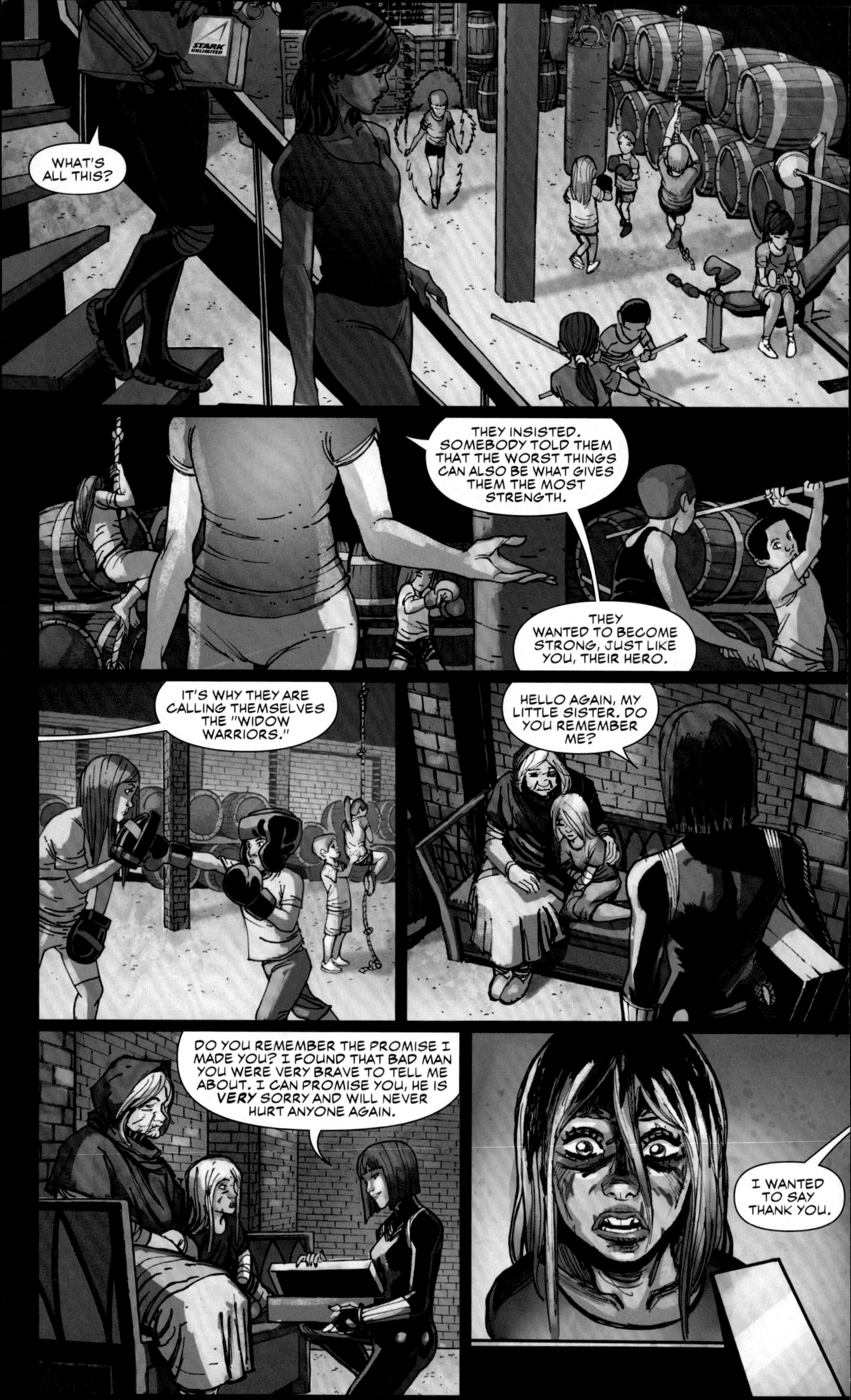
STARK UNLIMITED
WHAT'S ALL THIS?
THEY INSISTED. SOMEBODY TOLD THEM THAT THE WORST THINGS CAN ALSO BE WHAT GIVES THEM THE MOST STRENGTH.
THEY WANTED TO BECOME STRONG, JUST LIKE YOU, THEIR HERO.
IT'S WHY THEY ARE CALLING THEMSELVES THE "WIDOW WARRIORS."
HELLO AGAIN, MY LITTLE SISTER. DO YOU REMEMBER ME?
DO YOU REMEMBER THE PROMISE I MADE YOU? I FOUND THAT BAD MAN YOU WERE VERY BRAVE TO TELL ME ABOUT. I CAN PROMISE YOU, HE IS VERY SORRY AND WILL NEVER HURT ANYONE AGAIN.
I WANTED TO SAY THANK YOU.

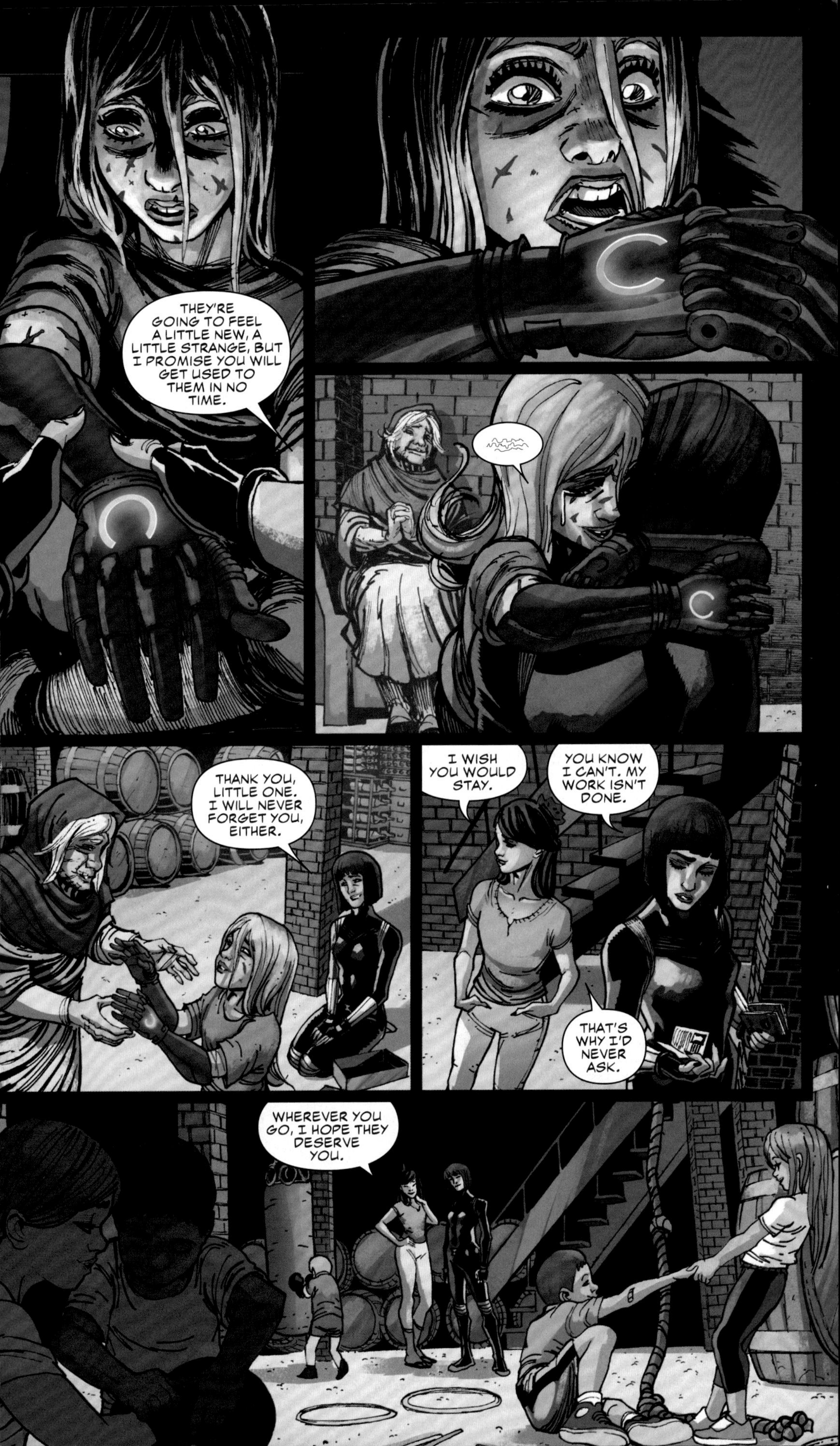
THEY'RE GOING TO FEEL A LITTLE NEW, A LITTLE STRANGE, BUT I PROMISE YOU WILL GET USED TO THEM IN NO TIME.
THANK YOU, LITTLE ONE. I WILL NEVER FORGET YOU, EITHER.
I WISH YOU WOULD STAY.
YOU KNOW I CAN'T. MY WORK ISN'T DONE.
THAT'S WHY I'D NEVER ASK.
WHEREVER YOU GO, I HOPE THEY DESERVE YOU.

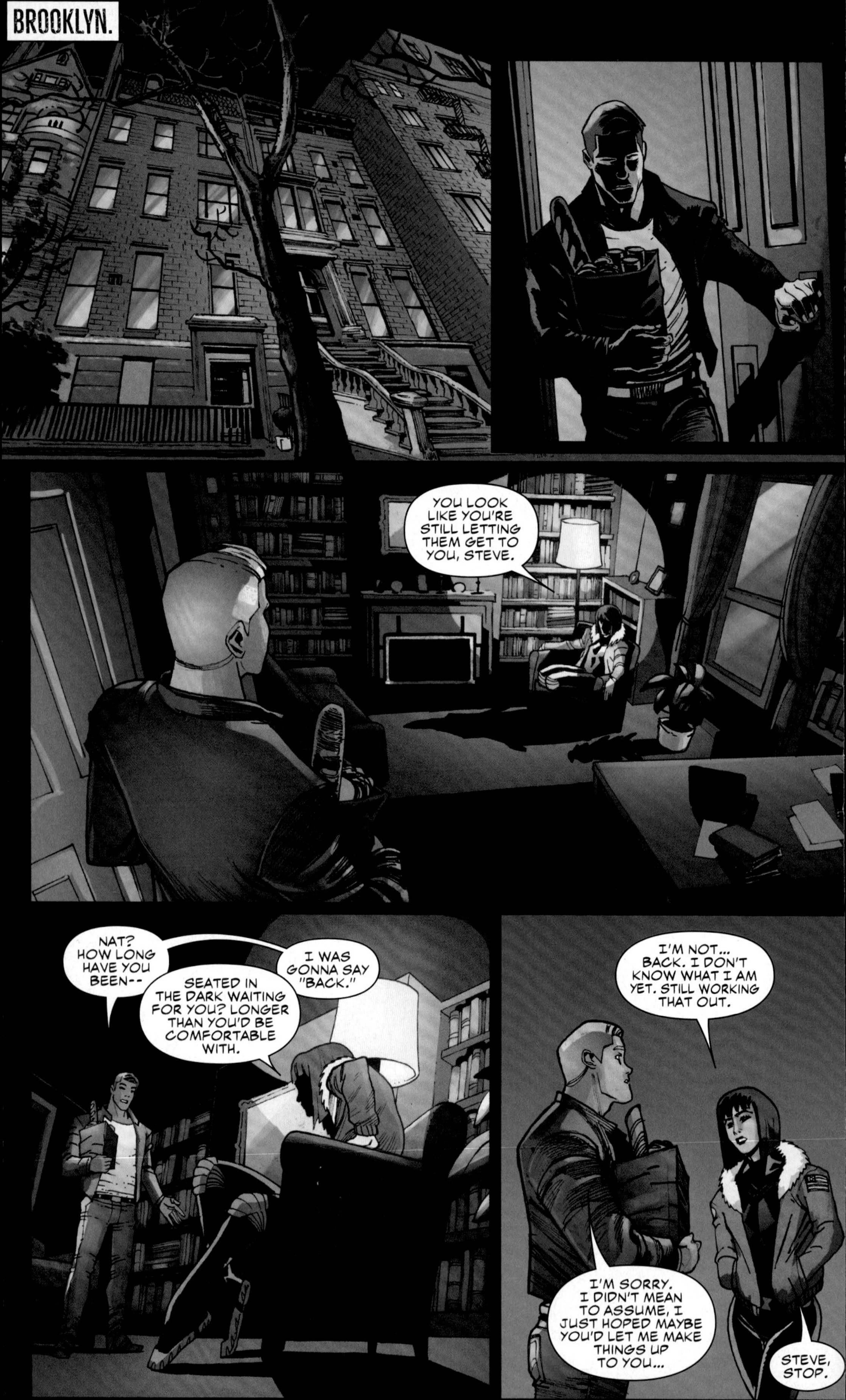
BROOKLYN.
YOU LOOK LIKE YOU'RE STILL LETTING THEM GET TO YOU, STEVE.
NAT? HOW LONG HAVE YOU BEEN--
SEATED IN THE DARK WAITING FOR YOU? LONGER THAN YOU'D BE COMFORTABLE WITH.
I WAS GONNA SAY "BACK."
I'M NOT... BACK. I DON'T KNOW WHAT I AM YET. STILL WORKING THAT OUT.
I'M SORRY. I DIDN'T MEAN TO ASSUME, I JUST HOPED MAYBE YOU'D LET ME MAKE THINGS UP TO YOU...
STEVE, STOP.

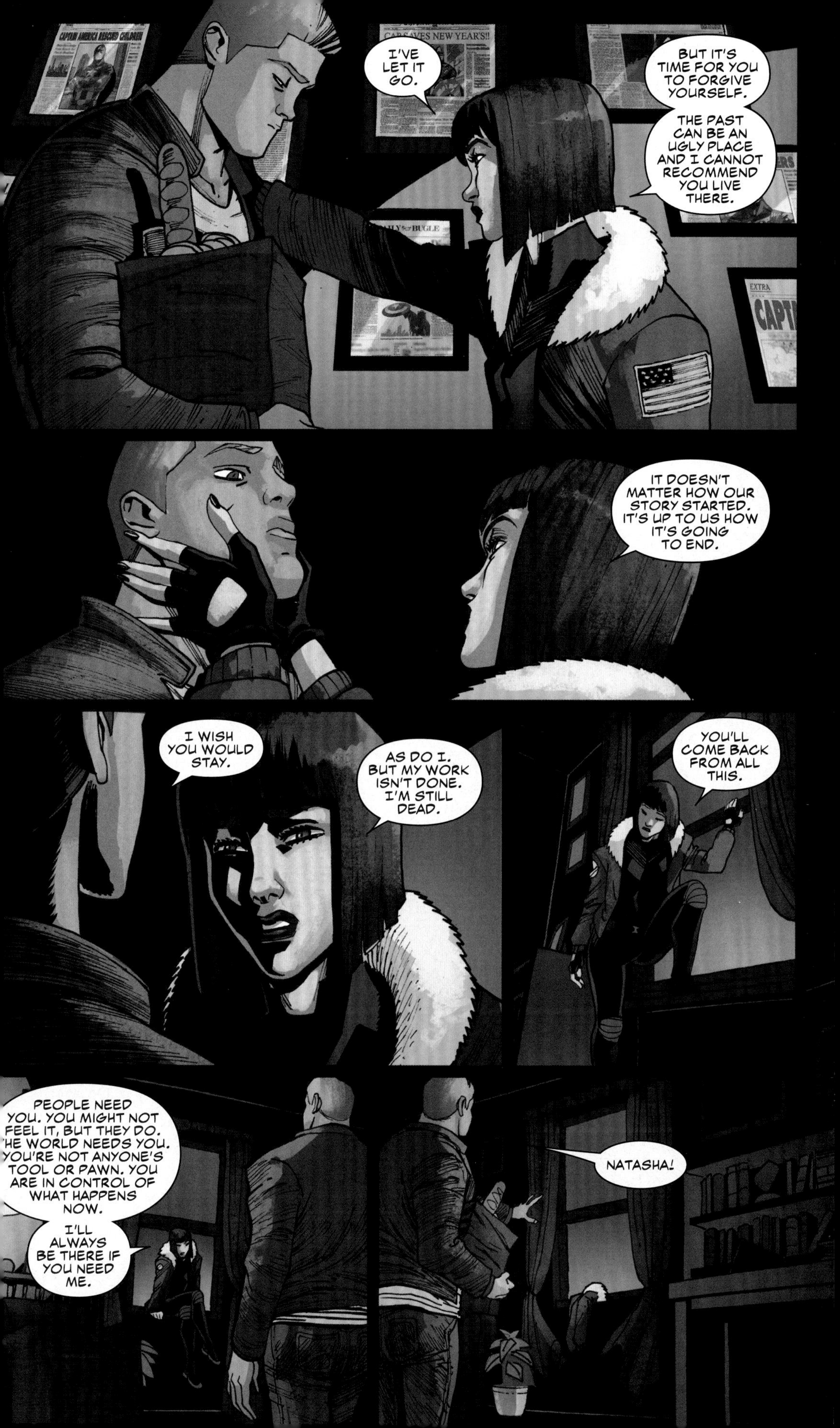
I'VE LET IT GO.
BUT IT'S TIME FOR YOU TO FORGIVE YOURSELF.
THE PAST CAN BE AN UGLY PLACE AND I CANNOT RECOMMEND YOU LIVE THERE.
IT DOESN'T MATTER HOW OUR STORY STARTED. IT'S UP TO US HOW IT'S GOING TO END.
I WISH YOU WOULD STAY.
AS DO I. BUT MY WORK ISN'T DONE. I'M STILL DEAD.
YOU'LL COME BACK FROM ALL THIS.
PEOPLE NEED YOU. YOU MIGHT NOT FEEL IT, BUT THEY DO. THE WORLD NEEDS YOU. YOU'RE NOT ANYONE'S TOOL OR PAWN. YOU ARE IN CONTROL OF WHAT HAPPENS NOW.
I'LL ALWAYS BE THERE IF YOU NEED ME.
NATASHA!

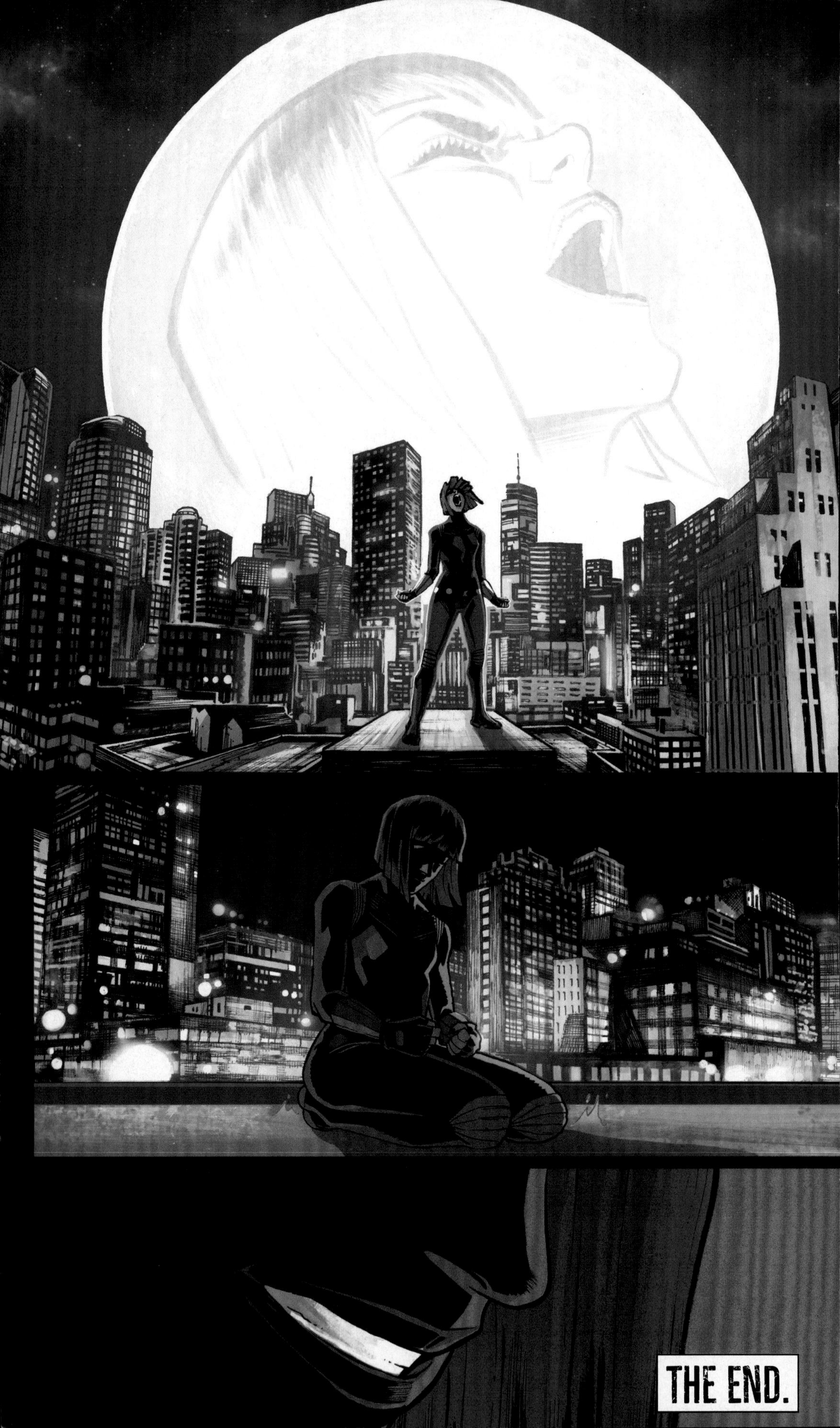
THE END.

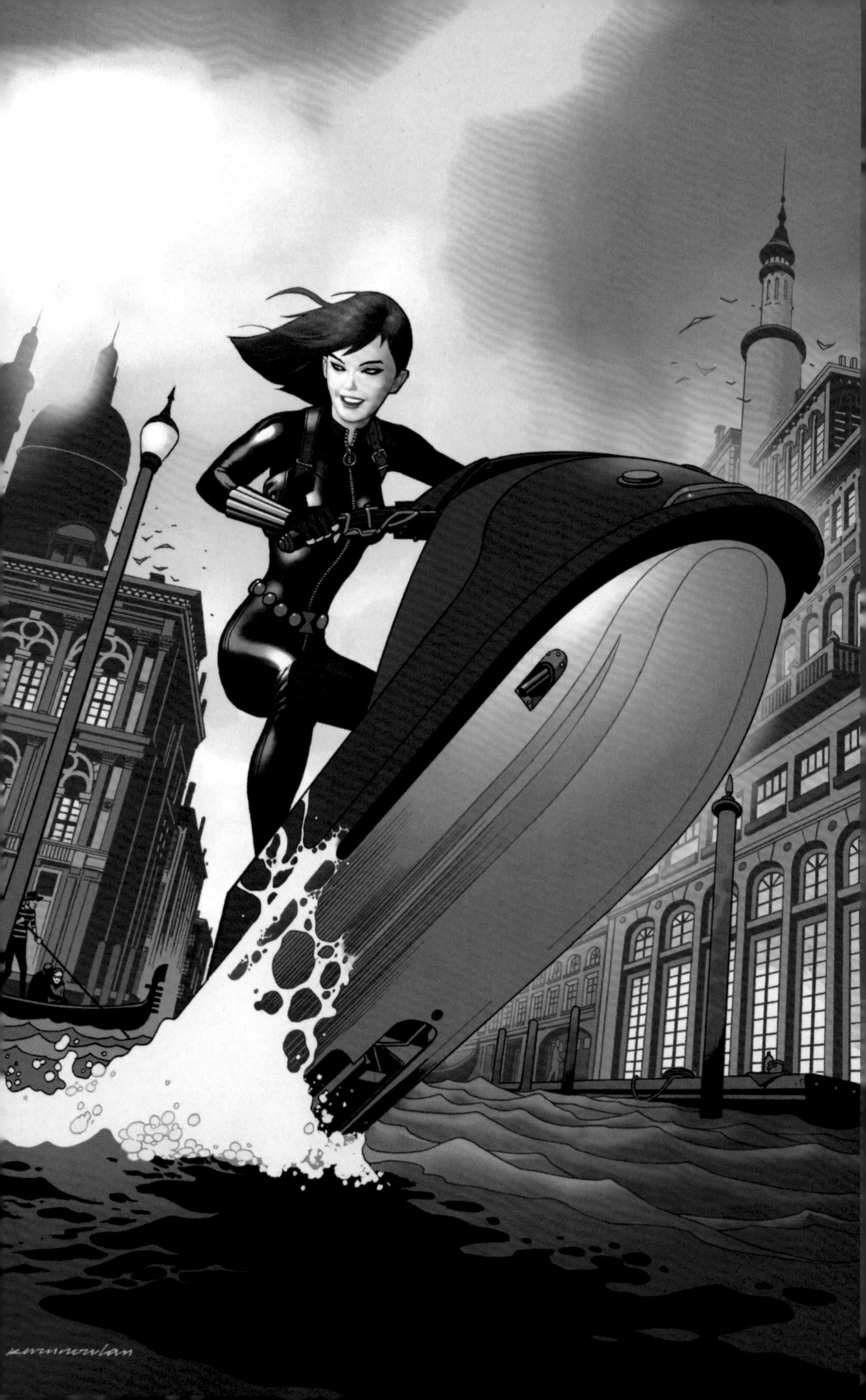

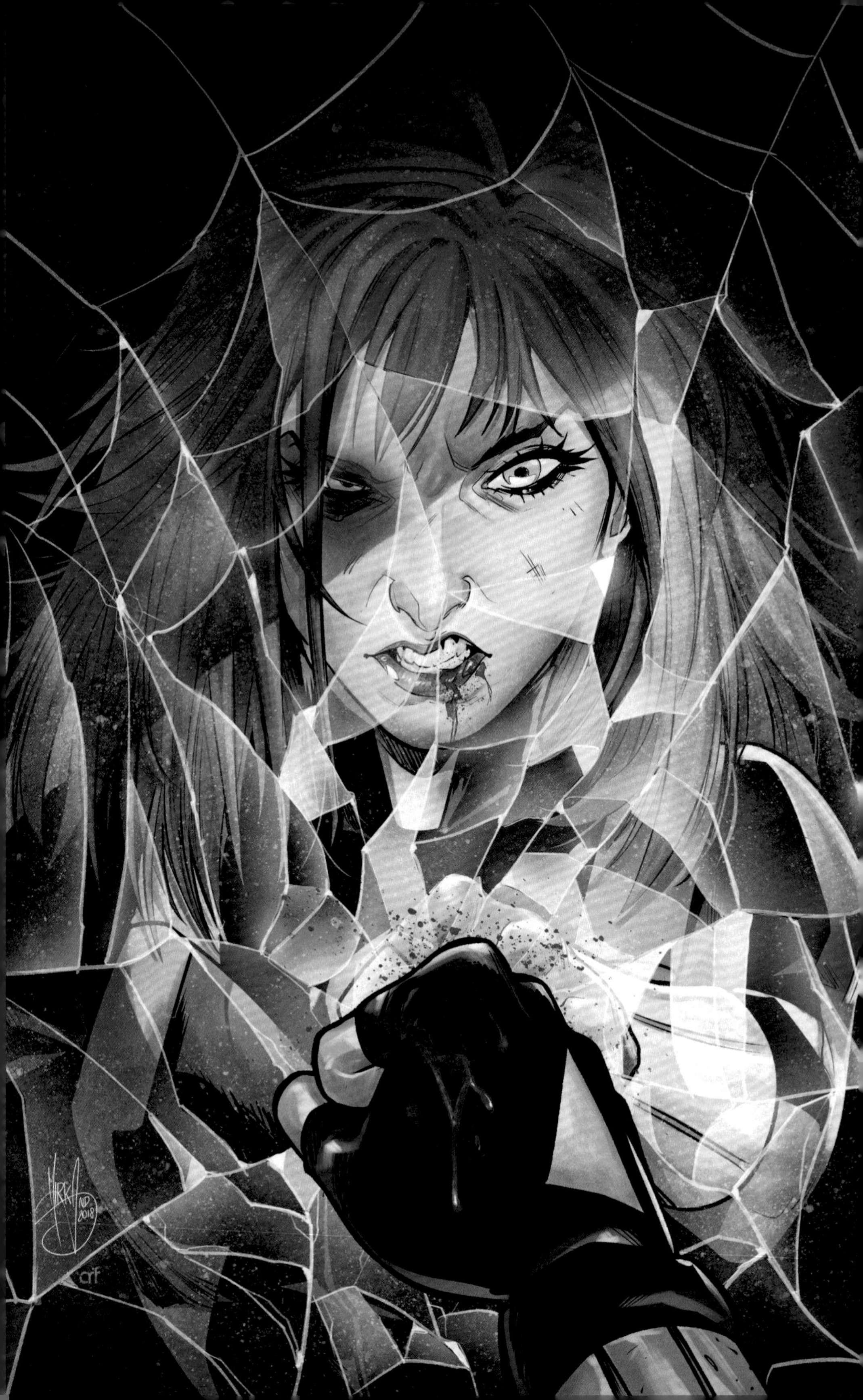

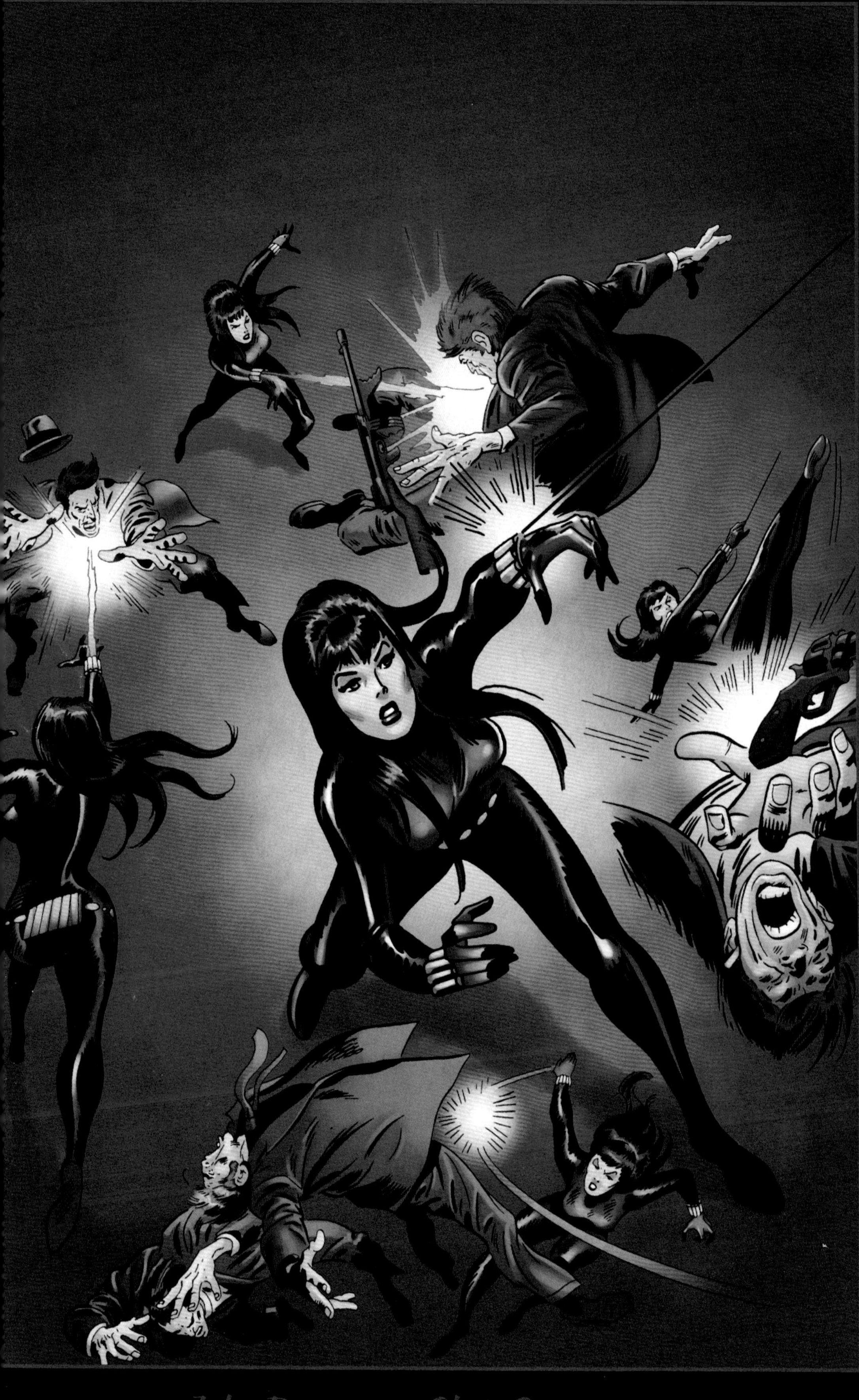

John Buscema & Chris Sotomayor

#1 REMASTERED VARIANT

ORIGINALLY PRINTED IN #1

Dear Reader,

We find it almost impossible to put into words what it feels like to be writing *Black Widow*. We grew up reading Marvel comics, and people like Nat, Tony and Steve were all very real to us. Nat is a close, personal friend who has been there for us throughout the years. Our strong friend who could more than handle her own with the fellas. It's a dream come true to be writing stories for an all-new generation of fans and readers. Some of you may have read every word Nat's ever uttered and some of you may be picking up your first copy ever. Whether you're a weathered Widow Warrior or you've found your way here from the wilds of fandom to see what tales we have in store for Marvel's most notorious spy, we're happy you came.

While we love Nat's journey to where she is right now, we've always felt she's been held back. Free from the Avengers--and with the supreme freedom granted a "dead woman"--Black Widow is unleashed. No regrets. No mercy. Exactly what you'd expect from a Black Widow. And we're just getting started. So thank you for joining us. Thank you for reading. Stick around. We're about to take you on one hell of a ride with some no restrictions play.

Anything goes...

Your Friendly Neighborhood Soska Sisters,

Jen and Sylv

ORIGINALLY PRINTED IN #5

Dear Reader,

Thank you for coming along with us for this ride. It was a privilege to get to write such a gritty story with one of the most recognizable super heroes in media today, with subject matter that is very real. Unfortunately, in real life we don't get a Black Widow to clean up the messes. We have to arm ourselves with education and critical thought. We have the power within ourselves to do great things.

We wish our grandmother were still here today because she loved grabbing us Marvel comics as kids, and she would have gotten a big kick out of knowing we are writing our own stories today. We never dreamed we would get such a brilliant opportunity on a book we are so incredibly proud of. We would like to thank our editor, Jake Thomas, who has always gone to bat for us and is the kind of collaborator who makes you do your best work; Flaviano, who created such a genuine, human Nat in a world of horror with his art; Veronica Gandini, whose brilliant colors brought everything to life; Clayton Crain, whose covers enticed people to pick up the book; Joe Caramagna and his beautiful lettering; and everyone at Marvel who worked hard to make this book the success that it has been.

If you're a fan reading this and you have dreams of writing these iconic characters, follow your dreams, because if you work hard and treat people with respect, you will find success. Living a life like that is success.

Thank you for reading, thank you for the kind words online, thank YOU for picking up this book. It was the thrill of a lifetime to get to write this series.

Anything goes...

Your Friendly Neighborhood Soska Sisters,

Jen and Sylv